American
JewBu

American JewBu

JEWS, BUDDHISTS, *and* RELIGIOUS CHANGE

EMILY SIGALOW

PRINCETON UNIVERSITY PRESS

PRINCETON AND OXFORD

Published by Princeton University Press
41 William Street, Princeton, New Jersey 08540
6 Oxford Street, Woodstock, Oxfordshire OX20 1TR

press.princeton.edu

ISBN 9780691174594
ISBN (e-book): 9780691197814

British Library Cataloging-in-Publication Data is available

Editorial: Fred Appel, Matt Rohal, and Jenny Tan
Production Editorial: Natalie Baan
Jacket/Cover Design: Amanda Weiss
Production: Erin Suydam
Publicity: Tayler Lord, Kathryn Stevens, and Nathalie Levine
Copyeditor: Cindy Milstein

Jacket art: iStock

This book has been composed in Arno

Printed on acid-free paper. ∞

Printed in the United States of America

10 9 8 7 6 5 4 3 2 1

To Uri, Naomi, Maya, and Micah:
For everything

CONTENTS

ILLUSTRATIONS

Figures

Tables

A NOTE ON THE SPELLING OF *JEWBU*

THE PORTMANTEAU USED to describe Jewish Buddhists has been spelled in various ways over the years. While conducting research for this book, I heard respondents identify themselves colloquially as JewBus, BuJews, and even BuddJews. In his popular 1994 book *The Jew in the Lotus*, Rodger Kamenetz spelled it JUBU, in all capital letters. However it is spelled, the term is of recent vintage and unknown origin. At the time of the publication of this book, it is not found in leading English-language dictionaries such as *Merriam-Webster's Collegiate Dictionary* or the *Oxford English Dictionary*. Yet it does appear in myriad forms—Jubu, Buju, Jewbu, and BuJew—in the *Urban Dictionary*, a crowdsourced online dictionary of neologisms and slang words.

In this book, I opted to use the spelling JewBu for two reasons. First, my hope is that the title *American JewBu* would make it clear to the casual book browser and those unfamiliar with the Jewish Buddhist phenomenon that this book is actually about Jews.

Second, my research reveals that Jewish Buddhists from the millennial age group, particularly those under the age of thirty, identify as Jew-Bus. Unlike many American Jews of the baby boomer generation who began practicing Buddhism in the 1960s and 1970s—who dislike the label and view it as a form of disparagement or condescension—millennials embrace this blended identity. As I suggest in the conclusion of this book, these young adults lay claim to this identity to demarcate themselves as more progressive and liberal than the mainstream American Jewish community. The title of this book takes its cue from these young adults who are charting the future of the Jewish Buddhist encounter in the United States.

ACKNOWLEDGMENTS

THIS BOOK was made possible through the support and encouragement of so many people to whom I am deeply indebted. My inspiration
for *American JewBu* came from a conversation with Wendy Cadge during my first semester in graduate school in winter 2009 after I read her
first book, *Heartwood: The First Generation of Theravada Buddhism in
America.* In it, she writes about how nearly a third of the people she interviewed at the Cambridge Insight Meditation Center in Cambridge,
Massachusetts, were of Jewish background. Intrigued, I spent summer
2009 poking around various different Jewish and Buddhist meditation
centers in the Boston area to see what I could find. By the end of that
summer, I was convinced that there was an interesting story there that
I wanted to tell. Wendy's dedication to this project, from its conception
to completion, has been beyond generous. She saw what this project
could offer a range of different audiences and encouraged me to expand
and sharpen my arguments accordingly. I am grateful to her for her support, guidance, and mentorship.

I am deeply indebted to all the wonderful Jewish Buddhists who
warmly accepted my presence, offered me their time, and shared their
personal stories with me. I want to especially thank Alison Laichter and
the other meditators at the Jewish Meditation Center of Brooklyn for
generously opening their doors to me. I cannot thank all of them enough
for their patience in answering so many of my questions. I hope some will
find these pages and recognize their tales within them. And even more,
I hope that these pages might help answer for them the question about
how their Jewish pasts mattered to their Buddhist trajectories.

I am grateful to my dissertation committee at Brandeis University for
encouraging me to think about my dissertation as a book from the beginning. Sylvia Barack Fishman served as a critical commentator on all
chapters of the dissertation and has been wonderfully supportive of me

and this project. She also has a keen editorial eye, for which I am immensely thankful. Jonathan Sarna's deep and broad knowledge has always inspired and challenged me—and continues to do so. I am greatly appreciative of his intellectual guidance and enthusiasm for this project. I am also deeply grateful for his mentorship and support more generally. And to David Cunningham, who joined my dissertation committee near the finish, and Tom Tweed, who read from afar, thank you for your probing questions, generous commentary, and support.

This book benefited enormously from the critical engagement of various friends and scholars. Nicky Fox, Casey Clevenger, and Dana Zarhin—three friends and colleagues from Brandeis—cheered me on throughout the writing of this book and helped me refine the arguments within it. I am grateful for the feedback and critical insights that Jeff Wilson, Shaul Kelner, Richard Seager, Janet Jacobs, Jaime Kucinskas, Cara Rock-Singer, Rodger Kamenetz, Jeff Guhin, and Shari Rabin offered on various chapters of this manuscript. I also want to thank Rachel Gordan, Jenny Caplan, Arielle Levites, Ilana Horwitz, Matt Williams, and Michelle Shain for their academic friendship and encouragement. The unwavering encouragement and support of two friends, Aisha Baruni and Ophira Stramer, has kept me anchored. I also want to thank Sydney Schweber for all her hard work formatting the citations in this manuscript. Finally, I want to thank Alicia Deane, Gladys Cazares, Deb Holmes, and Amparo Ulloa as well as Lexington Playcare Center and Old Hill Children's Day School for taking exceptional care of my children so that I had the time and quiet to focus on this book. This book would not have been possible without this village around me.

A number of institutions also generously supported the writing of this book. The Andrew W. Mellon Foundation, Research Circle on Democracy and Cultural Pluralism, Berman Foundation Dissertation Fellowship, and Hadassah-Brandeis Institute all provided generous funding for this project, for which I am deeply appreciative. The Perilman Postdoctoral Fellowship at Duke University gave me the time and space to focus on writing as well as revising chapters, enabling the transformation of my dissertation into this book.

At Princeton University Press, I have had the privilege of working with Fred Appel, who expertly shepherded this book into production. I am also grateful to Cindy Milstein for her fine copyediting, which sharpened the writing and structure of this book. This book owes a great debt to the two anonymous reviewers whose generous and incisive feedback substantively improved both its structure and arguments.

I owe my final and deepest thanks to my family. My parents, Susan and Steven Sigalow, have always believed in and supported me. My mother read each chapter as it appeared and the manuscript again in full with extreme care. She has both an uncommonly kind heart and a fine editorial eye. My siblings, Ian and Katie Sigalow, and their growing families have been sources of love and strength. My husband, Uri, has always been my staunchest supporter, living the joys and challenges of this book with me with encouragement and love. Finally, Naomi, Maya, and Micah, my dearest children: the three of you sustain and inspire me, brightening my life in every possible way. I am forever grateful for you.

American
JewBu

Introduction

AMERICAN BUDDHISTS like to tell a popular joke. A Jewish woman travels to the Himalayas in search of a famous guru. She heads east, traveling by plane, train, bus, and oxcart until she reaches a far-off Buddhist monastery in Nepal. An old lama in maroon and saffron robes tells her that the guru she is seeking is meditating in a cave at the top of the mountain and cannot be disturbed. She has traveled far and insists that she absolutely must see this guru. The lama eventually relents but requests that she not stay long, bow when addressing the guru, and say no more than eight words to him. With the help of a few lamas, monks, and Sherpa porters, she trudges up the mountain. Exhausted, she reaches the top and the cave where the guru is meditating. Keeping within the eight-word limit, she bows and says what she came to say: "Sheldon, it's your mother. Enough already, come home!" (Frankel 2013; Das 1998, 4).

This amusing story pokes fun at the widespread perception that American Jews have a particular affection for Buddhism. Past empirical research seems to support this view. In his sociological survey of seven Buddhist centers in North America, sociologist James Coleman (2001, 119) found that 16.5 percent of the Buddhist practitioners in his randomly generated sample were of Jewish backgrounds. Similarly, sociologist Wendy Cadge (2005) discovered that nearly a third of those she interviewed at the Cambridge Insight Meditation Center as part of her comparative ethnographic study of Theravada Buddhist organizations in the United States were of Jewish background. Through his research for his best-selling book *The Jew in the Lotus*, Rodger Kamenetz (1994) estimated that Jews represented about 30 percent of Western Buddhist groups in the United States.[1] While scholars do not have precise statistics about the number of Jews involved in Buddhist communities in the United States, it seems safe to assert that the proportion of Jews in Buddhist circles is disproportionate to the percentage of Jews in this country (Jews constitute about 2 to 3 percent of the population).

These numbers, and their insinuation that Judaism and Buddhism have a distinctive relationship in the United States, motivated this study. I wanted to know why Buddhism appeals to Sheldon and others like him and was curious how Sheldon arrived at the cave at the top of that mountain at all. I also wanted to know if the encounter between Judaism and Buddhism emerged out of the countercultural ethos of the 1960s, as popularly assumed, or if there were earlier antecedent encounters that required unearthing. This book wrestles with these questions by telling the story of how Judaism and Buddhism met and combined in the United States since the late nineteenth century, and how people incorporate these traditions in their daily lives today.

The distinctive relationship between Judaism and Buddhism has been part of public consciousness in the United States since Kamenetz published *The Jew in the Lotus* in 1994. His book chronicled the meeting between eight Jewish delegates—a group of progressive rabbis and scholars from across various wings of American Jewish life—and the Dalai Lama in Dharamsala, India. The book is now on its thirty-seventh reprint and even inspired a PBS documentary of the same name featured in film festivals around the world. It also popularized the term "JUBU"—a moniker for a Jewish Buddhist—for a wide audience (Van Gelder 1999; Chiten 1999; Kamenetz 1994, 1999).

Since the publishing of *The Jew in the Lotus*, countless popular articles, memoirs, books, and blog posts have cast attention on the special relationship between Judaism and Buddhism. Television stations, including PBS and ABC, have produced special programs about the Jewish-Buddhist relationship. Dozens of celebrities, including Goldie Hawn, Leonard Cohen, Steven Seagal, and Mandy Patinkin, have publicly extolled their Jewish Buddhist identities in print and on television. US newspapers—from broad publications like the *LA Times* to niche outlets like the *Jewish Daily Forward* or *Tricycle: The Buddhist Review*—have published articles about such topics as "JuBus—Embracing Judaism and

Buddhism," "Zen and the Art of the BuJu," and "At One with Dual Devotion."[2] Recently, *Tablet Magazine* even ran an article about the Jewish roots of mindfulness meditation in the United States, explaining how a group of four American Jews—Sharon Salzberg, Joseph Goldstein, Jack Kornfield, and Jacqueline Mandell-Schwartz—popularized mindfulness meditation in the United States, and how, in the words of journalist Michelle Goldberg (2015), they "turned a Buddhist spiritual practice into a distinctly American phenomenon—and a multi-billion-dollar industry."

Scholars, too, have expressed a curiosity about the Jewish-Buddhist relationship. In *The Transformation of American Religion*, religious studies scholar Amanda Porterfield (2001, 158) noted that Jews "took the lead" in the development of American forms of Buddhism, observing that "one of the most interesting aspects of Buddhism's merger with American religious and intellectual life is its disproportionate appeal to people with Jewish backgrounds." Similarly, in his book *Buddhism in America*, Richard Seager (2012, 225) pointed out the "important role played by Jewish Buddhists in the introduction and adaptation of the Buddha's teachings in America." And in the new volume *Buddhism beyond Borders: New Perspectives on Buddhism in the United States*, scholar Mira Niculescu (2015) writes about the rise of Jewish mindfulness as an offspring of Western Buddhism in the United States.[3]

Despite this popular and scholarly notice, we know comparatively little about the relationship between Judaism and Buddhism in the United States. We do not know how Jewish Buddhists experience and narrate their multireligious identities; based on these identities, how they have built institutions, new practices, and staked claims in their communities; and what broad social and historical factors explain how these two traditions came together over centuries to produce these identities in the first place. These are the questions at the heart of this book.

Threaded through the book is an argument that the distinctive social position of American Jews, or what I call the "Jewish social location," led American Jews to their engagement with Buddhism and fundamentally shaped the character of it. The Jewish social location is the set of orientations produced by the position of Jewish Americans as a distinctively left-liberal, urban, secular, and upper-middle-class religious minority in the United States. Jews occupy a distinctive place in contemporary US society in terms of residential patterns, class, education, occupation, and religious beliefs. More than any other religious or ethnic group in the United States, Jews live in and near the largest American cities, exceed all other groups in socioeconomic status, and surpass all other groups in educational attainment. In addition, Jews consistently fall at the bottom of measures of traditional religious beliefs. Compared to all other ethnic and religious groups (except "religious nones"), they are the least likely to be sure that God exists, to believe that there is an afterlife, and to say that the Bible is the exact word of God. A deep-seated appreciation of this particular sense of Jewish social distinctiveness rests at the heart of the stories in this book.[4] The American Jews in this book also relate deeply to the experience of being a religious minority living in a largely Christian society. The Jewish social location—itself a particular combination of a distinctive demographic, religious, and minority position—propelled Jews into their encounter with Buddhism and shaped the historical mark they left on it. Moreover, it defined the pathways through which Buddhism entered into American Judaism, and to this day, continues to structure how people interpret and knit together ideas from both traditions in framing their identities, creating religious practices, and building organizations.

Why Was Sheldon on the Mountain? An Overview of Past Arguments

Puzzled by the distinctive relationship between Judaism and Buddhism, scholars have offered explanations for the affinity between the two traditions and specifically for why Buddhism appeals to American Jews. Many of these arguments are based on some element of interview data combined with anecdotal evidence.[5] Broadly speaking, past explanations for the Jewish attraction to Buddhism fall into four categories: historical, religious/theological, demographic, and "pull" explanations.

The historical explanations include a number of different arguments, the most common of which is the claim that Judaism and Buddhism have a shared focus on suffering. Jewish people, the reasoning goes, dwell especially on the idea of suffering because the Holocaust forced them to grapple with the massive suffering endured by so many. Buddhism provides Jewish people with answers (and ways of coping) with that suffering (see Porterfield 2001; Linzer 1996; Rosenberg 2003; Sautter 2002; Brodey 1997). In another explanation, Coleman (2001) claims that since Jews traditionally played the part of outsiders in a US culture dominated by Christianity, they have been more willing to embrace ideas that mainstream society sees as deviant or foreign. He also suggests that Jews are more interested in new religious movements because Judaism has been more greatly eroded than Christianity by the processes of secularization. Other scholars contend that Jewish seekers were drawn to Buddhism because Buddhists had no history of prejudice toward Jews (see Linzer 1996; Rosenberg 2003).

The religious/theological explanations for the affinity between Buddhism and Judaism are many. Porterfield (2001) suggests that the intellectual training and study of religious texts serves as a bridge to connect Judaism and elite forms of Buddhism. Another argument claims that the Jewish conception of God proves an ideal fit with the nontheistic aspects of Buddhist philosophy (see Porterfield 2001; Linzer 1996; Weinberg 1994; Sautter 2002; Brodey 1997). Finally, other scholars contend that Buddhism does not make theological demands on its members, thereby making it accessible; Jews are frustrated with the emphasis on Jewish particularism or chosenness (see Porterfield 2001; Kamenetz 1994; Seidman 1998; Brodey 1997; Libin 2010), and the stress that many Buddhist teachers place on universal truth resonates with disaffected Jews; and the similarities between the mystical and meditative traditions of Buddhism and Judaism attract Jews to Buddhism (see Kamenetz 1994; Libin 2010; Linzer 1996).

Third, the demographic argument claims that Jews are overrepresented in the segments of society to which Buddhism appeals most strongly: the highly educated upper middle class, intellectuals, artists, and bohemians (see Coleman 2001; Rosenberg 2003). And finally, scholars base the fourth argument for why Jews are drawn to Buddhism on "pull factors," or the characteristics of Buddhism that pull in American Jews. Scholars reason that Jews are attracted to Buddhism because it is a body-based practice that lends itself to direct experience (see Porterfield 2001; Linzer 1996; Weinberg 1994; Sautter 2002; Brodey 1997; Kamenetz 1994; Libin 2010). Sheila Weinberg (1994), a reconstructionist rabbi, argues that Buddhist spiritual practices have been consciously and systematically tailored for the Western mind and vocabulary, making them appealing to American Jews (a discussion dealt with in more depth in later chapters in this book). Other scholars suggest that Jews are attracted to meditation because it allows them a means to "slow down and live" in a time of electronic media as well as a sense of collective breathlessness (see Green 2003), and they are attracted to the Buddhist approach to the elimination of war, poverty, racism, prejudice, environmental pollution, intemperance, and drug abuse (see Brodey 1997).

The many assertions presented above demonstrate the range of ways that scholars have thought about the appeal of Buddhism to Jews.[6] While all these assertions may touch on certain truths, they provide only partial explanations. For example, many Jews undoubtedly feel uncomfortable with the idea of God, but so do many other Americans, so why do Jews seem to look to Buddhism as a haven for their skepticism? Similarly, some American Buddhist traditions may well provide body-based experiential practice, but so do other traditions, so why do Jews seem to gravitate to Buddhism over other traditions? None of these past studies offers the sufficient empirical data that would allow scholars to evaluate their claims. In this book, I draw on over three years of ethnographic research—archival research, interviews, and participant observation—in order to discern how people understand their relationships to both Judaism and Buddhism, and why Buddhism appeals to many American Jews. I examine the various explanations for the affinity between the two traditions at various points throughout the chapters to come and tie them together in the conclusion. I repudiate any claim of an intrinsic affinity between these traditions; to understand how these two traditions came together, I argue that we need to understand instead the historical and social webs that connect them.

Toward a Sociological Perspective
on Religious Syncretism

At its most general, this is a book about religious syncretism in the United States, the history that produced it, and the way that individuals experience it in daily life.[7] Historically, the term "syncretism" has served as the conceptual bedrock across academic disciplines for the study of inter-religious mixing. Syncretism has a complex history and etymology, with its meaning dependent on the historical and political context in which it has been used.[8] Syncretism developed a pejorative connotation from its use within seventeenth-century theological debates about the degree to which illegitimate forms of religious mixture supposedly contaminated church doctrine. It implied an infiltration of foreign religious elements seen as belonging to other, incompatible traditions into a "pure" religious tradition (Stewart and Shaw 1994; Leopold and Jensen 2004). Thereafter the term continued to be polemically used within the comparative study of religions. This history has led many contemporary scholars of religion to feel that the term has been too tarnished to remain usable.[9]

Scholars have reclaimed the term syncretism over the past thirty or so years as it relates to themes central to postcolonial analysis, including creolization, hybridity, and interstitiality (Leopold and Jensen 2004; McIntosh 2009; Robbins 2011).[10] Anthropologists, in particular, invoke the term syncretism not to focus on the contrast between pure culture(s) and mixed ones, or the disorder caused by cultural mixing. Rather, they use the term to analyze the conditions, especially in the context of post-colonialism, in which cultures emerge, as Homi Bhabha (1994, 38) describes, "at the cutting edge of translation and negotiation, the in-between space." Scholars draw on the term to underscore the fluidity and heterogeneity in cultural and religious life, and deconstruct the broader cultural processes, discourses, and power relations surrounding religious mixing (McIntosh 2009).

Drawing on the concept of syncretism does not, however, overlook its charged history. Rather, as anthropologists Charles Stewart and Rosalind Shaw (1994, 2) note, "embracing a term which has acquired—in some quarters—pejorative meanings can lead to a more challenging critique of the assumptions on which those meanings are based than can its mere avoidance." In agreement with Stewart and Shaw, I specifically embrace the framework of syncretism to analyze the meeting and mixing of Judaism and Buddhism in the United States. Syncretism remains the concept central to the interdisciplinary study of religious mixing and raises broader questions about issues of boundaries and power, befitting an examination of the transformative encounter between these traditions. In this study, I broadly define syncretism as the mixing of various elements (including practices, beliefs, identities, communities, etc.) associated with different religious traditions.[11]

The use of syncretism as an analytic framework helps also to move sociologists of religion beyond the various metaphors—salad bar religion, religion à la carte, or bricolage—often used to explain religious mixing in the United States. These metaphors connote the idea that individuals pick and choose among religious options in highly individualistic and idiosyncratic ways and that the processes of religious mixing are steeped in arbitrary choice and random ordering.[12] This has led scholars to dismiss religious mixing as trifling and/or ephemeral, even as recent survey data have demonstrated the prevalence of religious mixing in the United States.[13] The framework of syncretism, as currently used in the literature, invites an analysis of the cultural and structural processes that shape religious mixing.

I also draw on the framework of syncretism to call attention to not only the presence but also the significance of religious mixing in the United States. The majority of the current work on syncretism emerges out of postcolonial contexts in the developing world, where religious blending holds harsh political or economic consequences. This has led syncretism to appear as a problem endemic to "traditional societies" in developing countries (see van der Veer 1994); it has created the impression among social scientists that religious mixing is not an important facet of religion in the West, even though historians of American religion have long underscored the significance of religious contact and exchange in the United States.[14] Examining religious syncretism in the United States throws into relief the salience of fluidity and heterogeneity in American religion, particularly in the current era of "new religious pluralism."[15] In doing so, it challenges the dominant paradigm within sociology that suggests that religions adapt and change in this country by assimilating into the majority and taking on the characteristics and organizational forms of liberal Protestantism.[16] The central contribution of this book is to demonstrate that minority religious traditions in the United States *also* reconfigure themselves by borrowing and integrating elements from each other through a process shaped by their specific social locations in society. They do not just adapt to the majority, I show, but also to each other.

Boundaries, Power, and Authority

Studying the Jewish-Buddhist encounter in the United States raises the issue of boundaries, and where to draw the line around who is (and is not) a Jew and who is (and is not) a Buddhist. Scholars of both Jewish and Buddhist studies have perennially wrestled with these definitions, without any agreed-on answers. Jewish studies scholars have long recognized that being Jewish is not only a matter of religion—the traditional, matrilineal definition of Jewish identity founded on halacha (Jewish religious law)—but also a matter of ancestry, ethnicity and cultural background. In this study, I consider anyone a "Jew" who identifies as such, even if they are also an ordained Buddhist priest who maintains little to no Jewish observance. In doing so, I depart from the convention in Jewish studies not to include as Jews those who have adopted another religious tradition. I examine the spectrum of Jewish and Buddhist engagements and identities, highlighting the involvement of both observant and "cultural" Jews in American Buddhist life, from the position of prominent Buddhist communal leaders (e.g., ordained monks, lamas, and roshis) to the position of casual meditators with little to no involvement in the Buddhist community.

By deliberately drawing attention to a broad range of Jewish engagements and identities, I seek to enlarge the historical analysis of American Jewry by adopting a "dispersionist" approach to American Jewish history (Hollinger 2009).[17] This dispersionist approach includes within its scope the lives of all American Jews regardless of their involvement with Jewish communal life and irrespective of their declared Jewishness.

American Jewish history has focused overwhelmingly on the stories and work of communal Jewry, organizations and institutions that the public identify as Jewish, and activities of individuals who proclaim themselves Jewish and/or are so identified by non-Jews. In the chapters to follow, I include the stories of those Jews who identify proudly and publicly as Jewish and those who see their Jewishness as seemingly irrelevant in their lives. In doing so, this book broadens the analytic scope of American Jewish history to include stories of those who have little to no involvement in communal life. It stakes a claim that upbringing and inheritance are impossible to entirely cast off, and the social locations of our past give shape to the religious possibilities of our future.

Buddhist studies scholars have similarly debated who counts as a Buddhist in the United States and how to categorize the various different Buddhist groups in this country.[18] Over the past several decades, scholars have offered various typologies using different criteria to categorize groups. Typically, they divide American Buddhists into two or three categories that distinguish between convert Buddhists, or those whose ancestry is not Asian and whose religious heritage is not Buddhist (most "converts" have European American ancestry), and "heritage" or "ethnic" Buddhists, or those who are typically immigrants and refugees from Asian Buddhist cultures, and their descendants. Although these categories help somewhat to clarify the differences among the various Buddhist groups in this country, they often reify artificial boundaries and fail to capture the diversity of Buddhism in the United States. They also rarely map onto people's self-identifications and frequently reflect and reproduce unconscious white privilege and power.[19]

The respondents in the chapters to follow largely think about themselves as "American Buddhists"—and in turn, I consider them as such—even while recognizing that "American Buddhism" is not a singular entity. These respondents do not view Buddhism as their inherited historic or ethnoreligious tradition, and few feel any connection to Buddhism as it is practiced and institutionalized in Asia. Rather, these Jewish Buddhists identify with a Buddhism that was constituted in and adapted to the United States—a process I describe in the chapters to follow. When I characterize Jewish Buddhists as a collective, I refer to them as convert Buddhists—a label I recognize as imperfect for all the reasons mentioned above but also necessary for the descriptive purpose of labeling those born in the United States who were not raised Buddhist, yet later came to identify or affiliate with Buddhism in some way.[20]

Related to the issue of boundaries is the issue of power, and who has the authority to exercise it over what counts as true, authentic religion (be it Judaism or Buddhism) and the decision-making power to decide what counts as allowable religious mixing. The issue of power is particularly important to the history of Buddhism in the United States, where the middle and upper-middle classes (including American Jews) have appropriated and recontextualized the tradition—and arguably exploited as well as fragmented it too—in order to commodify it and place it at the service of their needs. At different times and in different contexts, the exchange and mixing of Jewish and Buddhist forms will be shrouded in conflict, inherently unequal relations of power, and even the subjugation of ideologies and beliefs of Asian culture. When these issues of power and dominance surface, I call them out, and explain their context and ramifications. Broadly speaking, however, the encounter between Judaism and Buddhism largely occurred in a context defined by the inevitable transformations that arise when religions collide and remake themselves in response to each other and, unlike the early relationship between Buddhism and Christianity, was not mired in violence, missionization, or colonial oppression.[21]

Lastly, in narrowing in on these inevitable transformations, one of the final contributions of this book is to both excavate and illuminate the role that American Jews played in the project of Buddhist modernism. As Buddhist studies scholar David McMahan (2008, 6) has demonstrated, this project—a complex set of historical processes—sought to bring Buddhism into engagement with the dominant cultural and intellectual forces of modernity. In Europe and the United States, Buddhist modernizers have inserted the tradition into preexisting discourses and debates, interpreted it in terms of modern Western categories, and transformed it to accommodate to and/or resist European colonialism. These Buddhist modernists refashioned Buddhism in order to enhance its prestige and viability in an emerging global context (McMahan 2008, 70).

Throughout the chapters in this book, I discuss how American Jews, from Charles T. Strauss (1852–1937) in the nineteenth century to Joseph Goldstein (1944–) a century later, sought to reinterpret Buddhism to make it compatible with the norms and expectations of US society.

The Study

My arguments unfold across seven chapters, divided into two sections. They emerge from over three years of ethnographic fieldwork and historical research that I conducted about the relationship between Judaism and Buddhism in the United States. This research included over eighty interviews with Jewish practitioners of Buddhism, both teachers and lay practitioners, as well as archival work and extensive participant observation that I conducted in various Jewish and Buddhist meditation centers in New England, New York, and California.[22]

The first section of the book (chapters 1–4, organized chronologically) provides the history of the Jewish-Buddhist encounter in the United States, describing the broad social and political forces that brought Jews into contact with Buddhism, and then later Buddhism into contact with Judaism in the United States. Each chapter in this first section focuses on a specific time period from 1875 to today, demonstrating the various encounters between Buddhism and Judaism, and how American Jews have participated in the project of Buddhist modernism. This first section is an examination of the broad historical processes that sowed the seeds for contemporary forms of religious syncretism to occur. The second section of the book (chapters 5–7, organized thematically) moves from history to ethnography, and looks at how the encounter between Judaism and Buddhism led to the creation of new syncretic practices, spiritual discourses, and identities, respectively.

The first chapter opens at the World's Parliament of Religions in 1893 in Chicago, where Strauss—a wealthy haberdasher of Jewish descent—became the first person to convert to Buddhism on US soil. I tell Strauss's story—and his work to modernize and transform Buddhism—while also laying out the spectrum of ways in which American Jews encountered and engaged with Buddhism in the late nineteenth century from about 1875 to 1924. Chapter 2 describes the second period of Jewish-Buddhist involvement in the United States that began in the 1920s. In this period, the intellectual engagement between Judaism and Buddhism persisted, but it became augmented by a growing appearance of solo American Jews—largely from wealthy and prominent families—who received training by Asian teachers and pursued Buddhist practices in Asian-founded Buddhist groups. The chapter illustrates these developments through the stories of three prominent Jewish Buddhist modernizers: Julius Goldwater, Samuel Lewis, and William Segal.

The third chapter describes the period of intensive Jewish-Buddhist engagement that occurred within the American Left, from about 1966 to 1990. This chapter traces the trajectories that led many Jews in the second half of the twentieth century to Zen, insight meditation, and Tibetan traditions—three communities in which Jews have emerged as prominent teachers and leaders.[23] I argue that through their prominent positions as Buddhist teachers, Jewish Americans participated in the modernization of Buddhism in the second half of the twentieth century by elevating the practice of meditation, instilling within it an activist ethic, and increasing its psychotherapeutic orientation.

The fourth chapter describes the final period of Jewish-Buddhist activity in the United States, from about 1991 to the present. This chapter focuses on the involvement of American Jews, like Jon Kabat Zinn, in the promotion and popularization of a secular, psychotherapeutic Buddhism beginning in the early 1990s. It then discusses the important role that the Nathan Cummings Foundation played in creating new Jewish-Buddhist dialogues and systematically incorporating Buddhist ideas and practices into American Judaism.

In part II of the book (chapters 5–7), I move from the history of the Jewish-Buddhist encounter to an analysis of the syncretism of Jewish Buddhist practices, discourses, and identities. The fifth chapter explores the development and contours of the syncretism of religious practice, asking how the practice of meditation spread from Buddhism into Judaism and how it was reconfigured along the way. I show how meditation moved from Buddhism into Judaism through a process by which a prominent group of Jewish teachers and leaders de-emphasized its explicitly

Buddhist roots and repackaged it within a Jewish framework, thereby rendering it familiar and compelling, yet different and exotic to the American Jewish mainstream.

The sixth chapter probes the syncretism of spiritual discourse, asking how one group of Jewish Buddhists—those that I call the "spiritually enriched"—assign spiritual meaning to their Buddhist practices, and how that spiritual meaning in turn is charged with particular religious and political investments. This group of Jewish Buddhists maintains an active and practicing relationship to Judaism. They imagine Buddhism as an important means to enhance their sense of spirituality *and* complement their Judaism. I highlight four central frames of spirituality that emerged from my conversations with these respondents. Finally, the last chapter explores the syncretism of religious identities, investigating how Jewish Buddhists understand and narrate their relationships to both traditions. It draws on an analysis of thirty-two interviews with Jewish-born "Buddhist converts," or those who have turned their hearts and minds toward the teachings and practices of the Buddha and maintain a cultural identification with Judaism. I explain how respondents emphasize that they view their Jewish identities as ascribed and cultural and their Buddhist identities as achieved and enacted. I then describe four approaches that these Jewish Buddhists take to integrating their two identities into one syncretic Jewish Buddhist identity.

Finally, I conclude this book by discussing the broad threads that have carried through the history of the encounter in the United States between Judaism and Buddhism. I offer various speculations about *why* so many American Jews are attracted to Buddhism and provide a typology of three types of Jewish Buddhists in the United States. I also revisit the question of boundaries, power, and authority. The preeminent theologian Harvey Cox (1973, 121) once wrote that "few faiths ever escape modification when they collide or interact with others. Most profit from such encounters." My goal in these chapters is not to make an argument about who does and does not benefit from the encounter between Judaism and Buddhism but rather to describe how both traditions—and their people, organizations, discourses, and practices—were transformed as a result of their meeting.

PART I

Four Periods of Jewish-Buddhist Engagement

CHAPTER ONE

Breaking down the Barriers

ON SEPTEMBER 26, 1893, in the aftermath of the World's Parliament of Religions in Chicago, Charles T. Strauss became the first person ever to be initiated into Buddhism on US soil. Strauss traveled from his home in New York City to the Windy City to attend the parliament, a seventeen-day affair organized around the idea of bringing Eastern and Western religious traditions into contact with each other.[1] A serious student of Buddhism and "ardent admirer of the Buddha," he attended the parliament to learn more about Buddhism and hear teachings directly from the mouths of the parliament's various Buddhist representatives.[2]

A few days after the parliament concluded, Anagarika Dharmapala (1864–1933), a prominent Ceylonese Buddhist invited to the parliament to represent "Southern Buddhism," lectured about the topic in Chicago's Athenaeum Building under the auspices of the Chicago Theosophical Society.[3] Dharmapala, widely regarded as a charismatic speaker, drew a large audience and spoke at length about the fundamental principles of Buddhism. After his lecture, he introduced Strauss, a man of forty-one, to the audience as an earnest student of Buddhism. Strauss walked purposively up to the platform and, in front of the crowded room, gave a brief address declaring his intention to become a disciple of the Buddha. In a ceremony that newspapers characterized as "simple yet impressive," he took on the Five Precepts of Morality—vows to abstain from harming living beings, stealing, sexual misconduct, lying, and intoxication—as part of a lay Buddhist initiation rite called *Pansil*.[4] Dharmapala recited the precepts in Pali, and Strauss repeated after him. To those who witnessed the event, the recitation of these precepts made Strauss the first convert Buddhist in the United States.[5]

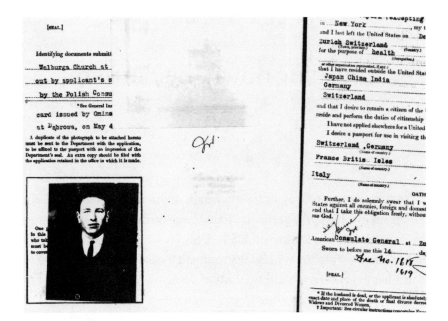

FIGURE 1.1. Passport photo of Charles T. Strauss. National Archives and
Records Administration, Washington, DC.

Strauss's passport indicates that he was born in Saint Gall, Switzerland,
in 1852. At age eighteen, he emigrated to the United States and worked,
along with his brother, in his father's lace goods business (see figure 1.1).
After his father died, Strauss and his brother inherited the business, and
carried it on under the firm name of Charles T. Strauss and Bro. At age
twenty-five, Strauss married Katie Agatz, a Jewish woman who had been
living in Hoboken, New Jersey. They had three children together before
Katie died young. At the time of Strauss's initiation to Buddhism, he was
a widower of four years with young children and a lace business that was
one of the oldest as well as largest wholesale lace curtain houses in New
York City.[6]

Though Strauss's initiation ceremony only lasted a few minutes, it created a stir in both Jewish and non-Jewish circles. In a note to one of the
leading US Jewish newspapers, the *American Israelite*, one reader con-
fessed, "Having traveled all over the world including the entire Orient,
this incident whereby one of our co-religionists became a Buddhist was

certainly novel and perplexing." He added, "I do not believe that such a ceremony has ever before taken place, and in order to have it recorded I will ask you if space admits to insert this letter in your paper" (*American Israelite* 1893b)." Other newspapers heralded the event as monumental; the *Galveston Daily News* (1893) described Strauss as the "first American to break down the barriers that have stood for centuries between Buddhism and the people of the west [*sic*]."

———

Strauss's turn to Buddhism marked the first time in history when converting to Buddhism became a serious religious possibility for Jews in the United States.[7] His conversion to Buddhism is the nineteenth century's most noted example of Jewish involvement in Buddhism, yet it is also indicative of a wider turn in that era toward Jewish interest in the tradition. As accounts from popular late nineteenth-century Jewish newspapers make plain, Buddhism captured the interest of many Jews just as it had of many Americans more generally.[8]

In this chapter, I lay out the spectrum of ways in which American Jews encountered and engaged with Buddhism in the late nineteenth century through to the end of the first quarter of the twentieth century (from about 1875 to 1923).[9] I begin with Strauss as an example of an early Buddhist adherent and modernizer, or someone who identified himself with the Buddhist tradition and sought to adapt it to the forces of modernity. Then I explain the other end of the Jewish Buddhist spectrum, which included a seemingly broad swath of American Jews who "sympathized" with Buddhism. Ultimately, I argue that the social position of liberal Jewish Americans like Strauss—financially successful, urban, and well established in the US social order—propelled them into their encounter with Buddhism in the late nineteenth century.[10]

Strauss: A Buddhist Modernizer

Before taking the stage at the World's Parliament of Religions, Strauss was said to have been a private man who read constantly and deeply about religious as well as philosophical matters. He had been briefly involved in the Ethical Culture Society, which was designed to replace theology with morality and ethical living (*Atlanta Constitution* 1893). Strauss never embraced Judaism as his religious tradition, explaining his relationship to Judaism and turn away from it in this way:

> The report that I was converted cannot be true, for the reason that I never was known as a [religious] Jew. Although my parents were Jews, I was brought up in a liberal way, and I do not believe that I have been in a synagogue more than half a dozen times in my life. In fact I am only a Jew in spirit when I hear that Jews are oppressed, and I try to defend them. (*New-York Tribune* 1893)

What Strauss meant by not being known as a Jew was that he did not abjure the Jewish faith in taking the Buddhist precepts because he never practiced Judaism as a religious way of life. In the United States, different than in Europe, religious affiliation was not passed down from generation to generation as an ascribed identity; instead, it was a conscious, voluntary choice. The voluntary character of Judaism in the United States allowed Strauss to claim that he was "only a Jew in spirit," whereas in Europe he would have been seen as unconditionally Jewish.

Strauss's emphasis on being brought up in a "liberal way" evokes the progressive and enlightened spirit of Reform Judaism, a movement to which many others in his social world—the commercial and professional urban elites of central European Jewish descent—belonged. The movement for religious reform emerged in the nineteenth century in central and western Europe, flourishing especially in Germany, after profound social changes transformed the external condition of European Jews and their understanding of themselves. The movement emphasized that Judaism, if properly interpreted, had a rational and universalistic character that was compatible with scientific discoveries as well as the premises of the European Enlightenment. It celebrated the pursuit of social justice, and rebelled against long-established modes of Jewish ritual observance and rabbinical authority. Transplanted to the United States, the Reform movement won large-scale adherence in the United States, where the government did not intervene in the religious affairs of its citizens like it did in Europe (Meyer 1995, 3–62, 225–64). Despite his disaffection from Judaism as a religious way of life, Strauss would nevertheless have been influenced by the liberal ethos of Reform Judaism—its stress on individualism, rationalism, and universalism—that circulated in the air around him.

Where Strauss first encountered Buddhism remains an open question, but it seems likely that his initial exposure came through books. By the late nineteenth century, a number of books about Buddhism circulated through the United States, particularly among the ranks of the educated elite.[11] Additionally, debates about Buddhism and Buddhist ethics reverberated within liberal and freethinking milieus in the United States and Europe, including among Unitarian and Universalist congregations, Theosophists, Spiritualists, New Thought groups, and various vegetarian and antialcoholic movements. These liberal circles praised Buddhism as the rational religion of modern times and found within it an imagined otherness that resonated with messages of tolerance, universal brotherhood, and justice.[12]

Although casual interest in Buddhism was popular in Strauss's liberal religious circles, he was decidedly not a Buddhist dilettante. Dharmapala's diaries made evident that Strauss was a serious student of Buddhism. Dharmapala wrote fondly of Strauss, calling him his close friend and "dedicated learner" of Buddhism.[13] Strauss studied Pali, the language of sacred Theravadan Buddhist texts, and was a donor and subscriber to the Pali Text Society.[14] After Strauss took on the Five Precepts of Morality, he went on to establish the New York branch of the Maha Bodhi Society, an international Buddhist organization dedicated to reviving Buddhism in Asia. Strauss lived in New York City until he left in 1906 to travel to India, China, and Japan.[15]

Strauss's story continued well beyond the United States, though. In 1908, he moved his permanent residence to Leipzig, Germany, which at the time was the center of the European trade market. He played a formative role in the establishment of the Buddhist community in Leipzig, the first Buddhist community in all of Europe. As a wealthy man, Strauss was able to travel to Sri Lanka (then Ceylon) several times, and established relations between the Buddhist community in Europe (Leipzig) and the Maha Bodhi Society.[16] Strauss fled Germany in 1916, just prior to the United States' entry into World War I, and lived out his final years in Zurich, Switzerland.

In 1923 in Zurich, Strauss authored a book, *The Buddha and His Doctrine*, that revealed his commitments to the principles of rationalism and religious liberalism, and emphasis on Buddhism's compatibility with these modern ideals.[17] In this book, Strauss strove to portray Buddhism as a progressive American religious tradition that was ethical, tolerant, and compatible with science and reason. Strauss (1923, 25) was especially attracted to Theravada Buddhism, referring to its writings as "original genuine Buddhism," echoing late nineteenth-century Orientalist notions that Theravada was the purest form of Buddhism, closest to the Buddha, while all other traditions had been adulterated by their cultural milieus. He imagined his book to be a treatise on Buddhism with the goal of providing a "short, popular description of the Buddha's life and doctrine," and admitted to writing the book to "refute some errors and prejudices which still exist very generally with regard to Buddhism" (v). In particular, he defended Buddhism against the disparaging nineteenth-century characterization of it as atheistic, nihilistic, and pessimistic. In response, he portrayed Buddhism as optimistic, fueled by activism, and scientifically oriented.

Strauss dedicated an entire chapter of his book to discussing Buddhist ethics and how they harmonized with the pursuit of social justice—a central principle of late nineteenth-century religious liberalism. He asserted that "the part of Buddhism which exercises the greatest attraction on those who begin to study it is its sublime ethics." Adding explanation, he continued, "Without postulating a God it gives prescriptions which suffice for all relations in life and which aim only at the welfare of all beings, not only of men, but also of animals and even plants." Strauss highlighted the teachings of the Buddha that emphasized the importance of compassion, self-restraint, good deeds, and frugality. These ethics, Strauss (1923, 73) claimed, made Buddhism a "living force which could be of use in solving many problems which trouble us in our social and political affairs." They also rendered Buddhism a religious tradition compatible with the liberal commitments of social betterment and improvement.

Defending Buddhism as an empirically oriented tradition, Strauss responded in his book to conflicts between religion and science that intensified around the turn of the twentieth century. He maintained that the Buddha "stood firmly on the foundation of reality" and "always insisted that things ought to be looked at as they really are." "Therefore," Strauss (1923, 44) concluded, "there never could arise in Buddhism a contradiction between religion and science, as in all other religions." Buddhism, in his estimation, was the only rational means of attaining religious truth.[18]

Strauss also demonstrated his commitment to portraying Buddhism as an empirical, rational tradition in his forceful criticism of esoteric Buddhism. He writes that it is "totally wrong to attribute to Buddhism any secret doctrines and label them 'Esoteric Buddhism,' as has been done in the presentation of some modern so-called religions . . . as, for example, Theosophy" (Strauss 1923, 104). He rejects unscientific and superstitious religious doctrines, upholding that "genuine Buddhism is the reverse of mystical, rejects miracles, and is founded on reality" (105). This reality, he writes, is comprised of the "facts of the world through natural laws and not through extra- and super-mundane interventions by a God or mystical forces" (106).

Like other religious liberals of his time, Strauss was individualistic in his understanding of authority, scorning creed and highlighting the value of self-reliance. He emphasized that he chose to take on the Buddhist precepts because he "freely indorsed [sic] the philosophy of the Buddha," feeling that it was the "best that had been given."[19] Explaining his religious choice, Strauss (1923, 115) noted,

> Buddhism teaches perfect goodness and wisdom without a personal God, the highest knowledge without a revelation, a moral world order and just retribution carried out with necessity by reason of the laws of nature and of our own being, continued existence without an immortal soul, the possibility of redemption without a vicarious redeemer, a salvation in which everyone is his own savior and which can be attained in this life and on this earth by the exercise of our own faculties without prayers, sacrifices, penances, and ceremonies,

without ordained priests, without the mediation of saints, and without divine grace.

Strauss was contemptuous of revelatory theology, arguing that Buddhism (particularly vis-à-vis Christianity) was tolerant and self-reliant, not needing an intermediary in order to obtain wisdom and salvation. Buddhism, in Strauss's interpretation, underscored the autonomy of the individual and a vision of emancipated souls.

Despite valorizing Buddhism as the doctrine that "satisfies both heart and mind," Strauss (1923, 116) admitted certain limits to his devotion to the tradition. He struggled, for example, to reconcile the ideas of rebirth and multiple deities, especially with modern science. Strauss also admitted that the mechanics of rebirth are not "easily grasped by us who have been brought up on entirely different ideas." That was not a problem, however, for he insisted that "one must accept in Buddhism only what one understands, and not adopt its teachings in blind faith" (72). Believing in rebirth, he ultimately concluded, was not necessary in order to live according to Buddhism's ethical precepts.

The multitude of deities in Buddhism posed another challenge to Strauss's rational worldview. Arguing that the deities served only as figureheads, Strauss legitimized their presence by desacralizing their role in Buddhism. The purpose of the many gods in Buddhist ethical stories, Strauss (1923, 50–51) claimed, was merely "to enhance the Buddha's good qualities and wisdom in comparison to them." Strauss contended that the teachings of the Buddha were corrupted by Asian cultural accretions, so he studied original Pali texts in order to liberate the truth of Buddha's teachings from their cultural appropriations (v–vi). His investigations led him to contend that "the [Buddhist] system of gods are entirely superfluous, therefore all prayers and sacrifices, in a word, all reliance on efficacy of religious rites and ceremonies is not only useless but a hindrance to spiritual advancement, as it awakens hopes which will not be fulfilled, takes up much valuable time, and diverts the mind from the right road" (53–54). Buddhist rituals, folk beliefs, and image worship as well as the cosmology of rebirth pushed the limits of his devotion. He remained unconvinced by and even critical of the aspects of Buddhism that did not harmonize with his rational, liberal worldview.

Strauss's de-emphasizing of Buddhist metaphysics, folk beliefs, and image worship—and stressing instead Buddhism's ethical and scientific nature—places him among the ranks of the earliest Buddhist modernizers in the United States. The Buddhist modernist movement began in the late nineteenth century and spanned geographic areas and schools of tradition, seeking to revive Buddhism by integrating it with the dominant cultural and intellectual discourses of Western modernity through a process that David McMahan (2008) describes as demythologization, detraditionalization, and psychologization. This movement sought to reinterpret Buddhism as a rational way of thought that was compatible with modern notions of reason, individualism, science, and tolerance. It underscored the importance of Pali texts, meditation, egalitarianism, and increased participation by laity, and minimized dogma that resonated with the discourses of modernity. At the same time, it minimized clerical hierarchy, traditional mythology and cosmology, gods, and icon worship that were inconsonant with modern science and liberal democratic values. Strauss's efforts to transform—even reinvent—Buddhism by emphasizing its compatibility with Western notions of science, activism, democracy, and individualism carried forward the perspectives of his teacher, Dharmapala, one of the central figures in the nineteenth-century Buddhist modernist movement.

Although Strauss never acknowledged his underlying impulse for refashioning Buddhism, presumably his modernizing efforts were motivated by the same deep resentment that Dharmapala held against the colonial rule of Ceylon and its suppression of Buddhism. Dharmapala sought to legitimate Buddhism not only in the eyes of its Western skeptics but also those of the colonized and downtrodden in Ceylon (McMahan 2008, 95). European colonization and Protestant missionization led to a loss of economic and political power among Buddhists in Ceylon, and Dharmapala fought back by promoting a Western representation of Buddhism that adapted it to the norms of a Western cultural context. Both Strauss and Dharmapala's alignment of Buddhism with rationalism and science are examples of what Richard Seager (1995, 96), following James E. Ketelaar (1991), calls "strategic occidentalism": "the selective and often highly politicized appropriation of western ideas, techniques, and critiques for use in undermining the claims of the West, asserting Asian independence, and negotiating roles in the emerging global society." Thus, Strauss's efforts to modernize Buddhism simultaneously resisted and accommodated the forces of the colonization and missionization of Buddhism in Asia.

Strauss's influence on the movement for Buddhist modernism is difficult to gauge. His book went through multiple printings in both English and German (seven editions in English and three in German), indicating that it sold well and likely made an impression on a wide readership. Additionally, his active participation in the Maha Bodhi Society and significant advocacy work on behalf of Buddhism in the United States, Europe, and Asia suggest that his efforts to reinterpret and recontextualize Buddhism likely had a consequential, transnational influence.

Finally, Strauss's public conversion to Buddhism—his taking on Buddhist vows and representing Buddhism as a series of beliefs—could also be interpreted as an act of Buddhist modernism, or at least as the consequence of the Western assumption that adherence and conversion to a religion was properly defined in terms of belief. Strauss's conversion ceremony—itself an invention of the West—reflected the perspective that the teachings of the Buddha could be distilled into a philosophical system rooted in the primacy of belief(s) rid of any extraneous cultural trappings accumulated over time and geographic spread. The ceremony was an early demonstration of how Buddhism adapted to—and was adapted for—the American religious context. In this sense, Strauss was not only the first convert to Buddhism in the United States but also one of the first to convert to Buddhism at all.[20]

Jewish Conversations about Buddhism: The Spectrum of Sympathizers

Strauss was the late nineteenth century's most famous example of a Buddhist adherent. He also seems to be the first and perhaps only case of a nineteenth-century Jewish person professing Buddhism as their faith. It is difficult to determine the religious identities of other Jews who were interested in Buddhism but did not publicly take on the Buddhist precepts. Yet it seems that the majority of American Jews who were interested in Buddhism could be classified as "sympathizers," or those who felt a certain attraction to Buddhism from reading about it in books or attending lectures on the topic, but did not embrace or profess it as their tradition (Tweed 2000, 42–77). Perhaps the most prominent late nineteenth-century Buddhist sympathizer was Felix Adler, the son of the prominent Reform rabbi Samuel Adler and founder of the secular Ethical Culture Society, with which Strauss had briefly been involved.

Born in Alzey, Germany, in 1851, Adler moved as a young boy to New York City, where his father assumed the distinguished pulpit of Temple Emanu-El, one of the leading Jewish Reform congregations in the country. Raised with considerable privilege, Adler attended Columbia Grammar School and then Columbia University before returning overseas for graduate study, intending to follow in his father's footsteps and pursue a career in the rabbinate. He first studied at the Hochschule für die Wissenschaft des Judentums in Berlin and then at Heidelberg University, where he received his PhD in 1873. While in Germany, he developed a serious interest in neo-Kantian philosophy, engaged in a broad study of comparative religions, and read deeply in the teachings of the Buddha (Kraut 1979).

After his return from Europe, the Jewish community in New York City assumed that Adler would succeed his father at Temple Emanu-El. Instead, he delivered a sermon at his father's synagogue preaching that the Judaism of the future would exist as a universal religion based on good works rather than creed. He could not accept a theistic God concept or the notion that the Jewish people were chosen by God to remain separate for the sake of a priestly mission (Meyer 1995, 264–96). The radically liberal views that Adler espoused in that sermon put an end to his future career as a rabbi. Adler (1905a, 1–2) believed that "spirituality is not indissolubly associated with any one type of religion or philosophy," and religions should do away with their trappings of ritual and creed, and unite through social action and good deeds. Rather than pursuing the rabbinate, he accepted a professorship at Cornell University, where he taught Hebrew and Oriental literature from 1874 to 1876 before going on to found the Ethical Culture Society in 1876.

As a man deeply committed to religious liberalism and rationalism, Adler—like Strauss—was attracted to the teachings of the Buddha. Adler (1876, 689) praised the Buddha, claiming that he should be counted "in the number of those whom the heart of humanity cherishes as its most loving if they be not its wisest benefactors." He gave frequent lectures on the life and teachings of the Buddha, in which he described Buddhism as a "system of ethics founded on sympathy, help of others, care for the sick, tolerance toward all men and their beliefs, and avoidance of cruelty, even to animals" (Werner 1877). Adler (1876, 687; 1905a, 79–81; 1905b, 176) seasoned his lectures and writings with Buddhist parables, and believed that the Buddhist ethical system was "productive of widely beneficial results." His views of Buddhism, like Strauss's, were another representative example of the late nineteenth-century rationalist-type approach to Buddhism.

Although the Buddha's ethical system appealed to his moral sensibilities, Adler found himself unable to accept Buddhist metaphysics in full measure as Strauss had. He was, for instance, deeply troubled by Buddhist explanations for suffering and the afterlife and concluded that the strength of Buddhism certainly did not lie in its "transcendental elements." He criticized the Buddha for borrowing the "supernatural doctrines of the Brahmans," which "opened the way for all that proved injurious to the future growth of his ideas." He repudiated the "pernicious effects" of nirvana, which led to "utter extinction," and neutralized "the active principle that inspires and invigorates Buddhist ethics." Adler (1876, 687) also found fault in what he saw as Buddhism's being "passive and indifferent to the concerns of the present." For Adler, a man who dedicated his life to the pursuit of social justice, he found the ethical teachings of the Buddha compelling, but the worldly indifference he saw in Buddhism presented an insurmountable barrier to greater sympathy for the Buddhist tradition.[21]

Newspaper accounts from the late nineteenth century demonstrated a broader Jewish interest in or sympathy for the rational and scientific nature of Buddhism. The *American Hebrew* published an article titled

"Eastern Religion: A Science," in which the writer, Jesse Linnell Greenbaum, argued that within Buddhism, as within other Eastern religions,
people "will find a wide field prolific of much religio-scientific truth." In
this article, Greenbaum (1890) presented karma as the notion of "ethical
causation," or the collective expression applied to a complicated group
of affinities for good and evil generated during life.[22] He couched karma,
rebirth, and other Buddhist concepts in scientific language, trying to harmonize them with the spirit of the late nineteenth century. Greenbaum
admitted that the tenets of Buddhism "will differ from the doctrines of
most creeds," and cautioned that only the "intelligent" and "intuitive" in
society will understand the true nature of Buddha's teachings.

Other newspaper articles published about Buddhism in Jewish newspapers conveyed a different romanticized Jewish interest in Buddhism.
In a review of Edwin Arnold's *Light of Asia* in the newspaper the *Jewish
Messenger* (1879a), the writer described the book as "an exquisite Buddhist Song of Songs," wherein "India, and the wealthy and magnificence
of Eastern life, the breath of its flowers, the rippling of its waters, and
music of its birds, and beauty of its maidens, find their harmonious expression." Similarly, the *Jewish Exponent* (1889) published an article about
the life of Buddha that waxed poetic about his sweeping influence. The
article romanticized,

> When Nebuchadnezzar broke down the walls of Jerusalem, destroyed
> the Temple and leveled the Holy City to the ground; when Israel de-
> spairingly exclaimed, Our hope is lost, we are quite cut off! . . . there
> arose on the horizon in the far distant land of India a new light des-
> tined to shine for ages for at least one-quarter of mankind—a light
> beneficent, kindly, like the beauteous radiance of the moon Siddhar-
> tha Gautama, holy Buddha was its name.[23]

Similarly, New York's widely read *American Hebrew* proclaimed that Buddhism had "awakened considerable interest among intelligent people,"
and "some deem it an unequivocal sign of culture to quote texts from the
Chinese and Indian scriptures" (Greenbaum 1890). An editorial note in
the *Jewish Criterion* (1896) was especially articulate about the rise of this
romantic interest in Buddhism. It observed that "one is thought

uneducated and behind the times who has not at his command a few utterances culled from the religious books of Buddha." The explanation for this Jewish interest in Buddhism, the editor concluded, is that "fashion has set the pace, the desire for novelty has sanctioned it, and the taste for the oriental has encouraged the dipping into the fountains of Eastern culture."

The rational and romantic interpretations of Buddhism presented in Jewish newspapers overwhelming extolled it, either as a religion for the sophisticated and intellectual members of society, or one of beauty. Not all late nineteenth-century Jewish periodicals praised Buddhism, however; various articles in fact proved voluble about their disdain for the faith. After Strauss took on the Buddhist precepts at the World's Parliament of Religions, the editor of the *American Israelite* sternly rebuked Buddhism as a chosen religious path for Jews.[24] He wrote,

> The novelty of the affair does not, in my estimation, consist in a Jew turning Buddhist as much as in the publicity surrounding this especial case. A good many people have a taste for making spectacles of themselves and Mr. Strauss seems to belong to that class. . . . Considering that Mr. Strauss has been such a profound student of old and new religious systems he has acted somewhat hastily. . . . [I]t is rather strange that he did not pause long enough to investigate the different aspects of Judaism. Had he done so I am sure he would have found what he was seeking, for between the extremes of ultra-Orthodoxy and agnosticism to be found in our synagogs [*sic*] and temples almost every soul in quest of anchorage can find a harbor. (Blumberg 2012, 63)

The editor readily dismissed Strauss's turn to Buddhism, suggesting that Strauss was merely looking to make a spectacle of himself. Although many individual Jews may have taken an armchair interest in Buddhism in the late nineteenth century, the editor's response demonstrates that other Jews, like other Americans more generally, did not view Buddhism as a real religious option in the United States.[25] The defensiveness that courses through the editor's response, particularly in his claim that Judaism offered ample religious possibilities for all Jews, seems to reflect a larger concern among American Jewish leaders at that time that their congregants and constituents were increasingly open to exploring other religious alternatives.[26]

Other letters to and editorials from American Jewish periodicals were more forthright in their criticisms of Buddhism and Strauss's adoption of it. In the *Jewish South* (1893), one of the few publications concerning Jews in the South in the late nineteenth century, Strauss's adoption became a lightning rod for controversy. In a letter to the editor, a reader asked how an enlightened Jew like Strauss could profess Buddhism. The newspaper responded with two charges. First, it railed against Buddhism, portraying it as an unsuitable religion for enlightened Jews and denouncing it as "the religion of negation," which taught "that the greatest boon that could be bestowed would be not to have been born . . . and the most desirable thing is annihilation." Second, it asserted that a Jew like Strauss could embrace Buddhism only for the "purpose of notoriety." In New York, the news of Strauss's "conversion" bewildered the Jewish community.[27] The *Chicago Daily Tribune* (1893) reported that Strauss's family was "astonished as well as indignant over Mr. Strauss' abjuration of the faith of his fathers, and they cannot understand his move toward the effete religious mysticism of the East."

Various Jewish newspapers leveled specific allegations about what they perceived as Buddhism's pessimistic, nihilistic, and idolatrous nature. A journalist for the popular *American Israelite* (1893a), in a summary of a speech about Buddhism given at the Jews' College Literary Society (presumably in London), characterized Buddhism as "atheistic pessimism," which "has proved a curse and not a blessing in all lands where it has taken root." The writer disparaged Buddhism as "a mass of incomprehensible metaphysics and mysteries akin to gross idolatry, and controlled by a powerful priesthood, and presided over by the Grand Lama in Thibet [sic]." Another article in the *American Israelite* condemned Buddhism for emasculating human nature by training men to be "patient slaves that suffer meekly like sheep while being preyed upon by wolves." The article described Buddhism as "the most consistent and gloomiest pessimism known to the student of thought" because it is based on the belief that "life is not worth living, that it is a pernicious illusion which mocks us with its vain joys and torments us with its innumerable evils" (Moses

1898). These acerbic condemnations of Buddhism, which existed incongruously alongside accounts acclaiming Buddhism's grandeur, mirrored popular American criticisms of Buddhism as pessimistic and passive (Tweed 2000, 133–56). They also demonstrated that the Jewish affection for Buddhism in the nineteenth century was far from universal; many Jews harbored a disdain for the tradition.

Other condemnations of Buddhism in Jewish newspapers reverberated with racist and xenophobic overtones. They revealed a larger Jewish concern about Chinese immigration, which as one Jewish reader warned in a letter to the editor, would bring about "swarms of Chinese invaders" as well as "usher in a mongrel and Mongolian era in American civilization" (*Jewish Messenger* 1879b). Beginning in the mid-nineteenth century, the Chinese—and later the Japanese—came to be seen as the chief racial threat on the West Coast, where Asians were the primary targets of nativist and racist groups. Anti-Asian sentiment in the United States culminated in the Johnson-Reed Act of 1924, which severely restricted the annual number of immigrants who would be accepted into the country and outright banned the immigration of Asians. Many Jews viewed these Asian groups as threatening to the white and Judeo-Christian complexion of US society.[28] And for those Jews who did not necessarily view Asians as a direct threat, the strength of anti-Asian sentiment discouraged them from identifying with or publicly promoting Asian culture or religions.[29]

The scope of the actual Jewish interest and involvement in Buddhism in the nineteenth century is difficult to gauge. Display ads in Jewish newspapers and advertisements about lectures given to Jewish audiences suggest a popular Jewish interest in Buddhism, which seemed to exist alongside the fearful or racist feelings that other nineteenth-century Jews harbored about Buddhism or Asians more generally. Various display ads promoted to their Jewish readership a number of "new releases" about Buddhism, including Paul Carus's *The Gospel of Buddha*, published in 1894, and *Karma: A Story of Early Buddhism*, also published in 1894 (*American Hebrew* 1896, 1897). Across the country, prominent Buddhist teachers also lectured about Buddhism to Jewish audiences. Professor T. W. Rhys-Davids of London, a renowned British scholar of

Buddhism, lectured at New York City's Reform citadel, Temple Emanu-El, on the subject "The Life and Teachings of the Buddha" (*American Hebrew* 1895). Liberal Jewish groups across the country invited Dharmapala to come and speak before their Jewish constituents, who hoped to learn about Buddhism directly from the mouths of Asian teachers. Dharmapala's diaries revealed that he spoke to Jewish clubs across the country during his US lecture tours.[30]

Rabbis also used their pulpits to lecture about Buddhism, introducing this new tradition to their congregations. The *Baltimore City News* reported that Rabbi Israel Joseph of Wilkes-Barre, Pennsylvania, preached at the Radical Reform Har Sinai Temple on "Buddhism, the Catholicism of the East" (*Jewish Exponent* 1893). In Cleveland, Rabbi Aaron Hahn gave a lecture on the topic of "Buddha" at Tifereth Israel's Huron Street Temple. The newspaper account of this Huron Street lecture—in a testament to the popularity of the topic—reported that the event was "largely attended" and "well delivered and proved very interesting to the throng of people that were present" (*American Israelite* 1886).[31] Other clergy spoke about Buddhism to Jewish groups as well. In Chicago, for example, Reverend J. L. Jones, a Unitarian minister with sympathies for Buddhism, spoke on "Buddha" to the Council of Jewish Women, and a Miss Hannah Schiff "read a paper on the same subject" (*Jewish Messenger* 1895).[32]

Although these lectures demonstrate a Jewish interest in Buddhism, the number of Jews turning to Buddhism was not great enough to elicit a response or reprobation from Jewish religious leaders—something that would have been expected if conversion to Buddhism had posed any threat to Jewish numbers. In her assessment of Jewish involvement in Christian Science, Ellen Umansky (2005, 23) estimated that the number of Jews involved in Christian Science at the turn of the century lay between four thousand and forty thousand.[33] This degree of Jewish involvement in Christian Science created a sizable stir in Jewish circles. Jewish newspapers of the time were replete with stories about Jewish defections to Christian Science, the threat it posed to Judaism, and arguments about the incompatibility of the two religions. Buddhism evoked no such large-scale communal response in nineteenth-century Jewish circles.

Principally it existed as a topic of fascination for many Jews who were looking to the East for ethical guidance, rational scientific truth, or romantic inspiration.[34]

What Explains Jewish Interest in Buddhism during This Time?

A combination of factors—related to the character of Buddhism, Judaism, and US life in the nineteenth century—produced and shaped the Jewish interest in Buddhism. First and most generally, a lively public conversation about Buddhism intensified in the United States between 1893 and 1907, as Buddhism became increasingly attractive to a broad swath of Americans who read about Buddhism in books and attended lectures on Buddhist topics (Tweed 2000). For the first time, Asian Buddhist teachers, like Dharmapala and Soen Shaku, visited the United States and spoke to predominantly white audiences of European descent. Many of these teachers presented Buddhism as tolerant, scientific, and ethical, heightening its appeal to the religiously liberal like Strauss. The World's Parliament of Religions, where Strauss took the stage in 1893, also brought increased attention to Buddhism and marked a watershed event between the East and West.[35] In short, the late nineteenth century saw Buddhism emerge as a new and alluring liberal religious movement in the United States, paving the way for new adherents and sympathizers to emerge.

Second, social circumstances specific to the late nineteenth-century American Jewish community also helped spur the Jewish interest in Buddhism. Between 1825 and 1875, nearly 250,000 Jewish immigrants arrived in the United States—the vast majority of them from German-speaking lands (Meyer 1986, 61). These central European Jews, like Strauss and his family, had established themselves in the United States by the late 1870s, largely in or around the largest urban centers of the time, and many had become commercially and financially successful. Well-established Jewish Americans sought to gain respect in this country, and adopted lifestyles and interests similar to their Protestant neighbors. During the late nineteenth century, Protestant highbrow culture included a romanticized appreciation of Asian culture—its art, drama, language, and even religion

(Tweed 2000). Sharing these cultural tastes, well-to-do Jewish Americans were attracted to Buddhism's exotic and distant aspects too, and they had the time, education, and means to pursue this interest (Tweed 2000). As the editorial note in the *Jewish Criterion* (1896) brought into relief, people were thought "uneducated and behind the times" in the nineteenth century if they did not have at their command a few utterances from the Buddha.

If well-established Jewish Americans were similar to their Protestant neighbors in their social tastes, they were different from them in terms of their religious activities and affiliations. The third factor that influenced the Jewish interest in Buddhism relates to the progressive and liberal ethos of Reform Judaism, a movement to which many nineteenth-century central European Jews belonged. As mentioned above, nineteenth-century Reform Judaism, like the liberal Protestantism of the time, saw itself as a rational and progressive faith compatible with the premises of the European Enlightenment. In addition to instructing their congregants on Judaism, Reform rabbis lectured on Darwinism, biblical criticism, and the latest scientific discoveries. Social justice and Jewish ethics emerged as the movement's major concerns, and the common liturgy of the movement emphasized broader universalistic and liberal values. The movement stressed the individual autonomy of rabbinical authority and a desire to restore Judaism to its classical form, stripping it of ceremony, ritual, and obligatory observance of Jewish law.[36] The ethos of Reform Jewish liberalism complemented that of the Buddhist modernist movement occurring at the same time, bridging what Jewish Americans might otherwise have perceived as incompatibilities between the two traditions.

Looming large in the late nineteenth century, and coursing through both Reform Judaism and the Buddhist modernist movement, the diffuse spirit of American religious liberalism also fostered a Jewish interest in Buddhism. Nineteenth-century religious liberalism emphasized a turn away from religions beset by authority and institutional oversight and toward new religions directed by the individual spirit (Schmidt 2005, 1–25). A variety of new liberal religions peppered the American landscape in the late nineteenth century—Spiritualists, Swedenborgianists, the

New Thought movement, Theosophists, Ethical Culture, and others. These liberal religions placed a cultural priority on individual religious experience, silence and solitude, an ethical pursuit of justice, and creative self-expression, all the while stressing religious ecumenism, pluralism, and universality.[37] The Jewish interest in Buddhism, when interpreted in the light of nineteenth-century religious liberalism, epitomized the spirit of the times.

Conclusion

This chapter explains the spectrum of ways in which American Jews— notably the financial and commercial elites of central European Jewish descent—encountered and engaged with Buddhism from about 1875 to 1923. On one end of the spectrum, Strauss exemplified a Buddhist adherent and modernizer, a person who professed an allegiance to the Buddhist tradition and sought to adapt it to the norms of a Western cultural context (Tweed 2000, 48–77). At the other end of the spectrum, a broad, if not well-defined, number of American Jews "sympathized" with Buddhism. These Jewish sympathizers felt an attraction to Buddhism but did not embrace or profess it as their tradition.

The particular social position of central European Jews in the late nineteenth century—financially successful, religiously liberal, and urban— propelled them into an encounter with Buddhism at that time. Like other Americans of their social class, Jewish Americans read about Buddhism in books and attended lectures on Buddhist topics. Some Jewish Americans, like Strauss, were attracted to the rational and intellectual aspects of Buddhism, viewing it an ethical system or rational means of attaining religious truth. Other Jewish Americans, influenced by the highbrow culture of the times, were attracted to Buddhism as part of a romanticized appreciation of Asian culture more generally. Both the rational and romantic admirers of Buddhism had the time, education, and means to pursue their interest in the tradition.

American Jews, however, seemed resistant to the esoteric or occult forms of Buddhism that attracted other nineteenth-century Americans. The esoteric or occult-type Buddhists consisted of those who emphasized the hidden sources of religious truth and meaning in Buddhism and believed deeply in a spiritual or nonmaterial realm populated by nonhuman or suprahuman realities. Often these esoterics were spiritually eclectic, blending Buddhism in particular with Theosophy and Spiritualism. The esoteric Buddhists were more likely to be found in rural areas, were less socially and economically prosperous, and had less formal education (Tweed 2000, 51). I found no evidence of an esoteric interest in Buddhism among late nineteenth-century Jewish Americans. I suspect this had to do with the fact that American Jews were not well represented in the social demographic from which most esoteric Buddhists were drawn.

The nineteenth-century encounter between Judaism and Buddhism casts light on how American Jews like Strauss participated in the selective appropriation and recontextualization of Buddhism, prefiguring a central theme in the twentieth-century Jewish-Buddhist encounter. The results of purging Buddhism of its traditional elements, and reconciling the tradition with the expectations and discourses of Western liberalism, led to profound changes in how Buddhism has been understood and represented in the United States (and the West more generally). Most significantly, this recontextualization has led to a distancing of Buddhism from Asian cultural systems and ethnic identities, effectively "whitening" Buddhism in order to reconcile it with the dominant cultural forces of the West.[38]

The Jewish interest in Buddhism in United States was temporarily halted by World War I, which disrupted most seeker-type religious activities. Beginning in the 1920s, however, the engagement between Judaism and Buddhism persisted as well as changed.[39]

CHAPTER TWO

Buddhist Paths to Self-Discovery in the Early Twentieth Century

THE LATE nineteenth century saw Buddhism emerge as a new and alluring liberal religious movement in the United States, but that Buddhist vogue waned in the second quarter of the twentieth century. Antipathy toward Asians—particularly the Japanese—gripped the United States in the decades leading up to World War II, which lessened, if not diminished, the popular Jewish interest in Buddhism. On the West Coast in particular, the strength of anti-Asian sentiment and desire for social acceptance discouraged Jews from identifying with or publicly promoting Asian culture or religions (Eisenberg 2008). While Jewish newspapers from the late nineteenth century were replete with articles romanticizing Buddhism and reports of Buddhist teachers speaking in synagogues packed with attendees, by the mid-1920s, few newspaper articles painted Buddhism in a positive light, or discussed any broad romantic or popular Jewish interest in Buddhism.[1]

Replacing the armchair Jewish interest in Buddhism of the previous century was the appearance of solo American Jews—mostly from wealthy and prominent families—who received training by Asian teachers and pursued Buddhist practices in Asian-founded Buddhist groups. These early Jewish Buddhists were spiritual seekers who explored many paths to self-discovery, and sought meaning in life beyond material or financial success. They followed in the footsteps of other Westerners, mainly Protestants. Yet unlike these Christian Buddhists, the Jewish Buddhists did not bring to Buddhism a Jewish vocabulary, set of theological assumptions, or interpretative framework.[2] These early Jewish Buddhists had little, if any, Jewish education during their childhood and none emerged from households immersed in Jewish observance, doctrine, or scriptural study. Rather than assimilating Buddhism into Jewish categories, these Jewish Buddhists understood Buddhism through a lens shaped by their social position, political context, and liberal sensibilities. These Jewish Buddhists all proffered modernized versions of Buddhism that sought to reconcile it with three of the central liberal religious perspectives of their time: universalism, perennialism, and romanticism.[3] This chapter illustrates these developments through the stories of three American Jews—Julius Goldwater, Samuel Lewis, and William Segal—who found their way to Zen Buddhism in the first half of the twentieth century.

From Prominent Political Family to Jodo Shinshu Leader in Hawaii (1908–31)

Goldwater (1908–2001) was born in Los Angeles to one of the most prominent Jewish families in the US West. Goldwater's paternal family arrived in California in the mid-1800s, just after the gold rush of 1849 that brought many Jews to the state for the first time (Clar 2002; Goldberg 1995). Shortly thereafter, the discovery of gold in Arizona in the 1860s lured his grandfather and great-uncles to the Arizona territory, where they set up small business enterprises around the sites of new mines. These small trading and mercantile businesses grew in size and influence, eventually becoming Goldwater's department stores, founded by Julius's great-uncle Michael Goldwater. These stores remained in family hands until 1962, when they were sold to Associated Dry Goods Corp. of New York (Barnes 1998).[4]

Before immigrating to the United States, Julius's grandfather and his family lived in Konin, a Jewish shtetl in Russian Poland. The son of Jewish innkeepers Elizabeth and Hirsch Goldwasser, he—like his brothers before him—left Poland, fleeing the revolution of 1848 and onerous restrictions placed on Jews by the Russian czars. Once in the United States, the Goldwassers anglicized their name to Goldwater. In addition to their success as merchants, the Goldwater family achieved political prominence in the United States. Most famously, Julius's second cousin, Barry Goldwater, who was born in 1909, just a year after Julius, served five terms as a US senator from Arizona (1953–65, 1969–87) and was the Republican Party's nominee for US president in the 1964 election.

On his maternal side, Goldwater's family emigrated from Germany. His mother, Ray Etta (possibly Rayette) Goldwater (nee Michaels), intended to raise him an observant Jew following her family tradition.[5] She tragically died when he was only two and a half. His father, Benjamin Goldwater, enrolled him in Jewish Sunday school for a few years, but Julius reported in an interview that "it didn't take" (Prothero 1997, 45). During his early years living with his father in Los Angeles, Goldwater took an ardent interest in mysticism and Eastern religious philosophies. He was particularly close to and influenced by Manly P. Hall, a charismatic writer, philosopher, and preacher who took over leadership of the Christian Church of the People in Los Angeles in 1923 (Prothero 1997; Kashima 1977). A world traveler and prolific author, Hall served as a figurehead for the Los Angeles subculture comprised of mystics, artists, faith healers, and spiritual visionaries (Sahagun 2008). He brought Goldwater under his wing, mentoring him, inviting him to services at his church, and granting him access to his extensive library about parapsychology, mysticism, and Eastern religions (Prothero 1997).

In his late teens, Goldwater left Hall's mystical world to follow his father to Hawaii, where he first encountered Buddhism (Kashima 1977; Prothero 1997). The dominant tradition of Buddhism in Hawaii in the 1920s when Goldwater arrived was Shin Buddhism, also known as Jodo Shinshu (True Pure Land), practiced by the island's Japanese American population. These Japanese immigrants had come to Hawaii to replace the Chinese laborers who were banned entry by the Chinese Exclusion Act of 1882 (Unno 2001). These first-generation Japanese immigrants (called issei) mostly worked on plantations but, like the Chinese before them, faced significant legal discrimination (Williams 2002, 192). They were forbidden from certain occupations, subject to miscegenation laws, and not eligible to become naturalized citizens (Unno 2001; Hill 2013). By 1924, the total population of Japanese in Hawaii had reached over a hundred thousand people (Ama 2011, 32).

Recognizing a need for Buddhist ministers to serve the issei, the Jodo Shinshu leadership in Japan sent Buddhist missionaries to Hawaii in 1889. For protection and mutual aid on the island, the missionaries and issei established a network of new Shin Buddhist temples, which served as community centers as well as places of worship. By the mid-1920s, there were more than 170 Buddhist temples in Hawaii (Hill 2013).[6] Up until the 1920s, the services that these missionaries conducted in these new temples were in Japanese, catering to the issei. Few, if any, Americans of non-Japanese descent attended these Japanese-language services. In an effort to adapt Buddhism to its new environment and minister to the English-speaking, second-generation Japanese Buddhists, Honolulu's Hompa Hongwanju Temple began to offer services and study classes in English, thus opening the door for non-Japanese participation in the temple (Ama 2011; Prothero 1997; Kashima 1977).

Goldwater attended one of these English-language Buddhist study classes as a teenager in 1924 at the recommendation of a friend.[7] At this study class, Goldwater met Reverend Ernest Hunt, a British-born teacher of Buddhism. As Goldwater later remembered,

> I didn't understand a thing and he [Hunt] spoke in perfect English, and I heard every word he said. I couldn't cognate his usage of words but it was very exciting, you know, and there were just a few people, about eight of us gathered, and of course I was the only kid. And gradually . . . I became more and more seduced. (Kashima 1977, 99)

The seduction that Goldwater described stemmed from Hunt's (1955) moral lessons about love, charity, kindness, respect, and service, all drawn from the teaching of the dharma, or the Buddha's teachings. Hunt emphasized that Buddhism and true Americanism shared a common purpose, both advocating for absolute religious freedom and equal opportunity for all people, irrespective of race, color, or creed (Ama 2011, 56). He also championed the creation of a broad, ecumenical Buddhist movement focused on active goodwill.

Captivated by Hunt's teachings, Goldwater committed himself to Buddhist study and became one of Hunt's prized students. In Honolulu in 1928, Goldwater, along with eight others in his study group, took the

Buddhist vows of *Pansil* in front of Bishop Yemyo Imamura and Hunt to "become publicly the first group of Occidentals to become Buddhist under the American flag" (Ama 2011, 99).[8] As to why Goldwater took these Buddhist vows (in a ceremony called *tokudo*), he later noted, "I began to realize that the doctrine, as well as the way of life of my English teacher, conformed exactly with my ideas of how a true gentleman should conduct himself." He continued, "The vital thing that is furnished by Buddhism, and lacking in other religions, is genuineness." Even after the initiation ceremony, Goldwater—like Strauss before him—did not envision himself a Buddhist convert but rather felt that becoming Buddhist was a process; "a true believer is determined by the way he lives" instead of the lines he recites or ceremonies in which he participates (*China Press* 1937).

Three years after the initiation ceremony, Goldwater married Pearl Wicker, a Lutheran, in a Jodo Shinshu ceremony in Hawaii. Both Imamura and Hunt officiated at the wedding (Prothero 1997, 45). Shortly thereafter, at the urging of his wife, Goldwater returned to Los Angeles to teach and minister at the Nishi Hongwanji Los Angeles Buddhist Temple affiliated with the Buddhist Mission of North America (the early Jodo Shinshu governing body in North America). The temple's Japanese elders feared that their US-born children were rejecting Buddhism as inconsonant with the American way of life and recruited Goldwater, one of the few white Buddhists in the tradition, to demonstrate to them that they could be both American and Buddhist (*Los Angeles Times* 1934).[9] Goldwater's return to Los Angeles marked his period of service to and leadership in the Buddhist community.

A Wartime Ally and Buddhist Minister in Los Angeles (1931–2001)

At Nishi Hongwanji in Los Angeles, Goldwater taught Buddhist doctrine to and interpreted Buddhist scripture for second-generation Japanese immigrants and Americans of European ancestry. He delivered sermons about the dharma in English and held study classes for English-speaking people. He also officiated at funerals and weddings, and fought to allow the Japanese children to participate in American youth dances that the issei did not find culturally acceptable (Ama 2011; Kashima 1977; Seager 2012, 100). As part of his mission to disseminate Buddhism, he introduced and translated the *Tannisho*, the best-known text in Shin Buddhism, to European Americans (Ama 2011). Goldwater's work extended beyond the temple as well. He visited Japanese American agricultural settlements on the West Coast, conducting outreach work that he saw as akin to "preaching the gospel" (Prothero 1997, 46).

In the 1930s and early 1940s, Goldwater received three different Buddhist ordinations. Although he had been ordained (tokudo) in Honolulu in 1928, he accepted ordination a second time in 1934 from Bishop Kenju Masuyama in Los Angeles at the Nishi Hongwanji temple. This ordination gave him formal recognition as a Buddhist "missionary" and American minister. Masuyama, the head of the Buddhist Mission of North America, was strict about whom he would ordain. He would only consider ordaining students if he supervised their practice and study for one year and found them satisfactory—a test that Goldwater passed (Ama 2011).

Goldwater thus became the first European American to be ordained as a Buddhist priest or minister in Los Angeles. The novelty of the ordination attracted the attention of the *Los Angeles Times* (1934). In an article titled "Buddhists Ordain American," the newspaper described Goldwater's ceremony in considerable, even flowery, detail, noting that, for example, "Buddha sat cross-legged . . . and with immutable gaze saw a fair-haired American don the robes of priesthood in one of the earth's oldest religions." The article reported on the scene of the ceremony as well as the nature of the vows and chants that Goldwater performed.

A few years later, Goldwater traveled to Kyoto, Japan, to take ordination in a *tonsure* ceremony like other Japanese priests. This ordination came at the urging of the leading Japanese priests in Los Angeles who wanted him to have the authority of an Asian Buddhist ceremony in order to better serve as a role model and leader to the Japanese youths back in Los Angeles. In an interview, Goldwater later explained that "I couldn't have been less interested in the priesthood . . . but their [the Los Angeles Japanese community's] need was so great" (Prothero

1997). Goldwater also took a third ordination in 1937 in Hang Chow, China.[10]

Goldwater rose to a position of increased significance in the Buddhist Mission of North America after the Japanese bombed Pearl Harbor in 1941. President Franklin Delano Roosevelt issued Executive Order 9066 in response to this bombing, removing Japanese Americans from their homes and incarcerating them in internment camps. Following this internment order, nearly all the Japanese American Buddhists from Goldwater's Los Angeles temple were sent to camps. Goldwater became the sole resident minister and volunteer caretaker at the temple during this time. He was also given power of attorney and full control over three other Los Angeles temples (Kashima 1977, 101).

Concerned about the plight of his fellow Buddhists, Goldwater became their wartime advocate in the Los Angeles area. He encouraged Japanese Americans to store their belongings and possessions in the temple so that he could safeguard them during the incarceration era. He traveled to every internment camp, including centers in Wyoming and Arizona, distributing coffee, candy, and Buddhist service materials, comprised of devotional and liturgical books and shrines (Tweed and Prothero 1999, 172–77; Prothero 1997, 47). He also watched over internees' homes, even preventing the illegal sale of one home by alerting the Federal Bureau of Investigation. Advocating for Buddhism during the war meant that he sparred with the police and federal authorities too in order to convince them that Buddhism was autonomous and separate from the Japanese government (*Los Angeles Times* 1934).

During the war, Goldwater raised funds for the Buddhist community by leasing the temple to black war workers at the Providence Baptist Church. When the Japanese internees were released at the end of World War II, Goldwater contentiously ousted the black church to turn the temple into a hostel where Japanese Americans could find temporary housing as well as assistance in obtaining a job, driver's license, and gas rations. Goldwater loaned his car to his fellow Buddhists, and when anti-Japanese grocers refused to sell them food, he would buy it for them (Kashima 1977, 102; *Los Angeles Times* 1934).

As he aged, Goldwater continued to support and raise funds for the Buddhist community in Los Angeles, particularly after the passage of the Immigration and Nationality Act of 1965. This new legislation opened the door to a new wave of Asian immigrants to the United States from Korea, Vietnam, Cambodia, Thailand, Sri Lanka, Laos, and other countries in Asia. Goldwater provided these Asian Buddhists financial support and aided the community in its establishment of new temples in Los Angeles (*Los Angeles Times* 1934). In one of his final enduring initiatives, he established the Buddhist Sangha Council in 1980, drawing together diverse representatives of the greater Los Angeles' growing Buddhist community in the pursuit of promoting more unity among Buddhists and Buddhism (Woo 2001).

A Buddhist Universalist

In terms of his approach to Buddhism, Goldwater crafted and advocated for a deeply modernized and nonsectarian version of the tradition that minimized differences among the branches or schools of Buddhism and emphasized its ecumenical character. Following in the footsteps of his teacher, Hunt, Goldwater endeavored to rid Buddhism in the United States of its sectarian roots—specifically the three broad schools of Theravada, Mahayana, and Vajrayana that have historically structured Buddhist thought and practice—in order to promote a broader and more inclusive Buddhism that he felt would appeal to Americans (Kashima 1977, 56). Goldwater saw the teachings of the Buddha as transcending their specific local contexts and cultural accretions. His personal practice grew increasingly eclectic as he aged, incorporating elements from Indian, Chinese, and Japanese Buddhism into a broader and more porous version of the tradition (Prothero 1997).

One prominent example of Goldwater's commitment to Buddhist universalism was his establishment of the Buddhist Brotherhood of America during the incarceration era. The brotherhood was a nonsectarian Buddhist organization dedicated to printing and distributing ecumenical Buddhist books and worship materials to the incarcerated Japanese

Americans. In a statement about the organization, Goldwater explained, "In this endeavor there can be no thought of discrimination in sect, race, or color; the teachings must be paramount, combining the best of both Hinayana [i.e., Theravada] and Mahayana School, and in doing so, reaching that equilibrium so necessary for completeness and growth" (Kashima 1977, 55). In addition to seeking a common ground among different Buddhist lineages, Goldwater used the Buddhist Brotherhood of America to transform Buddhism by adapting to Protestant categories, norms, and vocabularies. Aware of the pervasive anti-Japanese sentiment in the United States during the war, he strove to reconfigure Buddhism in order to make it seem more legitimate and less threatening to wartime America. He created and disseminated Buddhist worship materials in English that resembled Christian creeds and hymns in form as well as structure (Prothero 1997; Tweed and Prothero 1999). Goldwater had considerable knowledge about Christianity from his time in Hawaii, a territory that had experienced tremendous Christian missionary activity since the 1820s, and from Hunt, who was born Anglican and had a Christian upbringing, and who also endeavored to bring Buddhism more in line with the norms of American Protestantism.

Among the books that Goldwater created for and distributed at the internment camps was *A Book Containing an Order of Ceremonies for Use by Buddhists*, which contained two catechisms, responsive readings, numerous hymns, a liturgy for Buddha's birthday, and even a history of Buddhism in which Jodo Shinshu founder Shinran is likened to Martin Luther (Tweed and Prothero 1999, 172). In 1944, when the United States rallied around unity and nationalism in the final throes of the war, Goldwater urged the Buddhist Mission of North America to change its name to the Buddhist Churches of America in an attempt to better assimilate into and become accepted by Protestant America. Goldwater's efforts to Americanize and Protestantize Buddhism met with resistance from some of the temple elders after the war. These Japanese-born Buddhists disapproved of Goldwater's assimilationist agenda and even sued him for the mismanagement of temple funds during the war.[11]

Goldwater, like Strauss before him, shaped Buddhism into the mold of his own thought, dispensing with the vestiges of the tradition that he found incompatible with the norms and expectations of US society. He worked to erase sectarian differences essential to the constitution of Buddhism in Asia and forged an ecumenism within the tradition that rendered it more broadly accessible to Americans. In responding to the charged political climate that surrounded Buddhism during World War II, Goldwater recontextualized Buddhism by adapting it to Protestant categories and vocabularies. His efforts to Protestantize Buddhism could be seen as acts of both resistance and accommodation to a racist wartime nation. He refashioned Buddhism to resist the violence against the Japanese Americans during the war, but he did so by adopting (and accommodating to) the categories and conceptual resources of the oppressor. Goldwater's appropriation of Protestant ideas for the purposes of Buddhist resistance is another example of "strategic occidentalism" that American Jews (and other Buddhist advocates) used to negotiate the acceptance of Buddhism in US society.[12] Others might view Goldwater's efforts to Protestantize Buddhism as an example of Homi Bhabha's (1994) concept of "hybridity": formulations of resistance that employ the discourse, language, and forms of the oppressor. Bhabha conceives of hybridity in terms of the way that the colonized imitate the forms and discourse of the colonizer, yet Goldwater himself was neither colonized nor oppressed. Rather, he was a Jew who made Buddhism more Protestant in order to make it valid in the eyes of a wartime nation; he was an outsider who defended the oppressed by leveraging the tools of the oppressor.

Two Jewish Students of Zen Buddhism

In the aftermath of the World's Parliament of Religions, where Strauss professed his commitment to Buddhism, a wave of Buddhist teachers from the Zen tradition visited the United States to spread the teachings of the Buddha to an American audience. Three Japanese teachers in particular—Sokei-an Shigetsu Sasaki, Nyogen Senzaki, and D. T. Suzuki—effectively laid the foundations for Zen Buddhism through their tours in the United States (Seager 2012, 43). These Japanese teachers were critical of the institutional forms of Zen that they experienced in Japan, and sought to teach Buddhism to American students distanced from its traditional and institutional context. Because anti-Asian sentiment had a strong foothold in the United States during the second quarter of the twentieth century, these teachers did not enjoy a widespread, popular audience among Jews. Instead, they attracted a small number of eager students, including Lewis and Segal, two Jewish-born spiritual seekers who pursued Buddhism for its meaning and wisdom in the first half of the twentieth century.

A Religious Perennialist

Like Goldwater, Lewis (1896–1971) was born into an affluent American Jewish family. Lewis's father, Jacob Lewis, worked at Levi Strauss and Co., where he began as an elevator operator and then ultimately rose in rank to become a senior executive of the San Francisco–based company (Meyer, n.d.). He and his wife, Harriet (Rosenthal) Lewis, were of German Jewish descent, and they lived a life full of material prosperity, if considerable family dysfunction. Lewis's father had hoped that his son would follow in his footsteps by working in the family business and practicing Judaism, but Samuel displayed little interest in either.[13] Lewis had little in the way of a Jewish education, though reports from family members suggest that he became a bar mitzvah at age thirteen. From a young age, he felt an attraction to the world of mysticism and spirituality outside Judaism and rejected his parents' materialistic lifestyle, just as they had rejected his otherworldly interests.[14]

A pivotal moment in Lewis's spiritual life came in 1915, when, at the age of eighteen, he attended the World's Fair in San Francisco and was introduced to Theosophy. Its premise that all religions stem from the same God captivated him. After the fair, he ventured to read the scriptures from all religions in search of universal truths (Meyer, n.d.). A few years later, Lewis's formal mystical training began when he met the Jewish-born Sufi Murshid Rabia Martin, a disciple of Hazrat Inayat Khan, founder of the Sufi order and prominent teacher of Universal Sufism. Martin encouraged Lewis to study Sufism with Khan, and after the requisite training, Lewis was formally initiated as a Sufi. The teachings and worldview of the Sufi order remained central to Lewis throughout his life.

Shortly after he began studying Sufism, Lewis met Senzaki, a Rinzai Zen teacher and monk in California. Lewis studied Zen with Senzaki and became a committed student of his. In 1926, he assisted him in opening "the floating zendo," an informal group for Buddhist study and practice disconnected from the Japanese Zen establishment (Fields 1981; Lewis 2013). The floating zendo became an important outpost for the small group of Americans who expressed interest in Buddhism in the second quarter of the century. At the floating zendo in San Francisco, which was also called the Mentorgarten Meditation Hall, Lewis studied Japanese art and culture, practiced meditation, and listened to Senzaki lecture about the essence of Zen (Senzaki 1978; Fields 1981, 182–83). Lewis also traveled to New York to meditate with Sokei-an, another early Japanese Rinzai teacher in the United States and founder of the First Zen Institute of America. Sokei-an gave Lewis dharma transmission, a rite establishing a successor in an unbroken lineage of teachers and disciples, thus recognizing Lewis as an accomplished teacher of Zen.[15]

Sufism and Zen acted as important spiritual anchors during Lewis's life, and Lewis built new bridges and conversations between these traditions. In 1923, he introduced Senzaki to Sufi leader Pir-O-Murshid Inayat Khan. Reflecting on this meeting, Lewis (2013) said that they "both initiated each other, so to speak." Senzaki (2008, 242) reported that their exchange went as follows:

SENZAKI: "Murshid," I . . . said, "I see Zen in you."
MURSHID: "Mr. Senzaki, I see a Sufi in you," he replied.
Both of us then smiled at each other.

After this meeting, these two spiritual leaders established an important friendship and brought their two traditions, which had few, if any, encounters in the United States prior to this meeting, into direct contact and exchange (Lewis 2013).

While Goldwater endeavored to find unity among the various different Buddhist traditions, Lewis carried this universalist impulse one step further. Lewis believed in the essential unity of not just all Buddhist lineages but also all religions. He viewed all religions as paths pointing toward the same consummate reality, with every religion containing ultimate truth(s) and no religion owning them all. By viewing Sufism and Zen as paths toward the same ultimate end, Lewis proffered the view that they belonged to and could be accessed by all people.[16]

Influenced by Senzaki, Sokei-an, and his Sufi teachers—all of whom had a distrust of religious institutions and particularistic claims to truth—Lewis viewed sparks of the divine as present in all religions. His deeply universalist view of religion was reflected in the organization he created shortly before his death called the Sufi Ruhaniat International. In its mission statement, the organization describes itself as affirming a "desire for unity of heart with all spiritual seekers on all paths toward God," and striving "to establish a human unity with no consideration of caste, creed, race, nation, or religion," because "differences produce in harmony and cause all miseries in the world" (Meyer, n.d.).

Lewis's commitment to spiritual ecumenism also manifested itself in his creation of the Dances of Universal Peace, his best-known legacy. The dances set sacred scriptures, poetry, and chants from the world's spiritual and religious traditions to music and movement. The American dance pioneer Ruth St. Denis inspired Lewis to fashion these dances, which drew on sources from Sufi, Buddhist, Hindu, Native American, Celtic, North African, Christian, and Jewish traditions. Lewis intended the dances to promote harmony and solidarity among all people, and cast light on the commonalities among all the world's religious traditions.

Unlike Goldwater, Lewis did not purposefully reconfigure Buddhism to conform to the norms of American society; rather, he strove to link Buddhism (and for that matter, Sufism too) with other religions of the world, emphasizing their similarities and minimizing their distinctions. This religious perennialism diminished the practices, beliefs, and histories specific to any given tradition in pursuit of one common religious path. With antecedents dating back to the sixteenth century, this perennialist view of Buddhism was a quintessential discourse of Buddhist modernism that Lewis adopted and propagated in order to make it more readily acceptable to as well as accessible for Americans of all religious backgrounds.[17]

A Buddhist Romantic

Different from Goldwater and Lewis, Segal (1904–2000) was not born into a wealthy and prominent American Jewish family. Instead, his parents were poor Romanian Jews who immigrated to Macon, Georgia, to live near relatives of his mother's family (Segal 2003, 29).[18] His family ultimately left Georgia to move to the north, settling in the Bronx, where his mother had hoped her children could meet other Jewish children (31). Segal left his Bronx home at eighteen to attend New York University, where he received an athletic scholarship to play football.

After graduating from New York University, Segal entered into the magazine publishing industry in New York City. He started the garment trade publication *American Fabrics* in 1946 when the American textile industry experienced a boom in growth due to the development of new synthetic fabrics like polyester and nylon. He also founded *Gentry*, a men's fashion magazine, which sought to bring an innovative, European style to Americans. These magazines as well as his other business publications made him a millionaire by the time he was thirty (Lewis 2000).

For Segal, though, material gain and professional success were not sufficient for a meaningful and satisfying life. As his trade publications succeeded and made him wealthy, he increasingly sought meaning and greater self-understanding through various spiritual as well as religious explorations. This pursuit of self-awareness led him to study esotericism, metaphysical thought, and Eastern religion, and meet and learn from many of the important spiritual leaders of the twentieth century.

Although Segal widely explored various paths to self-discovery, two traditions influenced him most markedly. First, he was an earnest student of philosopher and mystic George Ivanovitch (G. I.) Gurdjieff and his approach to self-development, variously called the "the Fourth Way," "the Method," or "the Work." The Gurdjieff system of thought and practice combined a focus on mind, emotions, and the body. Segal viewed Gurdjieff as a spiritual master who taught him methods of attention and awareness training. Gurdjieff's student, the Russian esotericist P. D. Ouspensky, had a strong influence on Segal too. Segal met Ouspensky in the early 1940s, and developed a close friendship with him and his wife.

Ouspensky played an important role in helping Segal distill and apprehend Gurdjieff's ideas.[19]

Segal was also a serious student of Zen Buddhism. He first learned about Buddhism through the teachings of Suzuki, the prominent exponent of Japanese Zen Buddhism in the West. Suzuki had lectured at various American universities after the war, and Segal interviewed him for a philosophical article for *Gentry* while Suzuki was teaching at Columbia University in the mid-1950s. Suzuki and Segal quickly forged a close friendship, and Suzuki became one of his crucial spiritual teachers. Segal read widely about Zen thought, and began practicing Japanese Zen meditation (*zazen*) both in New York and Japan. Suzuki taught Segal about the romantic conceptualizations of nature, art, and creativity that he set forth in his Zen teachings. Suzuki, much like Segal, was critical of the lust of material luxuries, commercialism, and industrialization begot by the modern era, and sought a return to a simpler and more natural world.

Through introductions made by Suzuki, Segal also visited and spent time in many of the great Buddhist monasteries in Japan, befriending many of their priests and abbots. From his overseas trips, Segal developed an increased fascination with Japanese life, reminiscent of the romanticized Jewish interest in Buddhism of the late nineteenth century. Attracted to the aesthetic of Zen Buddhism, he held a deep appreciation of the architecture of the Zen temples, ceremonial dress, and Zen gardens and landscapes. He acquired a taste for Japanese culture more generally as well. Segal delighted in Japanese meals of fresh fish and warm sake, the culture of long baths in wide and deep tubs, and geisha performances. Although Segal (2003) visited India twice, and met various Tibetan masters there including the Dalai Lama, Japanese Zen remained the Buddhist tradition most dear to him.

Back in the United States, Segal collected Asian (especially Japanese) art and built a meditation house on his farm property in New Jersey. He led meditation sessions for friends and family at this country house, where he also had a painting studio. Segal dedicated himself to explorations of visual beauty through his paintings. He painted a Western version of *The Ten Oxherding Pictures*, which relate back to a Zen master in the Sung dynasty in China (1126–279 AD) and have roots in early Buddhist texts. These pictures symbolize the search for human meaning, from youthful aspiration to enlightenment and back to earthly self-awareness, through a series of illustrations depicting the spiritual development of a young man over his life's course. On his visit to the Ryoko-in Temple at the Daitokuji monastery in Kyoto, Rosho Nanrei Kobori, himself a poet and painter, told Segal, "Your own version of 'The Ten Oxherding,' which you showed me in New York, is the first one I know of the old man with western eyes" (Segal 2003, 239).

As part of his search for self-understanding, Segal also famously painted sixty years of self-portraits from his youth to old age.

Segal married twice, first in 1930 to Cora Segal (nee Carlyle), who came from a nearby neighborhood in the Bronx. After her death, he married Marielle Bancou, a French designer. In 1971, Segal lost his right eye in a terrible automobile accident that he barely survived, and for the rest of his life he had to wear a black eye patch. While Segal (2003, 8) was recovering from the accident, a Zen master told him, "Lucky man . . . one accident like yours is worth 10,000 sittings in a monastery." The accident brought gratitude and search for meaning to the fore for the remainder of his life.

Toward the end of his life and after his death, Segal—along with family and friends—published various books and films about his life as well as life's work. Segal collected interviews, writings, and poems that captured his religious philosophy, and published them as a book, *Opening*, in 1998. His wife, together with the editor Mark Magill, compiled various interviews and transcribed recollections about his explorations of Gurdjieff work, Zen Buddhism, and art, and published them posthumously in the book *A Voice at the Borders of Silence*. US filmmaker Ken Burns produced three short films about Segal and his search for meaning in life called *Seeing, Searching, Being: William Segal*, which he finished just days after Segal's death.

Segal did not draw parallels between Buddhism and other religious traditions (in the manner of Lewis) nor did endeavor to reconcile

Buddhism with American expectations (in the manner of Goldwater). Instead, Segal held a different, if nonetheless modern, view of Buddhism that was inflected by the currents of Western romanticism. Influenced by his teacher Suzuki, Segal cast a nostalgic gaze toward "the East," especially Japan, viewing it as superior to the industrialized, materialist West. Segal's exaltation of the rustic, natural world and cultivation of the interior experience owed much to Suzuki's teachings, which intertwined Buddhism and romantic-transcendentalist thought.

Conclusion

The stories of Goldwater, Lewis, and Segal reveal a distinct change in the Jewish-Buddhist relationship from the late nineteenth century to the first half of the twentieth. Whereas the nineteenth-century United States witnessed a popular Jewish interest in Buddhism (mirroring the larger American interest in Buddhism occurring at that time), the first half of the twentieth century saw the decline of the popular, armchair interest in Buddhism and emergence of a small number of Jewish spiritual seekers who explored various paths to self-discovery before pursuing Buddhism. These spiritual seekers largely came from wealthy and/or prominent American families, and their distinctive bourgeois social location led them to search for meaning in life beyond material or financial success. The most prominent Jewish Buddhist of this period was Goldwater, who ordained as a Buddhist priest, led his own Buddhist community, and advocated for Buddhist rights during World War II.[20]

These Jewish Buddhists all crafted their own modernized versions of American Buddhism that sought to reconcile it with the central liberal religious perspectives of their time: universalism, perennialism, and romanticism. The themes in the encounter between Judaism and Buddhism in the first half of the twentieth century foreshadowed the contemporary engagement between these traditions in these three particular ways. American Jews, as later chapters will demonstrate, continued to adapt Buddhism to the expectations and norms of US society by contending that it has a common, timeless essence. They also continued to make claims about and gravitate toward the exotic character of Buddhism, developing a romantic appreciation of the tradition precisely because they viewed it as foreign and Eastern. The next chapter will focus in greater depth on how Jews continued to Americanize and transform Buddhism in the third quarter of the twentieth century.

CHAPTER THREE

Jews and the Liberalization of American Buddhism

IN THE FIRST HALF of the twentieth century, a small number of American Jews—mostly spiritual seekers from wealthy and prominent families—studied the teachings, philosophy, and practices of Buddhism, a religion largely unknown to the average American at that time. Beginning in the 1950s and extending through to the mid-1970s, Buddhism grew in mass popularity in the United States as a result of the confluence of various factors. First, as mentioned in the last chapter, the postwar period witnessed a "Zen boom" as a result of the increased presence and availability of Zen Buddhist teachers, texts, and university-level classes, which made Zen more widely available to Americans interested in pursuing it. Second, the Beat movement, and the literary interest that many of its central members took in Zen Buddhism, helped propel Buddhism into the American consciousness while giving it a distinctive association with the American counterculture.

Third, in an effort to bring the teachings of the Buddha more in line with US expectations, a number of both Asian- and American-born Buddhist teachers reformulated Buddhism in more positive and humanistic terms, thereby increasing its popularity in the United States. And finally, the changing immigration laws in 1965 led to a new wave of Asian immigration in the United States, thus not only increasing the presence and visibility of Buddhism in this country but also introducing a range of new traditions, innovations, and institutions into American Buddhism. By the "sixties," or the period of time between the early 1960s and mid-1970s, these changes led Buddhism to emerge as an increasingly fashionable religious tradition in the United States that had distinctive ties to the American Left.[1]

During this time period, the community of native-born Americans interested in Buddhism expanded from a small group of seekers focused on Zen to a wider and more diverse community that explored many Buddhist traditions, including Nichirin, Tibetan, Theravada, and other forms of Buddhism (Seager 2012, 49). Different from earlier decades, the Jewish Buddhists of this period were not necessarily, or even largely, from prominent Jewish families, though some still were. Rather, they drew more broadly from the left-leaning sector of American society, where Jews were distinctively overrepresented.[2]

This time period in and around the 1960s' counterculture witnessed a turn away from a predominantly intellectual, literary, or romantic interest in Buddhism toward an attraction to the experiential practice of meditation. It also saw the emergence of a first generation of Buddhist teachers and leaders of Jewish descent at the helm of flagship Buddhist institutions as well as creators of innovative Buddhist communities and practices. Although some American Jews participated in Asian American immigrant Buddhist communities during this time, most gravitated to convert Buddhist communities, or those American Buddhist communities that consisted largely of Americans of European descent who came to embrace the teachings and practices of the Buddha.[3] These convert Buddhist communities have close ties to the insight meditation (or *vipassana*), Zen, and Tibetan traditions in particular, and share an emphasis on the practice of seated meditation, an association with the counterculture, and a similar educated, upper-middle-class demographic base.[4]

In this chapter, I first trace the trajectories that led many Jews in the second half of the twentieth century to Zen, insight meditation, and Tibetan traditions—three communities in which Jews have emerged as prominent teachers and leaders.[5] I then explore how American Jews have shaped the character and tenor of the Buddhist culture of these three communities through their leadership within it. I argue that through their prominent positions as Buddhist teachers, American Jews participated in the modernization of Buddhism in the second half of the twentieth century by elevating the practice of meditation, instilling within it an activist ethic, and increasing its psychotherapeutic orientation. Jewish Americans were not the first, only, or even necessarily most influential modernizers in these three regards, but they have had a clear influence on Buddhism in these arenas. Different from the Jewish Buddhists in the first half of the twentieth century, those in the second half had deeper relationships with Judaism, and occasionally brought ideas and concepts drawn from Judaism into Buddhism, sowing the earliest seeds of Jewish-Buddhist syncretism in the United States.

Jews and American Zen

The postwar years witnessed the emergence of a broad movement to revitalize and modernize Zen Buddhism for an American audience, thus sowing the seeds for the first significant encounter between Jews and Buddhists in the twentieth century (McMahan 2003; Seager 2012, 112–34). In an attempt to present Zen as an acceptable American religious faith, various Japanese Buddhist teachers and scholars in the early 1950s distanced it from its traditional background (particularly from the institutionalized rituals of Zen temples in Japan) and emphasized it as a universal path toward experiential spirituality. The renowned Japanese author and scholar Suzuki, the man whom Buddhist scholar David McMahan (2003, 221) suggests "did more than any individual to repackage Zen for the West," played a particularly important role in this process.[6] Through his popular writings, Suzuki presented Zen as a "pure experience of unmediated encounter with reality," accentuating individual experience rather than rituals, dogma, or institutional rites" (McMahan 2003, 220; Jackson 2010, 49). He jettisoned traditional elements of Zen that seemed incongruous to largely Protestant America (i.e., priestly rituals, monasticism, and hierarchies), and reformulated it as an "ahistorical essence of spirituality" available for any and all to sample (McMahan 2003, 221).

This ahistorical essence of Zen, eponymously called "Suzuki Zen," appealed to many Americans in the postwar years but loomed large in particular among the anticonformist, liberal-left subcultures of the 1950s.

Zen gained a strong foothold in these circles because the Japanese teachers presented it as an alternative form of spiritual expression that emphasized the authority of the individual over that of religious institutions. It also became a means of anticonformist protest against the middle-class values of the 1950s. Because American Jews have historically tended to participate in countercultural circles, they were overrepresented in the segment of society—namely the left-leaning subcultures—to which Zen Buddhism appealed most strongly.[7]

One particular countercultural group famous for its attraction to Zen was the Beat generation, the group of post–World War II writers and poets, congregated mainly in the Bay Area, who experimented with drugs (especially psychedelics) and sexuality, and rejected what they saw as a growing postwar materialism. Many of the Beat writers had a literary fascination with Buddhism, which included little in the way of meditation or disciplined practice. The central figure of the Beat generation, Jewish-born Allen Ginsberg, identified as both a Jew and Buddhist, giving a public face and countercultural cachet to this dual religious identity.[8] Raised in a Jewish socialist-communist house in Paterson, New Jersey, Ginsberg was introduced to Zen Buddhism by Jack Kerouac and Gary Snyder, two other Beat poets, in the 1950s.[9] Throughout the 1950s, Ginsberg studied Zen Buddhism from his armchair and only later in life began to practice meditation with the eminent Tibetan teacher Chogyam Trungpa Rinpoche.[10] In many ways, Ginsberg's poetry reflected his personal trajectory of West meets East, as both his Jewish background and self-taught Buddhism deeply informed his poetic works.

The Beats gave the Bay Area the reputation as the vanguard for aspiring artists, countercultural experiments, and explorations into Zen Buddhism. This reputation lured many artists and bohemians, who in various combinations sought artistic, literary, and Buddhist inspiration, to Northern California in the 1960s and 1970s. At approximately the same time that these Jewish Americans arrived in the Bay Area chasing the Beat boom, a new institutionalized form of Zen—or "establishment Zen"—took hold in California.[11] Japanese Zen teachers, most notably Shunryu Suzuki and Taizan Maezumi, arrived in California in the late 1950s looking to revitalize Zen by establishing new practice communities grounded in discipline and established procedures. These teachers saw the United States as a land of opportunity where Zen could freely take on new forms without the constraints of Japanese institutional oversight.[12]

This new wave of Japanese teachers introduced the formal practice of zazen (sitting cross-legged meditation) as the heart of the practice. This led to a shift in the central interest of American Zen from individual spiritual experience to disciplined, seated practice. For the most part, however, the Jewish Americans—like other counterculturalists more generally—who arrived in the Bay Area in the 1960s and early 1970s looking to experiment with Zen still imagined it as a free-form spiritual expression à la Suzuki Zen. They had little idea of the actual discipline involved in the Zen practice that they were chasing. Those early students of the newly established California Zen centers who ultimately committed to Zen practice found that it offered a path of radical sobriety, and indeed it afforded many a way out of the drug culture by replacing their psychedelic-induced highs with the natural highs of meditation (Weitsman 1999). Many Jews who came to Zen Buddhism in the 1960s followed a similar route through countercultural involvement, experimentation with psychedelic drugs, and committed political activism to Buddhism.[13]

This trajectory—from bohemian artist to eminent Zen teacher—typified the path that led Mel Weitsman, the founder and abbot of the Berkeley Zen Center, to Buddhism. Born in Los Angeles in 1929 to poor, Ukranian Jewish immigrants, Weitsman later moved to Northern California to attend the California School of Fine Arts (now known as the Art Institute of California). After college, he lived the life of the West Coast starving artist until joining the Soto Zen Mission called the Sokoji on Bush Street in San Francisco, where Suzuki led a group in sitting meditation early every morning.[14]

After only a few years of practice, he cofounded the Berkeley Zen Center with Suzuki across the bay—the first Zen meditation center in California established, at least in part, by a non-Asian practitioner. At this Berkeley zendo, he was ordained resident priest and received dharma transmission from Suzuki's son Hoitsu. Viewed through the lens of traditional Soto Zen history, it was a notable historical moment that

Weitsman succeeded Suzuki, whose priestly lineage traced back to Japan.

Weitsman was officially installed as abbot of the Berkeley Zen Center in 1985, ascending to prominence as a highly venerated American Soto Zen leader. In the late 1980s, he moved across the bay to serve as the leader and abbot of one of the largest Zen Buddhist communities outside Asia, the San Francisco Zen Center. He held the position of abbot there for ten years, and then he returned to his former role as abbot of the Berkeley Zen Center in 1997, where he currently resides. Weitsman's installation as an abbot of a major Zen center in the United States marked the first time such a Buddhist accession occurred for a Jew in this country. In terms of the story of the Jewish-Buddhist encounter in the United States, Weitsman is also important for transmitting the dharma to many prominent Buddhists of Jewish heritage who have gone on to become important leaders and innovators in Zen Buddhism, as discussed in more depth below.[15]

One of Weitsman's dharma heirs, Blanche Hartman, deserves special attention for her role in elevating the status of women in the Zen tradition. Born in Birmingham, Alabama, to nonpracticing Jewish parents, she arrived at the Berkeley Zen Center in 1969 disenchanted by the violence within the civil rights movement and seeking a practice to cultivate peace. She began sitting regularly from the first day she had meditation instruction, initially at the Berkeley Zen Center, and later in residence at the San Francisco Zen Center and its satellite centers. In 1988, she received dharma transmission from Weitsman, and by 1996, was installed as the first female abbess of the San Francisco Zen Center.

Hartman's installation as abbess of the San Francisco Zen Center— the first time a mother (or grandmother) *ever* in the history of the Zen tradition held such a prestigious leadership position—set a new precedent for the role of women in American Zen. She used her role as abbess there to pioneer new Buddhist teachings tailored especially to the needs of women practitioners. In 1992, she led an all-female meditation session at Suzuki's home temple in Japan, marking the first time in the five-hundred-year history of the temple that women conducted a training period there. She also led women's retreats at Green Gulch Farm in Mill

Valley, California. Hartman was especially known for her expertise in the ancient ritual of sewing a *kesa*, or the traditional Japanese priest's robes. She created and performed new rituals and ceremonies specifically for women, including one for women grieving miscarried or aborted babies. This ceremony drew on the bodhisattva (enlightened spirit) of Jiso Bosatsu, the traditional Japanese Buddhist savior of souls and protector of children (Keller and Ruether 2006, 643).

Jews have risen to important leadership roles in Korean, Vietnamese, and Chinese Zen lineages as well, though they have not had the same conspicuous involvement as innovators and social justice leaders as they have had within Japanese Zen.[16] A few examples of prominent Jewish-born teachers in these Buddhist traditions include the Korean Zen master Bon Soeng, born Jeff Kitzes, who studied beneath Zen master Seung Sahn and is now the guiding teacher of Empty Gate Zen Center in Berkeley; Korean Zen master Wu Kwang, born Richard Shrobe, who also studied beneath Sahn and is the guiding teacher of the Chogye International Zen Center of New York City; and Skip Ewing, who trained in the tradition of Vietnamese Zen master Thich Nhat Hanh and founded the Nashville Mindfulness Center. Aside from the prominent cadre of Zen teachers of Jewish descent, across all the different schools of Zen, there have been many more Jews who are everyday practitioners of the tradition. Some of these Jews seriously engaged in Zen practice, meditating in and affiliating with Zen centers across the country. Many more, however, more loosely incorporated Zen and Zen-like ideas into their daily lives.

Jews and Insight Meditation

While American Jews were studying Zen in meditation centers in California in the 1960s and 1970s, a different meeting between American Jews and Buddhism took place across the ocean in India. Beginning in the 1960s, American Jews joined other countercultural Westerners who traveled to the East on a "hippie trail" in search of new spiritual experiences and cheap, plentiful drugs (Nisker 1994). At the time, Bodh Gaya, India, had the reputation for having famous English-speaking Buddhist teachers interested in teaching Buddhist techniques to Western students. This reputation lured many Western travelers to the city.[17]

Anecdotal accounts suggest that many of the spiritual seekers in Bodh Gaya in the late 1960s were of Jewish descent. The actual numbers of Westerners, let alone Jews, to journey to Bodh Gaya during that time is difficult to determine, but enough Jews passed through the city for the Tibetans in exile to notice and remark on the Jewish presence. The moniker "Bewish" was born at that time and jokingly passed around among the Jewish travelers.[18] Winter 1970, in particular, drew many to Bodh Gaya because the renowned Theravada teacher from Burma, S. N. Goenka, arrived in town. Goenka, who had been touring around India leading meditation retreats, had a reputation for presenting Buddhism as an experiential, nonsectarian practice focused centrally on being in the present moment. This basic, accessible form of Theravada Buddhism appealed to many Westerners. A group of approximately thirty travelers, nearly all of whom were from the United States, signed up for Goenka's ten-day retreat in Bodh Gaya that winter, and many ended up staying a month or many months, completing one retreat after another.[19]

This first retreat—one that Jewish Buddhist teacher Wes Nisker described as the "meditation retreat that shook the world"—played a pivotal role in the story of the late twentieth-century Jewish-Buddhist encounter.[20] It brought together and connected a gathering of travelers—an inordinate number of whom were American Jews—who later became the pioneering generation of teachers of a new stream of Theravada-inspired mindfulness meditation that came to be called insight.[21] Some of the travelers who connected through this 1970 retreat included Joseph Goldstein, Sharon Salzberg, Jacqueline Mandell-Schwartz, Nisker, Barry Laping, and Stephen Levine—all American Jews who went on to become leading insight meditation teachers in the United States. The retreat also included other travelers who became leaders in other traditions, including Surya Das (born Jeffrey Miller), now the famous American lama ordained in the Tibetan tradition; Ram Dass (born Richard Alpert), the American spiritual teacher and author of the cult classic *Be Here Now*; Daniel Goleman, the internationally renown psychologist and author of the 1995 book *Emotional Intelligence*; and Krishna Dass (born Jeffrey

Kegel), a famous American singer of Indian *kirtan*-style devotional music.[22] Most of these Jewish travelers returned to the United States in the early to mid-1970s, either because their money had run out or their health was failing. They often lived a peripatetic life after returning stateside, traveling from one city to another trying to sustain their meditation practice.

Goldstein and Jack Kornfield deserve special notice for their role in marshaling the practices and teachings they learned in Asia into the insight meditation movement in the United States. They both grew up in East Coast Jewish families, graduated from Ivy League institutions, and served in the Peace Corps in Thailand. During their time in Asia, they practiced Buddhist meditation in famous monasteries, and studied with eminent teachers from India, Burma, and Tibet.[23]

Goldstein and Kornfield returned to the United States in the early 1970s and formed a partnership in 1974 during the inaugural summer session of the Naropa Institute, a recently established Buddhist school in Boulder, Colorado, designed to bring Eastern spirituality into conversation with Western intellectualism. After teaching together during that summer, they traveled around the country, offering retreats and courses in insight meditation that focused intensively on the practice of moment-to-moment mindfulness. Their courses achieved a rapid degree of popularity, bolstered by the rising wave of interest in Buddhism and Eastern spirituality more generally in the United States in the 1970s.[24] At that time, the United States was largely unconstrained by Buddhist institutions, allowing Goldstein and Kornfield license to be exceedingly creative and innovative in their teachings. They incorporated myriad new approaches to insight meditation based on their training and intuitions as well as their understandings of Theravada Buddhism. They distilled the essence of the Buddha's teachings and adapted them to what they saw as the cultural—and Protestant—expectations of American society. In doing so, they minimized the elements of Buddhism associated with the wider religious tradition of Southeast Asian Theravada Buddhism in favor of the simple practice of seated meditation that they thought would seem less ethnic and more appealing to US society (Cadge 2005, 28–31; Seager 2012, 29; Fronsdal 1998, 163–80).

In 1975, along with Salzberg and Mandell-Schwartz, two other American Jews who were Goldstein's friends from his days in India, Goldstein and Kornfield established the Insight Meditation Society (IMS), the first Theravada Buddhist meditation center founded by non-Asians in the United States and central hub for the teaching of vipassana.[25] Together, these American Jews are now considered the founding teachers of insight meditation in the United States. For a decade, IMS served as the cornerstone of the insight meditation movement.

In the early 1980s, Kornfield left IMS and moved to California, looking to focus the insight meditation movement more on integrating meditation into daily life and less on extended retreat practice. Working together with a small group of Buddhist teachers, many of who were American Jews, he founded a new meditation center that came to be called Spirit Rock Meditation Center in 1988 on over four hundred acres of land in Marin County, California.[26] Over the past two decades, IMS and Spirit Rock have graduated a second and even third generation of teachers, generating an expanding network of affiliated groups across the country in the insight meditation tradition. The insight meditation movement has become a new American tradition of its own, modeled after and indebted to the Theravada traditions of Burma, Thailand, and Sri Lanka. Largely through the work of American Jews who founded and directed its two cornerstone organizations, insight meditation has skyrocketed into one of the most popular traditions of Buddhism in the United States. Although the Jewish involvement in the insight meditation movement is the best-known story line of the encounter between American Jews and Theravada Buddhism in the second half of the twentieth century, Jews were occasionally leaders in other branches of Theravada Buddhism, both in and outside the United States, during that time period as well.[27]

Jews and Tibetan Buddhism

Tibetan Buddhism increased in popularity in the United States in the late 1960s and 1970s, when lamas, or spiritual teachers in exile from Tibet, began to attract groups of devoted followers, particularly from within the

US countercultural movement. These lamas built new communities and practice centers throughout the country, organized around the four main schools of Tibetan Buddhism.[28] Tibetan Buddhism arrived in the United States largely untouched by the modernization process that had transformed and Westernized Zen and Theravada Buddhism, and as a result, the Tibetan tradition has preserved more of its historical religious worldview, complex mythological perspectives, and devotional rituals (Seager 2012, 136).

One of the most famous Tibetan teachers to create a network of practice centers, many of which attracted scores of Jewish followers, was Chogyam Trungpa Rinpoche, a former Tibetan monk with a reputation for his charisma, flamboyance, and sexual indiscretions.[29] In the mid-1970s, Trungpa founded the Naropa Institute, the Buddhist-inspired center for learning in Boulder, where Kornfield and Goldstein first met. Naropa developed into a gathering place for many countercultural Jews and other spiritual-seeking bohemians of the time.[30] A number of famous Jews taught at Naropa the first summer it opened, including Ginsberg and Ram Dass, and other Jews rose up in the hierarchy of the Naropa community, including Robin Kornman and Nathan Katz, both now professors and scholars, and Sam Bercholz, the founder of Shambhala Publications, the foremost publishing house for American Buddhism. In addition to these famous examples, many more spiritual-seeking American Jews traveled to Colorado to receive training and study Tibetan Buddhism with Trungpa, and then followed him to his various outposts in Canada. The number of Jews involved in his communities puzzled Trungpa, and he reportedly commented that so many of his students were Jews that they could form the "oy vey school of Buddhism" (Kamenetz 1994, 8–9).

Pema Chodron (born Deirdre Blomfield-Brown) is perhaps Trungpa's most famous Jewish Buddhist student. She studied with him from 1974 until his death in 1987, but received the full monastic ordination in a Chinese lineage of Buddhism in 1981 in Hong Kong. Pema served as the director of the Boulder Shambhala Center (formerly called the Karma Dzong), until moving in 1984 to rural Cape Breton, Nova Scotia, to be the director and resident teacher of Gampo Abbey, a Western Buddhist monastery in the Shambhala tradition.[31] Pema has also written a number of famous books that explain Buddhist ideas to Westerners, including the best-selling *When Things Fall Apart: Heart Advice for Difficult Times*.

In addition to the American Jews who studied Tibetan Buddhism with Trungpa, other Jews studied with various prominent Tibetan teachers in Asia in the 1960s and 1970s. A number of American Jews trained for many years in Asia, eventually ordaining as lamas and lineage holders. Surya Das and Thubten Chodron (born Cheryl Greene) are two notable Jewish-born Tibetan lamas to have followed this path.[32]

Surya Das is one of the foremost American Buddhist meditation teachers and scholars ordained in the Tibetan tradition. In 1991, on his return from twenty years of study and retreat in India, Nepal, and France, he founded the Dzogchen Center in Cambridge, Massachusetts. One of the goals of the Dzogchen Center is to make the teachings and practices of the Buddha as accessible as possible to Westerners. The Dzogchen Center offers an egalitarian and nonsectarian meditation practice that is socially as well as ecologically concerned. Surya Das also helped establish the Western Buddhist Teachers Network, an affiliation of Buddhist teachers across different Buddhist lineages from the United States and Europe who aim to adapt Buddhism to the West. In addition, he has published a number of accessible and popular books designed to introduce Buddhism to Americans, including *Awakening the Buddha Within: Tibetan Wisdom for the Western World*.

Similar to Surya Das, Thubten studied and practiced Buddhism in the Tibetan tradition for many years in India and Nepal. In 2003, she founded the Sravasti Abbey just north of Spokane, Washington, the only Tibetan Buddhist training monastery for Western nuns and monks in the United States. Thubten, like many other Jewish Buddhist teachers, emphasizes the practical application of the Buddha's teachings in everyday life. She has published books on Buddhist philosophy and meditation in several languages, and coauthored a book with the Dalai Lama—*Buddhism: One Teacher, Many Traditions*.

Jews and the Modification of American Buddhism

The committed Jewish Americans who practiced Buddhism beginning in the 1950s and 1960s burgeoned into a first generation of Buddhist teachers and leaders of Jewish descent in both the Zen and insight meditation traditions. The collective work of Jewish-born teachers in the last quarter of the twentieth century has had a transformative influence on American Buddhism in three central ways. For one, these teachers elevated the importance of the privatized experience of silence and meditation. Second, they emphasized the ethical pursuit of social justice. And third, they also cast Buddhism with a distinctive psychotherapeutic orientation. Through these three processes, American Jews contributed to the liberalization of Buddhism in the United States.[33]

First, within the insight meditation tradition, the first generation of teachers individualized the practice of mindfulness meditation at the center of the movement and minimized the importance of the wider religious tradition of Southeast Asian Theravada Buddhism in which that practice was derived. In their teachings, these Jewish Buddhist leaders focused primarily on the practical details of meditation, and de-emphasized the framework of Buddhist cosmological ideas about renunciation and detachment that have historically scaffolded this practice.[34] In their teachings and writings, they also advanced the idea that mindfulness and meditation are universal as well as nonsectarian practices in which all people can participate. The teachers consciously abandoned various other traditional elements of Theravada Buddhism, including chanting, temple rituals, and ceremonies that they feared Americans would view as too foreign or ethnic. As Kornfield acknowledged of the founding teachers, "We wanted to offer the powerful practices of insight meditation, as many of our teachers did, as simply as possible without the complications of rituals, robes, chanting and the whole religious tradition" (Fronsdal 1998, 167).

In doing so, these Jewish Americans continued the work of their Asian teachers—including Mahasi Sayadaw, Anagarika Munindra, Sayadaw U Pandita, Goenka, and Ajahn Cha—who were all part of the twentieth-century Buddhist modernization movement. These Asian teachers

presented vipassana as a moral and scientific tradition, deliberately weed-
ing out various metaphysical elements of Buddhism not seen as in line
with the dominant cultural and intellectual forces of modernity. These
teachers seldom introduced their students to the wider Theravada religious world or its complex interrelationships with Southeast Asian society. As a consequence, when Kornfield, Goldstein, Salzberg, and others
returned to the United States, founded new Buddhist organizations, and
taught insight meditation, they presented it as a system of individual practices detached from its wider Southeast Asian historical and religious
context, just as their teachers had done.

The American Buddhist teachers of Jewish heritage, however, went
significantly further than their own Asian teachers in emphasizing meditation and mindfulness and muting the dogmatic, doctrinal, and mythological elements of Buddhism. The Jewish Americans who studied in
Asia returned from their travels to a United States largely unconstrained
by Buddhist institutions or established hierarchies. This freedom from
institutional oversight enabled them to be inventive in their teachings.
They incorporated myriad new approaches to their meditation practice based on their own intuitions and understandings of Theravada
Buddhism, working to distill the essence of the Buddha's teaching and
adapt it to the needs of a Western audience (Cadge 2004, 28–31; Seager
2012, 29; Fronsdal 1998, 163–80).

In elevating meditation to the center of the insight movement, the
Jewish American teachers also engaged in a doctrinal reorganization,
highlighting certain preexisting aspects of Theravada Buddhism while
minimizing others, thereby leading to the development of new, creative
Buddhist outcomes. For example, while the cycles of rebirth had a prominent place in many of the teachings of their Asian teachers, they are
virtually absent in the teachings of the Jewish Buddhist teachers. Similarly, these Jewish Buddhist teachers have largely abandoned the Buddhist teachings on realms of existence, merit making, and the four stages
of enlightenment that are all integral to Theravada teachings in Asia
(Fronsdal 1998, 167). In reorganizing the dharma to meet these American expectations, Jews engaged in what Buddhist studies scholar Jeff Wilson (2014) calls "mystification," or the minimizing or obscuring of the

historical as well as religious origins of mindfulness meditation in order to make it broadly appealing to an American audience.

In contrast to their jettisoning of various aspects of Buddhist mythology, the Buddhist teachers of Jewish heritage accentuated four teachings central to their understanding of Theravada Buddhism: mindfulness (*sati*), loving-kindness (*metta*), ethics (*sila*), and generosity (*dana*). Of these four, the teachers emphasized mindfulness the most, but presented all four as important to leading an awakened life. Much more so than their Asian teachers, though, the Jewish American teachers elevated the practice of loving-kindness. Virtually every book written by these Buddhist teachers of Jewish heritage features a lengthy discussion of metta, although this is not a central feature of vipassana practice in Asia. This is the primary theme in Salzberg's book *Loving-kindness: The Revolutionary Art of Happiness*, Kornfield's *The Art of Forgiveness, Lovingkindness, and Peace*, and Goldstein's *A Heart Full of Peace* (Wilson 2014).

Although challenging to discern precisely why these teachers stress metta practices, it could be a result of the emphasis on and familiarity with the idea of loving-kindness that came from these teachers' Jewish backgrounds—an example of Jewish-Buddhist syncretism par excellence. The practice of loving-kindness, or *gemilut hasadim*, is a central Jewish tenet across all wings of Judaism in the United States. In Jewish scripture, it is written that gemilut hasadim is one of the three pillars on which the world rests (Pirkei Avot 1:2). This explanation seems even more reasonable in light of the way that these metta practices are frequently combined with a forgiveness practice that is unknown in formal Buddhist practice in Southeast Asia but that bears a striking resemblance to the *selichot* (forgiveness) service, the series of penitential prayers and liturgy most widely known for their recitation during the period of the Jewish High Holidays. The Buddhist forgiveness practice, which appears in many different books and articles, and is outlined in depth in Kornfield's *The Art of Forgiveness, Lovingkindness, and Peace*, entails a series of meditative recitations asking forgiveness of others, the forgiveness of oneself, and the forgiveness of those who have caused a person hurt or harm. These three forgiveness practices are commonly recited as part of the High Holiday liturgy in American Jewish congregations throughout the country.

By casting mindfulness and meditation as a universally accessible practice, these teachers also largely abandoned the tradition of Buddhist monasticism in favor of a movement geared toward laypeople and householders. In the Asian Buddhist context and history, meditation has largely been a monastic practice of ordained monks and nuns who had a command of Pali and knowledge of ancient scriptures.[35] The first generation of insight meditation teachers laicized this practice to allow Americans to participate in meditation alongside the responsibilities of jobs, children, houses, and other duties of adults living in the everyday world. The teachers reckoned that by making meditation a lay practice, many more people could and would benefit from it.

In sum, the efforts of the Buddhist teachers of Jewish heritage led to a simplified and arguably secularized version of vipassana meditation that remains only tenuously connected to its traditional roots in the Southeast Asian context. Its praxis-oriented character has contributed greatly to its growing popularity, in part by making the practice readily accessible and attractive to people with little to no interest in Theravada Buddhism as a religious tradition (Wilson 2014).[36]

Although less visibly, American Jews have brought this emphasis on and elevation of meditation into the Zen tradition as well. Perhaps the most famous Jewish American to distance Zen from its moorings in doctrine and ritual while elevating the practice of seated meditation was Toni Packer (1927–2013). Packer grew up in Nazi Germany as the daughter of two scientists. Her mother was Jewish, and her family hid their religious identity in order to avoid the death camps. After the war, she emigrated to Switzerland and then the United States, eventually becoming a student at the Rochester Zen Center (Lion's Roar Staff 2013; *Tricycle* 1996). Her teacher at the Zen center was Philip Kapleau, one of the important early teachers of Zen in the United States. After practicing and studying at the Zen Center for over a decade, Packer rose through the ranks and was asked to take over the center when Kapleau retired. Having grown increasingly disenchanted with Asian forms, tradition, and lineage—feeling that they detracted from the essence of meditative practice—she broke with Kapleau and the Rochester Zen Center and took a number of her students with her to found the Genesee Valley Zen

Center, which she later renamed the Springwater Center for Meditative Inquiry and Retreats in central New York. She established herself as an independent teacher who emphasized the significance of meditative inquiry and practice (as reflected in the name of her organization), divorced from lineage, doctrines, and mythology.

To a lesser extent, this same stress on the inquiry and practice of meditation over the traditional elements of Zen Buddhism is apparent in the recent work of Norman Fischer. Fischer was born in a small town in Pennsylvania in 1946 to an observant Jewish family. He moved to the Bay Area in the early 1970s to study the practice of Zen and escape the climate of charged left-wing politics of which he had long been a part.[37] In 1976, after about five years of practicing Zen intensively in Berkeley, he and his family entered into a residential practice at Tassajara Zen Mountain Center, the first Zen training monastery outside Japan.

Fischer ordained as a priest in the lineage of Suzuki in 1980 and received dharma transmission from Weitsman in 1988. He served as the abbot and director at Green Gulch Farm (a Soto Zen practice center) in Marin County, California, and from 1995 to 2000, served as the coabbot at the San Francisco Zen Center, where he is presently a senior dharma teacher. In 2000, Fischer founded the Everyday Zen Foundation, a pioneering Zen community dedicated to adapting Zen Buddhist teachings to the needs of Western culture.

Fischer is one of the most influential US-born teachers of Zen in this country, renown for promoting an understanding of American Zen as detached from the traditional institutional context of the Japanese monastery. He created the Everyday Zen Foundation predicated on the belief that the essence of Zen exists in everyday experiences beyond temple life. Fischer established a network of *sanghas* (communities) committed solely to the pursuit of Zen meditation, rid of institutional hierarchy. He explained that the mission of his new organization is to allow people to just "show up and practice; it's that simple."[38]

In his work, Fischer integrates Buddhist contemplative practices into the fields of business, law, software engineering, care of the dying (including work with the Zen Hospice Project), and conflict resolution. He has worked for the US Army teaching mindfulness practices to chaplains and was one of the creators of the course on mindfulness, Search Inside Your-self, taught at Google in its program for employees (Everyday Zen Foundation, n.d.). Both Packer's and Fischer's approach to Zen carries forward the ethos and teachings of Japanese Buddhist modernizers, par-ticularly Suzuki, who, as noted earlier, encouraged an understanding of Zen as free floating and divorced from the doctrine, priesthood, and hi-erarchy common in the Japanese institutional Zen setting.

It is difficult to determine if and how the Jewish upbringings of these Buddhist teachers influenced their decisions to abandon many traditional elements of Buddhism and emphasize the centrality and universality of the practice of meditation. In my conversations with these teachers, most explained that their mindfulness-oriented approach to Buddhism sim-ply suited their temperaments, reasoning that they felt more interested in the direct understanding possible through practice than in the cere-monial or mythological elements of Buddhism. It does seem likely, though, that these teachers deliberately minimized the mythological and monastic elements of Buddhism because they felt especially unfamiliar to them both as Jews and Americans. Judaism is a religion of family cele-bration and ritual observance so these Jewish Buddhists were not brought up in homes that underscored the importance of worldly denun-ciation. And as Americans, these teachers did not identify with or find meaning in the cosmologies and ceremonies tied to the wider religious tradition of Japanese or Southeast Asian Theravada Buddhism because those were not the societies or cultural backgrounds in which they were raised or felt most at home.[39]

The second way that Jewish Americans influenced the character of Buddhism in this country is through their development of an activist ethic within the tradition. Beginning in the 1960s, a new movement within Buddhism emerged that focused on applying Buddhist insights to social issues confronting contemporary society. This movement, known as engaged Buddhism or socially engaged Buddhism, spans Bud-dhist traditions in the East and West, and is unified by the intention of Buddhists of different traditions to draw on the values and teachings of Buddhism to address the problems of society in a nonviolent way.[40] This movement takes traditional Buddhist beliefs, practices, and moral precepts and applies them to social projects such as stopping war, promoting human rights, ministering to the victims of disease and disaster, and safeguarding the natural environment. Although socially engaged Buddhism is comprised of many individuals and groups, Buddhist leaders of Jewish heritage constitute a visible and influential presence within the core of the movement.

One particularly prominent figure at the center of this movement is Alan Senauke. Born to a New York Jewish family with strong cultural and ethnic ties to Judaism, Senauke moved to California after graduating from Columbia University in 1968. He eventually arrived at the Berkeley Zen Center, where he studied beneath Weitsman and eventually rose through the ranks to his current position as vice abbot.[41] From 1991 to 2001, Senauke served as the executive director of the Buddhist Peace Fellowship, one of the largest Buddhist activist organizations in the United States dedicated to drawing on Buddhist principles to bring about social change. Together with his Jewish-born colleague Tova Green, he helped propel the fellowship to the center of engaged Buddhism in the United States.[42] Senauke also founded the Clear View Project and is now its executive director. This project provides aid and material relief to a variety of social justice projects in Asia and the United States, supporting schools, training programs, meditation centers, and clinics since 2007.[43] Senauke (2010) wrote the book *The Bodhisattva's Embrace: Dispatches from Engaged Buddhism's Front Lines*, which brings his Zen Buddhist perspective to issues such as globalization, imperialism, militarism, race, and privilege.

Like Senauke, another prominent Buddhist leader of Jewish heritage, Paula Green, has received recognition for her important leadership and participation in the movement for socially engaged Buddhism. Green was born in 1937 and grew up in New Jersey in a secular, progressive Jewish family. She was a second-generation Jewish American; her grandparents fled the pogroms of eastern Europe. As a young adult, she was active in the civil rights and antiwar movement and eventually began practicing Buddhism at IMS in Barre. After considerable travels and activist work in Asia, Green returned to Massachusetts to found and serve as the director of the Karuna Center for Peace Building. At Karuna (which means compassion in Pali), she directed, designed, and implemented various training programs in nonviolent social change rooted in Buddhist teachings (Queen 2000, 128–56). The film *Communities in Conflict, Healing the Wounds of War* documents her multiyear peace-building efforts in Bosnia.[44] Currently, Green serves on the boards of IMS and Buddhist Peace Fellowship.

A number of other Buddhist leaders of Jewish backgrounds have played an important role in the movement for socially engaged Buddhism in the West. Bhikkhu Bodhi, who was born Jeffrey Block, is an American Theravada Buddhist monk of Jewish heritage. Bodhi was born to a Jewish family from New York and ordained in Sri Lanka. He founded and serves as the director of Buddhist Global Relief, an organization dedicated to combating chronic hunger and malnutrition by providing food to the hungry.

The Buddhist teacher of Jewish heritage most renowned for catalyzing, in the words of Buddhist studies scholar Christopher Queen (2013), "a worldwide shift in the practice of Buddhism—from a religion of contemplative retreat and devotion, to one that plunges into direct engagement with society's discarded people, places, and problems" is Bernard Glassman.[45] Glassman (1939–2018) grew up in Brighton Beach, New York, in a family of eastern European Jewish immigrants with a strong socialist orientation. After graduating from college with a degree in aeronautical engineering and then briefly living on a kibbutz in Israel, he moved to the West Coast to work for McDonnell-Douglas and pursue a PhD in applied mathematics from the University of California in Los Angeles. In 1967, he discovered a small Soto Zen temple, Zenshu-ju, nearly in his own backyard in Los Angeles, where he began practicing meditation beneath the Japanese Zen teacher Maezumi. He eventually left his job as an aeronautical engineer to become a full-time monk, and in 1976, advanced into the role of his teacher's first heir and most senior student.[46]

By the early 1980s, Glassman established a network of organizations called the Greyston Mandela dedicated to transforming the teachings and principles of Zen into a force for social change. This network included various social enterprises that provide housing, employment, job training, childcare, after-school programs, and a host of other supportive programs for inner-city communities.[47] A decade later, he established the Zen Peacemakers International, an interfaith network dedicated to promoting peace and social justice. One of the Zen Peacemakers International's well-known programs, called the Bearing Witness Retreats, takes participants to contemporary and historical sites of great suffering (ranging from inner-city neighborhoods to Auschwitz-Birkenau to Rwanda) in order to bear witness and encourage the process of healing. As a result of his work, Glassman emerged as arguably the most famous and influential American Buddhist leader to engage Buddhism with pressing social issues.

The visible and important presence that American Jews have had in the movement for socially engaged Buddhism mirrors the historical overrepresentation that American Jews have had more generally in the area of politics dedicated to alleviating social and political injustice.[48] Since the late nineteenth century, American Jews, working individually and in self-defined Jewish organizations, have been at the helm of efforts to eradicate discrimination and prejudice from US society. They have been important leaders in the campaigns against bigotry and prejudice as well as for civil liberties and human rights. The notable involvement of American Jews in the movement to engage Buddhism with pressing social issues fits within this larger historical pattern of Jewish social and political activism in the United States. From my conversation with many of these Buddhist leaders, they have spoken openly about how their commitments to social justice are shaped by their Jewish upbringings. In my conversation with Senauke, he explained that his Buddhist activism carries forward and is fueled by the spirit of his liberal Jewish upbringing, crediting Judaism for instilling within him his concern for social justice. Similarly, Glassman credited the seeds of his activism to his upbringing in a left-wing, socialist Jewish family that was deeply concerned about poverty and social engagement. Glassman openly drew on his Jewish identity in his Zen peace work, employing rabbinical tales in his dharma teachings, holding his Bearing Witness Retreats at Auschwitz-Birkenau, and assisting in peace efforts in Israel and Palestine.

Finally, the third way that American Jews have shaped the character of Buddhism is through their work to assimilate psychological and therapeutic assumptions, language, and practice into Buddhism, particularly into the insight meditation movement. In his book *Jews and the American Soul*, historian Andrew Heinze (2004) demonstrated how Jews have played an indelible role in shaping the field of modern psychology in the United States. By the second half of the twentieth century, American Jews brought this same conspicuous interest in the psychic condition of the individual to the development of insight meditation in the United States. All the first-generation insight meditation teachers promoted—to varying extents—a distinctive psychologized Buddhist practice, but Kornfield, who holds a doctorate in psychology, has most explicitly incorporated psychotherapeutic ideas into his written work and teachings. His book *A Path with a Heart* (Kornfield 1993), for example, includes a chapter called "Psychotherapy and Meditation," dedicated to bringing together psychotherapeutic techniques and the practice of meditation.

Much of Salzberg's and Goldstein's teachings and writings, striking a tenor reminiscent of self-help literature, also deal with psychological awareness. Their writings cover topics that include navigating feelings of unworthiness, guilt, and jealousy; coping with difficult times and suffering; and breaking the habit of anger. As a result of the interweaving of Buddhism and psychology, insight meditation has come to resemble a psychological technique that promotes mindfulness and awareness through the use of the Buddha's teachings.

Unlike the insight meditation movement in the United States, Theravada Buddhism in Southeast Asia does not hold these various psychotherapeutic goals, such as combating depression, mitigating anger, and managing stress; these are, traditionally speaking, extra-Buddhist concerns (McMahan 2003, 52; Fronsdal 1998, 170). The reconceptualization of Buddhism in psychological terms, however, has long been a framework that Westerners have used to interpret Buddhism. As such, American Jews can be understood as following in the footsteps of other Buddhist modernizers who integrated Buddhism with Western psychology (McMahan 2003, 52). Why American Jews played such an important role in the psychologization of insight meditation is difficult to determine, though it is most likely that Jews have a demographic overrepresentation in the field of psychology in the United States more generally, so one seems to reflect the other.

The collective influence that American Jews have had on the Tibetan tradition is more difficult to gauge than the influence that Jews have had on the Zen and insight meditation traditions. This has largely to do with the way that the leadership has been transmitted and structured within these three communities. Within the last quarter of the twentieth century, the leadership of the insight meditation community and various Zen (specifically Japanese Zen) communities passed to a generation of native-born teachers, of which a significant and visible number were Jewish Americans. In contrast, Tibetan practice centers took root in the United States in the 1970s and were led by lamas brought over from Asia who served as guiding teachers. Only recently have a new generation of American-born lamas assumed leadership positions within the Tibetan tradition. As a consequence, American Jews, and Westerners more generally, have not had the same opportunity to lead and effect change within the tradition as they have had in the Zen or insight meditation traditions.

Conclusion

The liberal ethos of American Judaism paved the way for Jews to encounter, embrace, and ultimately reconfigure Buddhism in the second half of the twentieth century. This liberal ethos drove many Jews, particularly artists, writers, poets, and bohemians, to study Zen in California. It led other countercultural Jews to follow the "hippie trail" through India in the late 1960s and 1970s, where they completed one Buddhist retreat after another before returning to the United States. And it inspired other Jews to travel to Boulder in the 1970s to learn about the wisdom of Tibet from Trungpa at his newly founded Naropa Institute.

The American Jews who committed to Buddhism in the 1960s and 1970s burgeoned into a first generation of Buddhist teachers and leaders of Jewish descent in the Zen, insight meditation, and, though to a lesser extent, Tibetan tradition. Across all three traditions, American Jews adapted the teachings of the Buddha to the US cultural context, just as

Strauss and Goldwater did before them. In doing so, they carried forward a modernizing agenda—a process of demythologization, detraditionalization, and psychologization—that was already at play for over a century (McMahan 2008).

Yet the Jewish backgrounds of these Buddhist leaders shaped this modernizing agenda in particular ways. In the Zen tradition, American Jews emerged as important leaders in the movement to engage Buddhism with pressing social issues. The socially engaged ethic currently present within US Zen thus owes a great deal to the innovative efforts of these American Jews, whose liberal Jewish upbringing instilled within them a concern for social justice. American Jews were the founders and architects of the insight meditation movement, shaping it by centralizing the practice of mindfulness meditation, engaging in a process of doctrinal reorganization, and incorporating psychotherapeutic insights into the tradition. American Jews were not the first or only reformers in these three regards, but they had significant influence on the movement in these areas. And in all three of these areas, these teachers minimized or jettisoned aspects of Buddhism that felt unfamiliar to them as both Jews and Americans (e.g., metaphysical and monastic elements of the tradition), and accentuated those aspects that resonated with their Jewish American background (e.g., metta practices, psychotherapeutic techniques, and social activism).

Understanding both how Buddhism has been (re)constituted in the United States and how American Jews participated in that process gives context to how Jews engage with Buddhism in the contemporary United States. In the chapters in part II, we will see that many American Jews today centrally view Buddhism as "a way of practice," and distance themselves from many of the traditional and cosmological elements of Buddhism. They frequently relate to meditation as a psychotherapeutic practice detached from a broader historical and institutional context. Their relationship to Buddhism, and fundamental understanding of it, is shaped and made possible by the historical processes delineated in this chapter. Through their efforts to adapt Buddhism to American society, the first generation of Buddhist teachers of Jewish descent made it more broadly attractive to the next generation of Jewish Buddhists that followed.

The Jewish involvement in Buddhism in the 1970s did not go without notice from the American Jewish community. The Lubavitcher Rebbe, for example, called his major students together in the mid-1970s to rebuke what he saw as the dangerous trend of many Jews meditating (Brill 2009). Similarly, scholars and Jewish leaders from various wings of Judaism began to probe Judaism for its own contemplative inheritance, looking to unearth practice-based models of meditation that resembled (or possibly could compete with) those from the East. Modern publications about traditional meditative or contemplative practices within Judaism are likewise fairly recent, dating back to Gershom Scholem's scholarly article "Meditation," first published in the *Encyclopedia Judaica* in 1972.[49] Since then, a small but growing number of books have been written about the ancient roots of Jewish contemplative practices, thereby generating both a historiography about contemplative Judaism and practical tool kit for Jewish teachers looking for meditative techniques rooted in the ancient Jewish tradition (see, for example, Verman 1996; Kaplan 1978, 1982, 1985). The 1990s, though, saw the rise of a systematic movement designed to bring Judaism and Buddhism into conversation with each other for the purpose of creating a more contemplative Judaism, as described in the next chapter.

CHAPTER FOUR

Buddhism and the Creation of a Contemplative Judaism

IN THE 1970S, at approximately the same time that American Jews were exploring Zen on the West Coast and attending Theravada retreats across the ocean in India, a new Jewish spiritual movement was taking hold in the United States. This movement, which came to be known as Jewish Renewal, emerged from the counterculture of the 1960s and 1970s, and combined elements of Kabbalah—the tradition of Jewish mysticism— with the charisma of Hasidism, the eighteenth-century Orthodox movement founded in eastern Europe.[1] It was built on a rejection of conventional synagogue worship and disappointment about the lack of "authentic" religious experience in American Judaism. Its charismatic founder and central thinker, Rabbi Zalman Schachter-Shalomi, whom his followers affectionately called Reb Zalman, founded ALEPH: Alliance for Jewish Renewal in 1976, formally inaugurating this new movement to revitalize American Judaism.

The Jewish Renewal movement attracted many American Jews who were disaffected with the staid, suburban Judaism of the time. Grassroots and experiential, Jewish Renewal offered a free-form style of worship that included dancing, chanting, drumming, and various contemplative practices. Schachter-Shalomi widely embraced other spiritual traditions— Buddhism, Sufism, monastic Christianity, and even Native American religions—and incorporated them into his Jewish Renewal celebrations and worship. Buddhist-inspired forms of meditation in particular had a prominent place in his worship services. This heterogeneous-style worship infused Jewish Renewal with a spirit that celebrated diversity, liberalism, and religious fluidity. In developing a deeply and intentionally pluralistic Judaism, Schachter-Shalomi created a movement where religious boundaries were intentionally crossed, mixed, blurred, and eventually transformed.[2]

Many Jews who had "gone East," or traveled to Asia to study with various Buddhist (and other Eastern teachers), returned to the United States and found a home in the Jewish Renewal movement, which valued and welcomed their past experiences. Schachter-Shalomi became an important teacher and friend to those who had explored, or continued to explore, Buddhism.[3] He consistently emphasized that different religions had much to teach each other, and that they grow and strengthen through cross-fertilization. This gave Jewish Buddhists in particular the license to explore Buddhism while also observing Judaism, and then to fashion a new Jewish-Buddhist syncretism that incorporated Buddhist techniques and practices into Jewish worship—a subject discussed in more depth in the next chapter (Kasimow, Keenan, and Keenan 2003, 85–99).

The rise of the Jewish Renewal movement in the United States marked an important moment of change in the Jewish-Buddhist encounter. Up until the 1970s, the direction of influence between Judaism and Buddhism had been decidedly one way. American Jews had risen in stature within various Buddhist communities, and through their leadership, made an imprint on Buddhism in the United States in the various ways described in previous chapters. The interreligious mixing spurred by the Jewish Renewal movement in the 1970s allowed the two traditions to begin to more mutually transform each other. The Jewish Renewal movement—with its broad-minded and universalist leanings—emerged as a meeting place and incubator for Jewish-Buddhist syncretism and a crossover space on the US Left where Buddhism entered into and reconfigured American Judaism.

Beginning in the early 1990s, Buddhism's encounter with and influence on American Judaism moved from the left margins to the center of American Jewish life due to the veritable explosion of popular interest in meditation and ideas of mindfulness in the United States. The Jewish-born scientist Jon Kabat-Zinn pioneered the effort to link meditation with stress reduction and management, furnishing it with scientific and evidenced-based value.[4] The scientific and clinical application of meditation enhanced its popularity and thrust it into the mainstream of American society.[4] This kindled a new interest in Buddhism within the mainstream of American Jewish life, ultimately giving rise to a series of new Jewish-Buddhist dialogues along with the outgrowth of new contemplative Jewish organizations, communities, and practices.

The Medicalization and Mainstreaming of Buddhist Meditation

The transformative force behind the application of Buddhist meditation to the fields of psychology and medicine came from the work of Kabat-Zinn in the last two decades of the twentieth century.[5] Born to a Jewish family of eastern European heritage, Kabat-Zinn studied Buddhism with Vietnamese Zen teacher Thich Nhat Hanh and other Asian Buddhist teachers, including Korean Zen master Seung Sahn. Kabat-Zinn helped found the Cambridge Zen Center (in Sahn's tradition), and also trained at IMS with Kornfield, Goldstein, and Salzburg.

After years of Buddhist study, he felt convinced that psychology and Western science would benefit from Buddhist teachings and practices.[6] In 1979, Kabat-Zinn, who held a PhD in molecular biology from MIT, founded the Stress Reduction and Relaxation Program at the University of Massachusetts Medical School. This program reformulated the teachings of mindfulness and practice of meditation into medical terms. The first of its kind, it also presented mindfulness—or a basic attention to the present moment achieved most commonly through the practice of meditation—as a therapy for alleviating stress and illness as well as a complement to traditional medical treatments. He renamed the program the Stress Reduction Clinic in the 1980s in an effort to normalize it as a clinical service. By the early 1990s, he rebranded the program once again, this time as Mindfulness-Based Stress Reduction (MBSR). Through his clinical application of mindfulness meditation at the University of Massachusetts Medical School, Kabat-Zinn paved the way for meditation to enter into the mainstream of American society as a widely popular therapeutic tool (Wilson 2014, 75–103; Center for Mindfulness, n.d.).

Anxious that Americans would view meditation as too ethnic or foreign, Kabat-Zinn repackaged the teachings of mindfulness in clinical, psychotherapeutic terms in order to render them more appealing and familiar. He also intentionally downplayed any connection between mindfulness and Buddhism. Kabat-Zinn (2011, 282) explained that

> from the beginning of MBSR, I bent over backward to structure it and find ways to speak about it that avoided as much as possible the risk of it being seen as Buddhist, "New Age," "Eastern Mysticism" or just plain "flakey." To my mind this was a constant and serious risk that would have undermined our attempts to present it as commonsensical, evidence-based, and ordinary, and ultimately a legitimate element of mainstream medical care.

Since MBSR's inception, nearly twenty-five thousand people have completed the program, making it one of the longest-running, academic-based mindfulness practice and training programs worldwide (Center for Mindfulness, n.d.). The MBSR program has been the subject of television documentaries and received broad newspaper coverage, enhancing its visibility in the United States. Kabat-Zinn also wrote the best-selling book *Full Catastrophe Living*, based on his work and experiences with the MBSR program.

The central focus of the program is an eight-week intensive training in mindfulness meditation and its application to everyday life, with one session a week for about two hours. The program claims that its training leads to reductions in medical and psychological symptoms across a wide range of medical diagnoses, including many different chronic pain and anxiety conditions (Center for Mindfulness, n.d.). Over the past two decades, the MBSR clinics have given way to a whole new family of what are now called mindfulness-based interventions, which include such topics as mindful eating, mindful work, mindful parenting, and more.[7]

The work of Kabat-Zinn has resulted in a refitting of meditation as a nonsectarian, universal practice, divorced from its Buddhist roots, and linked instead to stress reduction and management. The MBSR clinics created a precedent that enabled meditation to enter into the cognate fields of neurobiology and cognitive science too—fields that have further furnished it with evidenced-based value. The scientific and therapeutic application of meditation and mindfulness have propelled them not only into the mainstream of American science but also into mainstream American society.

Although Kabat-Zinn is the foremost leader in integrating meditation and Buddhist-inspired ideas of mindfulness into the fields of medicine and psychology, two other American Jews—Mark Epstein and Goleman, both longtime practitioners of insight meditation—were also leaders in introducing mindfulness meditation as a psychological technique.[8] Epstein trained as a psychiatrist at Harvard Medical School, and studied Buddhism with Goldstein and Kornfield. He wrote a number of popular books about the meeting of Buddhism and psychotherapy, including *Thoughts without a Thinker, Going to Pieces without Falling Apart, Going on Being,* and *Open to Desire and Psychotherapy without the Self.* In these books, he brought Western and Eastern ideas about the self into conversation with each other, and demonstrated how Buddhist perspectives could strengthen Western psychiatry.

Goleman studied meditation in India in the 1960s alongside Goldstein, Salzberg, Ram Dass, and other American travelers mentioned in the last chapter. He returned to the United States after his travels to complete his doctorate in psychology at Harvard on meditation as an intervention in stress arousal. Afterward, he received a postdoctoral grant to return to Asia and continue studying Buddhist thought, spending time in both India and Sri Lanka. He wrote his first book, now called *The Meditative Mind,* summarizing his research on meditation in Asia. Goleman (1995) has since authored nearly a dozen other books, including the internationally best-selling *Emotional Intelligence,* which argues, among other things, that mindfulness, or what he calls self-awareness, is a key tool to increasing a person's emotional intelligence. *Emotional Intelligence* was on the *New York Times* best seller list for over a year, and has sold more than five million copies worldwide and been published in forty languages. After publishing *Emotional Intelligence,* Goleman organized a series of intensive conversations between the Dalai Lama and scientists, resulting in the books *Healthy Emotions* and *Destructive Emotions* (*Daniel Goleman*, n.d.). The Jewish involvement in popularizing mindfulness and incorporating it into Western psychology fits within a larger pattern of the Jewish involvement in psychotherapy more generally. As noted in the last chapter, in his book *Jews and the American Soul*, Andrew Heinze (2004) has demonstrated how Jews have played an indelible role in shaping the field of modern psychology in the United States.

Nathan Cummings Foundation and the Rise of Jewish-Buddhist Dialogues

The work of Kabat-Zinn and others to recast meditation as nonsectarian and universal, and rebrand it in medical and/or therapeutic terms, dramatically increased its popularity in the United States.[9] It also made meditation attractive to a wide swath of American Jews who had little to no interest in practicing Buddhism, but like other Americans, were interested in learning about meditation as a stress-reduction technique. Recognizing the budding national interest in meditation and mindfulness, and the concomitant Jewish attraction to these practices, Jewish leaders began to look for opportunities to bring these Buddhist practices and teachings into conversation with Judaism. At the center of this movement for Jewish-Buddhist dialogue was the Nathan Cummings Foundation (n.d.). Nathan Cummings, founder of the Sara Lee Corporation, formed the foundation in 1949. After his death in 1985, the foundation received most of his estate, creating an endowment of more than four hundred million dollars.

In 1989, Charles Halpern was appointed the inaugural president of the Nathan Cummings Foundation (n.d.), an organization "rooted in the Jewish tradition and committed to democratic values and social justice, including fairness, diversity, and community." The foundation invested in "Jewish Life" as a focus area, and sought to fund programs with a stress on spiritual and contemplative practice out of a concern that in the postwar years, American Judaism had grown into a tradition deeply committed to rational intellectualism and family celebration but lacking the spiritual means to respond to pain and grief.[10] Under Halpern's leadership, the foundation financed dozens of Jewish-Buddhist collaborations and generated new conditions for Jewish-Buddhist mixing to occur. Halpern was a longtime practitioner of Buddhism and close friend of many of the insight meditation teachers of Jewish descent, particularly Goldstein and Salzberg.[11] Although not a practicing Jew, Halpern was connected to the American Jewish community and sought to fund programs that worked in the area of Jewish meditation and Jewish contemplative practice as a means to encourage spiritual renewal within Judaism.

One of the Nathan Cummings Foundation's first initiatives in this respect was to give money to various Jewish-Buddhist dialogues, the most famous of which was the dialogue between American Jewish leaders and the Dalai Lama in Dharamsala in 1990, written about in Kamenetz's *The Jew in the Lotus: A Poet's Rediscovery of Jewish Identity in Buddhist India*.[12] The Nathan Cummings Foundation gave the financial support that enabled the meeting in Dharamsala to occur and funded Kamenetz to write the book about it on his return to the United States. In *The Jew in the Lotus*, Kamenetz chronicled the meeting between eight Jewish delegates—a group of progressive rabbis and scholars from across various wings of American Jewish life—and the Dalai Lama. The meeting came about at the request of the Dalai Lama, who was grateful for the aid that the American Jewish World Service gave to Tibetan refugees in southern India in the 1980s. Curious about the Jewish religion from which many of his new followers were born, the Dalai Lama met with a group of Jewish rabbis and scholars in New Jersey during the course of his 1989 visit to the United States. This meeting led to the more famous one in Dharamsala in 1990 (Kamenetz 1994, 5–17; Goldman 1989).

The Jewish delegates to Dharamsala included Schachter-Shalomi; Irving and Blu Greenberg, both Modern Orthodox leaders (with Irving notable for his progressive leadership and theological writings, and Blu for her pioneering efforts on behalf of Orthodox feminism); Reconstructionist rabbi Joy Levitt, the first president of the Reconstructionist Rabbinical Association; Jonathan Omer-Man, the founder of Metivta: A Center for Contemplative Judaism in Los Angeles; Moshe Waldoks, now the rabbi and spiritual leader of Temple Beth Zion in Brookline, Massachusetts; Nathan Katz, a professor of Indo-Judaic studies at Florida International University; and Paul Mendes-Flohr, a professor of Jewish history and thought at the University of Chicago. As Kamenetz recorded the meeting of these delegates and the Dalai Lama, he wrestled with a number of larger issues that surfaced during the trip. One such issue, which the Dalai Lama raised, was how the Jewish people maintained their religion as a people in exile for over two thousand years. The Dalai Lama wanted to learn strategies to help his people preserve their Tibetan religion and culture through their period of exile.

Another question that emerged was how the Jewish mystical teachings compared to the Tibetan esoteric teachings and practices. Kamenetz also explored why a seemingly disproportionate number of Jews were attracted to Buddhism, and what this defection said about the problems within American Judaism. Kamenetz suspected that the lack of spiritual possibilities within American Judaism led many to look to Buddhism for spiritual fulfillment. Ultimately, his book pushed for a spiritual renewal of mainstream Judaism that would more substantively incorporate ancient Jewish contemplative techniques, like Jewish meditation, so that Jews seeking deeper spiritual practices might find it within their own tradition.

Several years after writing *The Jew in the Lotus*, Kamenetz started another Jewish-Buddhist dialogue called Seders for Tibet. Kamenetz sought to link the hardship of the Tibetan people suffering under Chinese oppression with the seder, a ritual Passover meal that celebrates freedom. He organized a seder to take place in Washington, DC, in 1997, that reframed the Jewish holiday in universal terms to recognize the plight of Tibet in exile. Seders for Tibet received sponsorship from prominent Jewish and Buddhist organizations, including the International Campaign for Tibet, Religious Action Center (the political arm of the Reform movement in the United States), leaders in different Jewish denominations, and various different Jewish student groups on campus. More than fifty people attended the first seder, including representatives of Washington's Reform, Conservative, and Orthodox communities. Other prominent guests included Supreme Court justice Stephen Breyer and

Adam Yauch of the Beastie Boys. The guest of honor for the evening, however, was the Dalai Lama, who attended the event while on a visit to the capital.[13]

The event closed with an altered version of the traditional Passover prayer that combined the hopes of the Jewish and Tibetan people: "*L'Shana Haba-ah B'Yerushalayim* [next year in Jerusalem]. . . . *L'Shana Haba-ah B'Lhasa* [next year in Lhasa. Next year may they be a free people]" (International Campaign for Tibet, n.d.). The event was such a success that the 109th annual convention of the Central Conference of American Rabbis (1998), the yearly gathering of rabbis from the Reform movement, passed a resolution urging the participation of Reform synagogues in the Seders for Tibet in years to come. By drawing widespread attention to the Jewish-Buddhist dialogue movement, *The Jew in the Lotus* and Seders for Tibet laid the groundwork for other interreligious conversations to develop.

In addition to funding Tibetan-Jewish dialogues, the Nathan Cummings Foundation brought leaders from the Zen and insight meditation traditions into conversation with Jewish leaders in the early 1990s in the hope of spiritually rejuvenating liberal Judaism. The foundation cosponsored (along with the Barre Center for Buddhist Studies and Jewish Community of Amherst) a series of annual Jewish-Buddhist conferences beginning in 1992, held at the Barre Center for Buddhist Studies in Massachusetts. These conferences, which inspired other similar conferences and groups in New York City and on the West Coast, brought together leading Jewish and Buddhist teachers, including Rabbis Michael Strassfeld, Joy Levitt, Marcello Bronstein, Nancy Flam, Rachel Cowan, Arthur Waskow, Mordechai Liebling, Sheila Weinberg, Joseph Goldstein, Sylvia Boorstein, and others. The purpose of these conferences was to provide a space for Jewish practitioners of Buddhism to examine why so many Jewish-born Americans were drawn to Buddhism, and why so many teachers of Buddhism in the United States were Jewish. The conferences also explored how Jewish Buddhists found fulfillment and nurturance in both their inherited and adopted traditions, and why some Jews have found spiritual nourishment within the Jewish fold while others have not.[14]

The Barre Center conferences were important to the movement for Jewish-Buddhist dialogue because they marked the beginning of the interfaith efforts of Boorstein, perhaps the best-known Jewish Buddhist in the contemporary United States. Boorstein was born in 1936 in Brooklyn, New York, to an observant Jewish family with eastern European roots. She earned a PhD in psychology and for many years practiced as a psychotherapist. Boorstein first began practicing mindfulness meditation in 1977, and relatively soon thereafter, dedicated herself to the practice, studying beneath Kornfield, Salzberg, Goldstein, and others in the insight meditation tradition. By 1985, she began teaching her own meditation classes and cofounded Spirit Rock Meditation Center.[15]

At the Jewish-Buddhist conferences at the Barre Center for Buddhist Studies, Boorstein met and then paired up with Weinberg (2010), a Reconstructionist rabbi and practitioner of insight meditation, to offer classes in meditation for American Jews. Boorstein and Weinberg transformed the conference from the traditional model of interreligious dialogue to a weekend dedicated to blending insight meditation and Shabbat (the Jewish Sabbath) celebration. Their hope was that by introducing American Jews to the teachings and practices of Buddhism, they could bring together strands of Jewish and Buddhism healing, mysticism, and mindfulness that would help American Jews lead more spiritually fulfilling lives.[16] In 1996, Boorstein and Weinberg (who had in the interim years begun to study insight meditation beneath Boorstein) led a Jewish-Buddhist venture, first under the name Contemplative Intersearch in Jewish and Buddhist Traditions, and later as Awakening in Buddhist and Jewish Traditions: A Contemplative Intersearch (*Insight* 1996). Though under different names, both retreats focused on how meditation could be taught and practiced through a Jewish lens. Boorstein led the group in meditation practices, and Weinberg led the group in Jewish prayers; both teachers concentrated on how the teachings of the Buddha could be understood using a Jewish framework.[17]

After teaching with Weinberg, Boorstein paired up with other Jewish leaders to teach meditation classes to Jews. She co-led retreats across the country with numerous American rabbis, including Shefa Gold, Miles Krassen, Joanna Katz, and Jeff Roth, to name just a few. From her experiences teaching to both Jews and Buddhists, and identifying as a "dual citizen" of both traditions, she wrote the book *That's Funny, You Don't Look Buddhist: On Being a Faithful Jew and a Passionate Buddhist.*[18] In this book, Boorstein (1997, 1) talks about Judaism and Buddhism as her "two vocabularies of response," and how she moves between both traditions' modes of thinking and expression as if she were speaking two languages.

The Nathan Cummings Foundation also supported Jewish-Buddhist dialogues, like those that Boorstein and Weinberg co-led at the Barre Center for Buddhist Studies on the West Coast in the 1990s. The most famous of these interfaith dialogues took the form of a conversation between two longtime friends—Alan Lew, a Conservative rabbi, and Norman Fischer, the Jewish-born Zen teacher discussed in the last chapter. Lew and Fischer facilitated these dialogues, which they called Translating Judaism, Translating Buddhism, at Green Gulch Farm, a Zen practice center near Muir Beach, California.[19] Lew and Fischer, both from East Coast Jewish families, met as graduate students in the Iowa Writers' Workshop in the late 1960s. They both traveled to California after obtaining MFA degrees and studied Zen Buddhism at the Berkeley Zen Center beneath Weitsman. As described in the last chapter, Fischer received dharma transmission from Weitsman in 1988 and went on to hold the position of abbot at Green Gulch Farm and coabbot at the San Francisco Zen Center with Hartman.

After studying beneath Weitsman at the Berkeley Zen Center, Lew took a different life trajectory than Fischer. When it came time for him to take ordination as a Buddhist priest, he decided to leave the Berkeley Zen Center. Shortly thereafter, he reengaged with Judaism.[20] He was ordained as a Conservative rabbi in 1988 and became the spiritual leader at Congregation Beth Sholom in San Francisco from 1991 to 2005.

At the Translating Judaism, Translating Buddhism workshops, Lew gave talks about Judaism, and then Fischer taught lessons about Buddhism, after which the participants would meditate, participate in an abbreviated Jewish prayer service, and study Jewish and Buddhist texts.[21] Lew (2001, 288–93) had hoped that Buddhist meditation techniques would help Jews deepen their Jewish practice, and Fischer wanted to use these workshops as a way to reach out to Jewish Buddhists who wanted to reconnect with their Jewishness. These meetings marked one of the first times that Zen Buddhism and Judaism came into intimate and deliberate conversation with one another in the United States.

After these dialogues at Green Gulch Farm, Lew and Fischer formed a partnership that placed them at the center of the Jewish-Buddhist dialogue movement in the United States. Driven by the conviction that Buddhist meditation techniques could reinvigorate normative Jewish practice and enhance its spiritual potential, they continued to offer classes together and work side by side for more than a decade.

Beginning in the early 2000s, a movement to create new Jewish practices, organizations, and communities that draw selectively on Buddhism came to replace the model of Jewish-Buddhist interreligious dialogues and workshops. Boorstein, Weinberg, Lew, and Fischer were at the forefront of this movement in its early years, though over time many other leaders joined in the work to recontextualize Buddhist teachings and practices for American Jews. Fueling this movement was the conviction that Buddhist practices and teachings could and would serve as a source of spiritual renewal for Jewish communities and congregations.

The Creation of New Jewish Contemplative Organizations, Communities, and Practices

The Jewish-Buddhist dialogues that took place in the early 1990s laid the foundation for new Jewish contemplative practices, organizations, and communities to develop in and around them. In January 2000, after the Translating Judaism, Translating Buddhism workshops, Lew and Fischer cocreated a new practice that they called Jewish meditation, drawing on basic Zen meditation practice as a way to reinvigorate normative Jewish worship. They imagined using this new practice as a preparation for Jewish worship. They would lead Jews in a mindfulness meditation sit before the start of a traditional Jewish synagogue service, generating a heightened spiritual state in which to pray.[22] Lew secured funding from the Nathan Cummings Foundation to support the growth of this Jewish meditation practice. From there, Lew and Fischer built a formal Jewish meditation program called Makor Or: A Center of Jewish Meditation, housed within Temple Beth Sholom in San Francisco. Makor Or became one of the first Jewish meditation centers established in the United States. Currently, it offers morning meditation classes, daylong retreats several times a year, and occasional classes on various topics relating to Jewish meditation.

At approximately the same time that Lew and Fischer began teaching classes in Jewish meditation, Boorstein and other teachers started to offer similar classes in Jewish meditation drawing from the tradition of insight meditation rather than Zen Buddhism. In the late 1990s, Jewish meditation developed into a nationwide movement through various efforts to organize and codify the practice—a process described in much more depth in the next chapter. As the next chapter demonstrates, Jewish meditation currently tends to consist of a practice that integrates Jewish language, texts, and interpretations with sitting in silence, being mindful of the present moment, and engaging in concentration and awareness exercises.

Over the past two decades, a host of new Jewish organizations have developed around this practice of Jewish meditation. New Jewish meditation centers have started in Chicago (Center for Jewish Mindfulness), Montclair, New Jersey (Jewish Meditation Center of Montclair), Washington, DC (Jewish Mindfulness Center of Washington), New York City (Makom), and Boston (Nishmat Hayyim) to name just a few. In addition to these organizations, Roth, a leading teacher of Jewish meditation in the United States, created the Awakened Heart Project for Contemplative Judaism, an online clearinghouse for resources and tools about Jewish meditation and contemplative prayer.[23] Roth and many of the other Jewish meditation teachers, including Lew, Weinberg, Gold, Cooper, Jonathan Slater, Jay Michaelson, and many others have also written popular books and articles about their teachings.

In addition to the growth of new Jewish meditation centers in the United States, other new contemplative organizations have developed as a result of the cross-fertilization between Judaism and Buddhism. For example, Roth and Katz, both rabbis and students of Schachter-Shalomi and Boorstein, founded Elat Chayyim Center for Jewish Spirituality in the Catskill Mountains of upstate New York in 1992, loosely based on a Buddhist retreat mode. Elat Chayyim, the first Jewish spiritual retreat center in the United States, was a year-round center that integrated Jewish learning, worship, and cultural programs. In its early years, many of the spiritual teachings at Elat Chayyim deliberately synthesized Judaism with various non-Jewish practices, including Buddhist practices. Ram Dass, Glassman, Boorstein, and other Buddhist teachers have all co-led sessions with various rabbis at Elat Chayyim, creating an intentional Jewish-Buddhist synthesis.[24] Additionally, David and Shoshanna Cooper, a prominent teaching pair at Elat Chayyim (which merged with and is now a part of the Isabella Freedman Jewish Retreat Center in Falls Village, Connecticut), offer courses on meditation from their training in both the Hasidic and Buddhist worlds. The different teachers and teaching pairs at Elat Chayyim have their own meditation style, retreat practice, and even dedicated groups of followers.

Different from the new communities and centers that have sprouted up across the country that deliberately seek to connect Judaism and Buddhism, other organizations have developed in an attempt to thwart, or at least decelerate, the mixing of Judaism and Buddhism in the United States. In 1991, for instance, Omer-Man, a rabbi ordained by Schachter-Shalomi, received money from the Nathan Cummings Foundation to establish Metivta: A Center for Contemplative Judaism, a nondenominational community dedicated to renewing and unearthing traditional Jewish meditation. Based in Los Angeles, Metivta focused on contemplative study and practice, especially Jewish meditation, as rooted in Jewish sources and texts. Omer-Man sought to uncover, translate, and pass on ancient Jewish techniques to contemporary Jews so that Jews did not have to turn to Buddhism or other Eastern religions for meditative practices.[25]

Similarly, Avram Davis, a scholar and rabbi, received money from the Nathan Cummings Foundation in 1999 to found Chochmat HaLev, a congregation and practice center for Jewish meditation in Berkeley, California. Davis felt that the mixing of Judaism and Buddhism threatened the integrity of Judaism because it brought foreign practices into the tradition. Like Omer-Man, he taught Jewish meditation as a practice rooted in ancient Jewish sources, particularly in Hasidic teachings and theology—a topic discussed in more depth in the next chapter.[26]

Conclusion

The mainstreaming and medicalization of meditation in the United States sparked a new Jewish interest in Buddhism that led to a pronounced shift in the encounter between the two traditions. Beginning in the early 1990s, Buddhism entered into and reconfigured the center of American Jewish life by infusing it with a contemplative spirit. The encounter between Buddhism and Judaism culminated in the development of a series of new Jewish-Buddhist dialogues and the creation of new contemplative Jewish practices, organizations, and communities. The Nathan Cummings Foundation played a pivotal role in facilitating this meeting between the two traditions in the last decade of the twentieth century. The foundation provided the capital that drove various dialogues and large-scale Jewish-Buddhist events. It also financed new innovative organizations designed to bring the traditions into conversation with each other. The role that the Nathan Cummings Foundation played in fostering a more contemplative American Judaism provides compelling evidence of the impact and significance of philanthropy on American Jewish life.[27]

This chapter closes the historical overview of the Jewish-Buddhist encounter in the United States. The broad historical processes that brought Judaism and Buddhism into interaction and conversation with each other also sowed the seeds for the rise of Jewish-Buddhist syncretism. By the end of this period, new forms of syncretism started to take hold, including a syncretism of Jewish-Buddhist practices, spiritual discourses, and identities. The next three chapters, taken together, probe these forms of syncretism through exploring the lived experience of everyday Jewish Buddhists in the United States. In the next section of this book, the story moves from the past to the present, from history to ethnography, and gradually from teachers to lay practitioners. Despite all this movement, the next chapter begins right where this one leaves off by narrowing in on the creation and contours of Jewish meditation.

PART II

Lived Experience of Jewish Buddhists in the United States

CHAPTER FIVE

Making Meditation Jewish

ON A COOL Wednesday evening in October, Jacob arrives at the Hannah Senesh Community Day School, a private Jewish school in Brooklyn. He walks up a flight of stairs to the school's multipurpose room, where the Jewish Meditation Center of Brooklyn (JMC) holds its meditation class, or "meditation sit." He takes off his shoes and places them on the shoe rack outside the door to the room, as the sign above the rack instructs him to do.

During the day, when thirty-one-year-old Jacob works as a grassroots organizer, this room serves as the school's *Beit Knesset*, or prayer space. A Torah ark prominently stands at the front of the room, and the back wall of the room contains large bookcases full of prayer books, bibles, and other Jewish sacred and liturgical books. Children's artwork containing illustrations of biblical stories and Jewish symbolism colorfully decorate the side walls of the room. Shortly after entering the room, Jacob begins to transform this multipurpose room into a "sitting" space.

Jacob clears the rows of chairs in the center of the large rectangular room to the perimeter, leaving much of the interior space of the room empty. As other community members and I slowly saunter in, we help Jacob with the room preparations. A few community members arrange black meditation cushions—*zafus*, as they are called in the Buddhist tradition—in a circle on the floor. We also set up a half circle of chairs behind the zafus for those meditators who prefer to sit with back support. From a cabinet, Jacob takes out a "Jewish blessings flag," modeled after the Tibetan prayer flag. I help him use it to festoon the Torah ark. Like the Tibetan prayer flag, the Jewish blessings flag contains a string of rectangular shapes that are connected along their top edges to a long

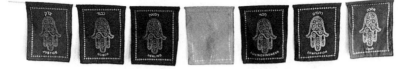

FIGURE 5.1. Jewish blessings flag. Photo courtesy of Fair Trade Judaica
(http://www.fairtradejudaica.org).

string. The center of each rectangle on the Jewish blessings flag features a *hamsa*, an image of an open right hand, which many contemporary Jewish people refer to as the "hand of Miriam" in remembrance of the biblical Miriam.[1] A set of blessings, written both in Hebrew and English, surround the hamsa image (figure 5.1).

Jacob places a small meditation bell from India and matching mallet on the floor next to a meditation cushion. He also pulls out a basket of heavy wool Mexican yoga blankets from a closet and places it near the door. He and other community members set up a folding table outside the multipurpose room. On it, they set a little box for donations (the suggested donation is ten dollars per sit), flyers about upcoming events, and a sign-up sheet asking for meditators' names and email addresses. More and more people arrive, take off their shoes, and enter the room. They greet each other quietly and warmly, often with silent hugs. Many community members grab a wool blanket from the basket near the door. We all begin to take a seat.

Of the approximately twenty participants, most sit cross-legged on the zafus; only a few sit on chairs. Some fold the heavy blanket, using it as an extra cushion to sit on. Others drape it over their bodies, shrouding themselves in the warmth of the wool. Most of the participants are in their twenties and thirties, with men and women in roughly similar numbers. Although typically the Wednesday evening meditation sit begins at 8:00 p.m., tonight's sit, a beginners' sit, starts at 7:30. The beginners' sit offers a broad introduction to Jewish meditation, teachings, and practice. These sits are open to people of all levels of experience and backgrounds, though most of the members present in the circle are regular rather than new members of the community.

One of the JMC cofounders, Alison Laichter, leads the sit for the evening. She sits on a dark zafu at the top of the circle near the Torah ark. An urban planner in her early thirties, Alison begins by welcoming us to the JMC. She asks that we go around to, if comfortable, share our name, why we came, and our prior experiences with meditation, if any. About half the participants speak about their experiences with meditation in the Buddhist tradition, and many mention how a search and desire for a welcoming Jewish community led them to the JMC. After we finish speaking, Alison briefly shares her biography with the group. She mentions that she first started meditating in high school, and over the course of the past ten years, has practiced meditation in many different contexts and traditions. She explains that she cofounded the JMC (with her friend Yael Shy) to bring meditation and mindfulness practices to the Jewish community.

Moving from the personal to the professional, she introduces the practice of Jewish meditation to the group. She emphasizes that Judaism has a long historical meditative tradition, so meditation is not a new Jewish practice. The Amidah, she notes, is a central part of the Jewish synagogue service, and is often considered an opportunity for silent prayer or meditation. She explains that Jewish meditators take off their shoes before entering the meditation space as a way to separate the sacred from the profane. When Moses encounters the burning bush, God tells him "Take off your sandals from your feet, for the place where you are standing is holy ground" (Exodus 3:5). Thus, she says, taking off one's shoes is a way to mark the space as holy. Alison offers suggestions for various different sitting positions: cross-legged on cushions or upright on chairs. Hands, she says, could rest face up, down on knees, or in the lap; each position signifies different things in different meditative traditions. She ends her instruction on posture by suggesting that we "sit as we would like to be." Sitting with the shoulders back opens up the heart. Sitting with straight shoulders connotes carrying ourselves with dignity.

Alison underscores that meditation is about being awake and in tune with the present moment. It is about cultivating mindfulness. She warns us that during a meditation exercise, we should expect and accept that our minds will wander. She explains that different people use different strategies to help anchor thoughts. Some people focus on breathing while paying attention to the rhythm of the inhaling and exhaling of the breath. Other people use chanting or mental visualizations. Imagine a murky lake with a lot of sediment, she says. Meditation helps the sediment to settle so that the clear water can take form.

Alison suggests that in this beginners' sit, we first try the basic strategy of paying attention to the breath, to each inhale and exhale. She asks us to sit for one minute in still silence with our eyes closed, paying attention to our breathing. She rings the bell to indicate that the minute of silence has begun. A minute later, she rings the bell again, indicating that the minute has come to a close. She asks us how the experience felt. A few new members speak about how hard it was to sit without fidgeting or moving. Other meditators lament that their minds kept wandering away from their breath. Some meditators feel that quiet sitting made them sleepy.

Alison offers us a second meditation tool or strategy. She explains that there is a Jewish technique of meditating on the letters that spell God's name in Hebrew (the letters Yud, Hey, Vav, and Hey). Meditating on these letters, she remarks, is an anchor that can help to return our focus to our breath. She encourages us to inhale saying "Yud" and "Hey," and exhale on "Vav" and "Hey." She rings the bell again, announcing the second round of silent sitting has begun. Murmurs of "Yud, Hey, Vav, Hey" fill the room as each of us quietly chants these letters while we inhale and exhale. After the second round of sitting, Alison again asks us to share our experiences. One woman speaks about how sitting on a cushion makes her back hurt. Alison observes that there are different ways to approach the pain and discomfort of sitting. In some traditions, a person is taught to sit with the pain until it becomes bearable. By concentrating on the pain and thinking about what hurts, she instructs, we can work through it. A second approach, she notes, is a more "Jewish" one to pain: just move our body around to find a more comfortable sitting position.

As the sit goes on, Alison introduces a variety of what she calls "anchors" or different tools to help us focus on our breath. She teaches us a mantra of saying "Modeh Ani" or (for women) "Modah Ani," phrases that mean "I give thanks" in Hebrew. This mantra, which she recently learned at a Jewish meditation teacher-training workshop, comes from the Jewish prayer recited on waking up in the morning. She rings the bell again, asking us to try to use this mantra during our minute of silent sitting. We continue to do several more one-minute sitting exercises—some with our eyes closed, some with them open, some with chanting, and some in complete quiet.

In between the sits, Alison shares with us various different stories from her own past. She tells us that she has practiced meditation with the "superstar Buddhist," Boorstein, who feels to her like a great Jewish grandma. Often during Wednesday evening sits, the sit leader will provide a *kavanah*, or intention, based on the week's Torah portion or upcoming Jewish holiday. We are in the period of time between Rosh Hashanah and Yom Kippur, a period known as Aseret Yemei Teshuva, or the Ten Days of Repentance. Because of this special time of year, in lieu of a kavanah, Alison says she wants to read us some excerpts from Rabbi Lew's book, *This Is Real and You Are Completely Unprepared: The Days of Awe as a Journey of Transformation*. After the reading, Alison talks for a few minutes about the idea of *teshuva* (repentance), and how this time of year allows us to take stock of the year past and look forward to the year ahead.

Alison then proposes that we try sitting for a full five minutes, but this time she asks that we imagine that our breaths are part of a larger ecosystem of breaths. Our inhale, she says, connects to someone else's exhale. In this way, we are all connected to a universe of breaths. She rings the bell, and we all sit for a full five minutes in silence, focusing on the connectivity of our breaths. Finally, Alison closes the evening sit by introducing us to a loving-kindness meditation. Loving-kindness, she teaches, is talked about in the Buddhist tradition as metta, and in the Jewish tradition is called *Hesed*. She asks us to cultivate loving-kindness by visualizing friends and family in our meditation. As we visualize different people, she instructs us to pair our inhales with "may you be blessed with," and our exhales with "peace, love, and *rachamim* [compassion or mercy]." She asks us to first imagine the people we love, then the people we find challenging, and then, last, ourselves. The bell rings, and we all begin our final five-minute sit, inhaling and exhaling, wishing others and ourselves peace, love, and compassion.

At 9:00 p.m., the sit draws to an end. We all slowly stand up, stretch our arms and legs, and wish each other a good rest of the week. Alison tells us about different options for Yom Kippur services for those who might be looking for a community. Many of the members of the group hang around after the meditation session concludes, talking and acquainting themselves with each other. Some members of the group decide to go out for dinner and drinks after the sit. I speak briefly with Jacob after the sit ends. He tells me that he likes to meditate at the JMC because it makes him feel kinder to himself. He also appreciates that as a new transplant to Brooklyn, this community allows him a way to meet other like-minded Jews. It's like therapy with friends, he says with a bit of a chuckle.

———

This Wednesday evening meditation group at the JMC is part of a burgeoning network of Jewish meditation offerings in the United States.[2] Jewish meditation classes are taking place in Jewish community centers, synagogues, and day schools, or informally in Jewish homes. At the same time, Jewish meditation retreats are sprouting up in centers from Asheville, North Carolina, to Garrison, New York, to San Francisco. Across these different spaces, Jewish meditation typically involves periods of silent meditation joined with a range of different practices, teachings, and ideas from both the Jewish and Buddhist traditions.[3]

This chapter explores the development and contours of the syncretism of religious practice, asking how the practice of meditation spread from Buddhism into Judaism, and how it was reconfigured along the way. I draw on personal interviews that I conducted with many of the first generation of teachers of Jewish meditation in the United States as well as an analysis of these teachers' books, blogs, and other writings, and participant observation in over a dozen different Jewish meditation offerings across the country. In examining the transformation and spread of religious practices, I draw on the insights from the social scientific theories on cultural diffusion. Diffusion studies broadly explore how practices—construed to mean behaviors, strategies, beliefs, technologies, or structures—are transmitted, adopted, and reconfigured by a recipient population. Within sociology, most of the research on diffusion focuses on its structural aspects. These structural approaches look at the social mechanisms, networks, and points of contact that lead to the diffusion of practices across different organizations and social movements.[4]

Over the past two decades, a growing body of research has taken a more culturally minded approach to diffusion. These cultural approaches to diffusion examine the interpretative process that underlies how practices spread and transform. Cultural theories of diffusion have demonstrated that practices are most likely to spread and become adopted when they are first made congruent with local cultures or frames of understanding.[5] As sociologists David Strang and Sarah Soule (1998, 276) summarize, "The argument is that practices diffuse as they are rendered salient, familiar, and compelling."

In this chapter, I first briefly explain the structural forces that enabled meditation to enter into mainstream American Judaism. Specifically, I highlight the importance of the first generation of Buddhist teachers of Jewish descent who actively sought to teach meditation to Jews, rise of a popular Jewish interest in meditation, and availability of financial resources and organizational support that enabled the movement for Jewish meditation to launch. Next, I delve more deeply into exploring the cultural and interpretative work that made meditation accessible as well as appealing to American Jews.

I argue, as noted earlier, that a prominent group of Jewish teachers and leaders repackaged Buddhist meditation within a Jewish framework, rendering it familiar and compelling to the American Jewish mainstream.[6] I imagine that the founding teachers, consciously or not, engaged in a syncretism of religious practice by creating a new "cultural container" around the central experience of meditation. They did this by overlaying Jewish and Buddhist forms, practices, and teachings of meditation, thereby making it enticing to American Jews.[7] In doing so, these teachers emphasized certain elements from both Judaism and Buddhism that they felt were compatible with as well as culturally accessible to liberal

American Jewish culture. They wanted to create a new practice in which American Jews would feel comfortable and safe participating. These teachers, however, also selected elements from Buddhism that were distinctly Asian, and elements from Judaism that were sometimes distinctly Kabbalistic and mystical, so that this new practice of Jewish meditation would feel different, new, and perhaps even exotic or romantic to American Jews. And it is this blend of familiar and different, Jewish and Asian, that gives this new syncretic practice its particular appeal, thereby enabling it to spread to and become adopted by a wide swath of American Jews.

The Historical Context Surrounding the Rise of Jewish Meditation

As described in the last chapter, beginning in the 1990s, the United States experienced a veritable explosion of interest in meditation. The work of Kabat-Zinn and others linked meditation to stress reduction and management, and furnished it with scientific value. The rebranding of meditation in medical and/or therapeutic terms dramatically increased its popularity in the United States generally, and increased its popularity specifically among Jews who sought out the practice as a stress reduction technique.[8]

Around the same time that meditation exploded in popularity in the United States, a number of American Jews who had practiced Buddhism since the 1960s and 1970s rose into prominent leadership positions in the Zen and insight meditation traditions. A few of those teachers, like Fischer and Boorstein, retained a practicing relationship with Judaism as well as Buddhism, situating them in a unique position to create cooperative ventures between these traditions. Thus, the 1990s witnessed the marriage of two complementary interests: the presence of a handful of Jewish-born Buddhist teachers interested in teaching meditation and a growing openness among practicing Jews to learning about meditation.

The Nathan Cummings Foundation and Institute for Jewish Spirituality (IJS) wedded those two interests together. In partnership and with seed money from the Nathan Cummings Foundation, IJS transformed Jewish meditation from a series of disparate offerings and retreats into a nationwide movement in the late 1990s. IJS (2019) emerged in reaction to the observation among some Jewish leaders that there was a growing number of Buddhists of Jewish heritage who were teaching Buddhism in the United States and many of their students were Jewish. It invited a number of prominent Jewish and Buddhist leaders to come together to create a Jewish meditation curriculum in the hope of spurring growth in practice-based spirituality within American Jewish congregations. After establishing its Jewish meditation curriculum, IJS launched a Jewish mindfulness teaching training program in which it invited rabbis, cantors, Jewish educators and leaders, and others from across the country to come to New York City to study and practice Jewish meditation. The teacher-training program aimed to educate Jewish leaders in Jewish meditation, and arm them with the skills necessary to teach and disseminate the practice to their local communities and congregations.

Through the work of IJS, the first generation of Jewish meditation teachers has gone on to train a second generation of Jewish meditation teachers, many of whom have only studied meditation from within the Jewish tradition. IJS has led three cohorts of Jewish leaders in mindfulness meditation teaching since 2000, creating a veritable explosion of Jewish meditation offerings across the country. Thus, through a combination of the first generation of Buddhist teachers of Jewish descent who actively sought to teach meditation to Jews, rise of a popular Jewish interest in meditation, and Nathan Cummings Foundation's financial resources and IJS's organizational support, the movement for Jewish meditation has skyrocketed in the United States.

Currently, classes in Jewish meditation are offered nationwide in synagogues, Jewish community centers, and various retreat centers. The teachers of these classes are largely students of the IJS mindfulness meditation program, and many, like Laichter in the opening vignette, have studied meditation in Buddhist communities as well. In addition to these classes, a number of grassroots initiatives have sprouted up, with the goal of creating intentional Jewish meditation communities.

Although Jewish meditation varies across different centers and groups, through the work of IJS's teacher-training program, books that the first-generation teachers have written, and close-knit social network of Jewish meditators, today more commonalities exist across Jewish meditation spaces than differences. Yet it was the interpretative and cultural work of Jewish leaders who reimagined Buddhist meditation for Jews, like those leaders at IJS, that made meditation a popular and attractive Jewish practice in the United States.

The Construction of a New Cultural Container

The founding teachers of Jewish Meditation—Boorstein, Fischer, Lew, Weinberg, and others—had significant experience meditating in Buddhist centers or on Buddhist retreats before becoming Jewish meditation teachers. The teachers largely understood meditation to be a universal technique rather than an explicitly Buddhist practice—a view that they learned in the Buddhist centers in which they studied and saw as supported by the entrance of meditation into both secular and medical contexts. In wanting to bring the experience of meditation that they learned in Buddhism into the Jewish community, these teachers engaged in a syncretism of religious practice by creating a new cultural container for it, or layers of Jewish and Buddhist forms, practices, and teachings that Jewish meditation teachers used to supplement the central experience of meditation. Below I describe the contents of this container, which include the various teachings, practices, and ideas from the Jewish and Buddhist traditions that the founding teachers felt were compatible with liberal American Jewish culture as well as beneficial to the progressive wings within the American Jewish community.

Buddhism: What's Brought in and What's Left Out?

First and most centrally, at the heart of a Jewish meditation class, as portrayed in the opening vignette, is a silent meditation practice that typically consists of various breath-awareness exercises, or exercises to pay attention to thoughts, feelings, and sensations. Though many of these exercises are modeled on the Buddhist practice of vipassana meditation, they are almost always talked about using the English word "mindfulness" practice rather than vipassana meditation in order to make these exercises seem more culturally accessible to American Jews.[9] Most often the silent meditation practice takes the form of a sitting meditation in which meditators either kneel or sit cross-legged on cushions, although sometimes they will sit on chairs. Some classes will also offer Buddhist-inspired slow walking or stretching meditations in which participants are encouraged to pay attention to their bodies in motion.

Jewish meditation classes tend to incorporate various Buddhist symbols, rituals, and ideas that the teachers do not feel are incompatible with Jewish law (halacha) or customs. For example, Jewish meditation classes, like those at the JMC, will frequently use Buddhist meditation cushions (zafus and *zabutans*) or an Asian bell to designate the beginning and ending of sitting periods. They will also draw on Buddhist teachings about mindfulness and presence, but will do so by presenting mindfulness as a largely secular, therapeutic tool useful for reducing stress and anxiety. At the end of a Jewish meditation class, usually the teacher will encourage participants to give a voluntary donation in a box or envelope if the participants have the financial means to do so. This voluntary donation offering closely resembles the act of dana, or giving, that occurs after a Buddhist meditation class. Jewish meditation classes and meditation centers also tend to maintain the aesthetic of many of the Western Buddhist centers: a physical space that privileges a feel of orderliness and simplicity.

Classes in Jewish meditation tend to exclude Buddhist practices or ritual items that might be interpreted by practitioners as incompatible with Jewish law in an effort to make participants from different Jewish backgrounds and levels of observance feel comfortable. In all the Jewish meditation classes in which I participated, I never saw a statue of a Buddha, any form of bowing, or the presence of an altar or shrine. Many of the founding Jewish meditation teachers view bowing to the Buddha as a gesture of humility or practice of mindfulness. The teachers, however, recognize that the biblical prohibition against bowing before images, idols, statues, or deities (Exodus 20:3) has left many Jews deeply uncomfortable with—and perhaps even suspicious of—Buddha imagery and bowing. The teachers abandoned the metaphysical elements of Buddhism too, including any discussion around the cycles of rebirth, realms of existence, or four stages of enlightenment that are all integral to Buddhist teachings in Asia.

Many of the founding teachers of Jewish meditation have explicitly written and spoken about concealing Buddha statues in closets during Jewish meditation sits, and/or creating spaces free of Buddha imagery and bowing in order to make them feel more welcoming to Jews.[10] Boorstein tells the story about coteaching a mindfulness meditation retreat for rabbis with Weinberg held at the Barre Center for Buddhist Studies. She worried about the presence of the Buddha statue in the meditation hall and struggled to decide where in the room to put the Buddha so as to not make the Jewish participants uncomfortable (Boorstein 1997, 137–39).

Jewish meditation as a cultural container also includes various elements that were Buddhist in origin, but were reinscribed in Jewish forms or translated into Jewish terms. Examples of physical reinscriptions of Buddhist material culture include the Buddhist cushion pictured below, which has been reinscribed with a Star of David (figure 5.2), or the reformulation of the Tibetan prayer flag as a Jewish blessings flag (figure 5.1).

Jewish meditation classes also include various teachings and ideas from Buddhism that have been translated into Jewish terms. In the introductory vignette, for instance, Laichter—who studied meditation in the Tibetan and Zen traditions—introduces the practice of loving-kindness meditation to the group of new meditators. She explains, as mentioned earlier, that loving-kindness is talked about in the Buddhist tradition as metta, and in an act of translation, notes that this same practice is called Hesed in Judaism. Moreover, she draws on a verse from Exodus to explain that meditators take off their shoes before entering the meditation space as a way to mark the sacred from the profane. This is an act of translation too, as taking off shoes before entering a meditation space is ritually rooted in the Buddhist tradition. In my interviews with Jewish meditation

FIGURE 5.2. Jewish prayer cushion. Photograph by the author.

teachers, nearly all of them described themselves as "translators" who interpreted Buddhism for a Jewish audience.

In her memoir, Weinberg (2010, 85–87), a rabbi and IJS founder, has written about the translation process that occurs during her teaching:

> As the days unfolded [while on retreat at IMS] I started to translate the teachings into a Jewish spiritual language. I understood that the Buddhist reference to suffering, craving, and the conditioned "I" that always wants attention and amusement was equivalent to what Judaism refers to as false gods and idolatry. . . . I begin to teach mindfulness to Jews using the language of Jewish story and symbol.

Weinberg takes the teachings and practices that she has learned from studying with Buddhist teachers, and as she writes later, communicates them in a "vocabulary of Judaism." In IJS's mindfulness teacher-training manual that Weinberg authored, she provides various examples of how this translation happens during a Jewish meditation class. In one instance in this manual, she introduces Jewish leaders to the mindfulness practice of vipassana meditation. She encourages these leaders to pay attention to their breathing, and feel wherever their bodies make contact with the ground or chair. Weinberg (2008, 4) then translates this mindfulness practice into Jewish terms: "You can think of this as the verse in Song of Songs, '*ani yesheinah v'libi air* [*sic*]' (I am asleep but my heart is awake). In this practice we are trying to realize the awakened heart."[11]

In other cases, Jewish meditation teachers translate between the traditions by substituting Jewish symbols for Buddhist symbols in order to convey a Buddhist teaching. Roth, one of the leading Jewish meditation teachers in the United States, explained to me, "If you're only talking about reminders to pay attention, you can use a *mezuzah* instead of a Buddha statue. A *mezuzah* reminds you to pay attention, like touch this thing, pay attention now. Every time you go through a doorway, stop, pay attention." He added, "So the symbols, the external symbols, just use whatever. Jews are more comfortable using Jewish symbols, and there is no reason to use stuff that does not add anything. . . . So we use anything that is Jewish that helps you wake up to the truth of what is."[12] As Roth observed, Jewish meditation teachers recognize that Buddhist symbolism and imagery might feel alien or uncomfortable to American Jews, so they substitute Jewish symbols in order to convey different Buddhist intentions, which in this example, was the message to wake up, pay attention, and focus on the present moment.

Judaism: What's Brought in and What's Left Out?

Jewish meditation as a cultural container also includes elements explicitly drawn from the Jewish tradition. Classes might include a discussion of the weekly Torah portion (*parsha ha'shavua*) interspersed between periods of silent meditation. At the JMC, for example, the sit leader typically provides a kavanah based on the week's Torah portion. Often, teachers will also reference the Jewish calendar and discuss upcoming

Jewish holidays in their talks. Some Jewish meditation classes will draw on Jewish prayers as meditative chants or sources of intentionality. In the opening vignette, Laichter used some of the language from the Jewish prayer recited on waking, "Modeh Ani" (for women, "Modah Ani"), as a meditative mantra. These prayers frequently serve as "anchors" (to borrow Laichter's terminology) that teachers offer to ground and guide the silent meditation periods. Because Judaism does not have strict rules that govern how a person should or should not meditate, Jewish meditation teachers, as mentioned above, generally encourage people to take a "Jewish" approach to pain and move around to find a comfortable sitting position.

Jewish meditation teachers, particularly those who have a background or interest in the Jewish mystical tradition, commonly include the teachings and practices from different Jewish mystical traditions in their teaching of Jewish meditation. In his book *Jewish Meditation Practices for Everyday Life*, Roth (2009) teaches Jewish meditation by weaving together the mindfulness practices that he learned in the Buddhist context with visualizations, chants, and body movements that draw heavily from Jewish mystical sources.[13] Rabbi Slater, another prominent Jewish meditation teacher in the United States, is also widely known for his integration of Hasidic spirituality and mindfulness practice. In Slater's (2004) book *Mindful Jewish Living: Compassionate Practice*, he teaches Jewish meditation through the lens of Hasidic teachings and theology. Even Laichter, who does not have a formal background in the Jewish mystical tradition, weaves the Jewish mystical practice of meditating on the letters that spell God's name in Hebrew (Yud, Hey, Vav, and Hey) into her Jewish meditation classes too.

Different teachers have different comfort levels, though, with incorporating the practices and teachings from the Jewish mystical tradition into their meditation classes. And some Jewish meditation teachers try to avoid bringing Jewish mystical practices into their meditation classes. In his book *Be Still and Get Going*, Rabbi Lew (2007, 6) writes,

At Makor Or, the meditation center I established in San Francisco at the turn of the millennium with my dear friend Norman Fischer, we have emphasized the considerable spiritual power of traditional, normative Jewish practice—prayer, Torah, study, and a deep immersion in the Sabbath—and the equally impressive capacity of mindfulness meditation to open us to this power. The practice we have developed at Makor Or is not based on dubious re-creations of Kabalistic meditation practices that may or may not have ever existed, but rather on the rock-solid certainly of two intact traditions—mindfulness meditation and normative Judaism.

Lew avoided incorporating Jewish mystical practices into Jewish meditation because he felt that these practices were extremely complex and often arcane, requiring a mastery of Jewish texts and sources to really understand.[14]

Jewish meditation classes also exclude various elements of Judaism that conflict with the ideal of egalitarianism in order to make the classes appealing to liberal American Jews. In contrast to Orthodox Jewish communities, Jewish meditation centers permit men and women to meditate and worship next to each other; both have full and equal opportunity to participate in as well as lead meditation sessions. The teachers are careful to avoid male-centric language and liturgy. And across the board, Jewish meditation teachers frequently speak about God and/or draw on God language (i.e. Divine Presence, Source, Oneness, etc.), but do so in gender-neutral terms and avoid talking about God in the third-person masculine. They often discuss meditation as a means to cultivate an awareness of or connection with the Divine Presence. In the JMC's (n.d.) mission statement, the group describes Jewish meditation as "a way to find relaxation, stillness, healing, and a sense of peace, as well as personal transformation and a deep connection to our Source."

Jewish meditation classes take place across a range of spaces, but frequently occur within established Jewish organizations. Many classes take place in Jewish community centers, synagogues, and even Jewish day schools. All these explicitly Jewish spaces contribute a certain Jewish character to the meditation class. Some of the Jewish meditation classes, like at the JMC, include social activities along with time specifically geared toward strengthening and building a Jewish community. On extended Jewish meditation retreats, like those that occur at the Isabella Freedman Jewish Retreat Center / Elat Chayyim Center for Jewish Spirituality, time each day is set aside for Jewish morning prayer services. For those retreats that run through the weekend, often a Kabbalat Shabbat service will take place on Friday nights as well as a Saturday morning Torah service.[15] Taken together, these Jewish elements of the meditation classes are intended to make it feel welcoming and familiar to the participants.

Deciding What Is and Isn't a Kosher Mixture

Nearly all the Jewish meditation teachers described a process by which they incorporated different elements from Judaism and Buddhism into their meditation classes based on the metric of "whatever works." The Jewish meditation teachers rarely expressed a concern about acceptable versus transgressive religious mixing, or selectively borrowing only certain aspects from Buddhism while discarding the rest. They also felt little pressure to maintain or police firm religious boundaries between Judaism and Buddhism.

Rather, Jewish meditation teachers all saw themselves as creating a practice that they felt simply benefited Jewish people. When I spoke to Shoshanna Cooper, another founding Jewish meditation teacher who frequently coleads retreats with her husband, David, I asked her how they decide what Buddhist practices to incorporate within their Jewish meditation classes.[16] She explained,

> I mean the truth is somewhat subjective. We're bringing in anything that seems to work toward making people wiser and more compassionate, and living more kindly, acting better in their lives. . . . So we bring in anything that works. We need to stop with the nonsense on this fear of being infiltrated from the outside. Take what's good [from Buddhism], leave the rest, and move on.

When I asked Cooper how she decides what is good or not good in Buddhism, she answered,

Just take whatever you want. . . . And if it works for you, great; if it doesn't work for you, OK, well then you are going to have to go someplace else and find it. I don't like bowing down. I think they [Buddhists] have, just as I think Judaism has, and any other tradition has, a lot of fixations on silly ideas. I don't need to pick, but some of those [practices] I like, so I like to do them. I like kissing the Torah. That feels really good to me. Is it ultimately true? No, but do I want to go in and kiss the Buddha? No, I don't. And I don't want to bow down to it. That doesn't feel good to me. Is that right or wrong? Who cares? I don't want to do it. . . . So I pick and choose what I want, but I'm not going to claim any of it is truth.[17]

Ultimately, Cooper described that the metric "whatever works" fundamentally means a process by which she incorporates the practices, teachings, and ideas from both Buddhism and Judaism that resonate with her and that she feels "work" to make people wiser, kinder, and more compassionate (her mission). And she discards elements from these traditions that do not feel relevant, comfortable, or useful to her in achieving those ends. At play here is a politics of appropriation in which Cooper, like other teachers of Jewish meditation, felt empowered to decide what to take and what to discard from both Judaism and Buddhism. In doing so, these teachers assert personal authority over their religious lives, relying on individual discernment rather than prescriptions or obligations from their collective tradition, sacred texts, or community.

This flexibility to "pick and choose" (using Cooper's words) among the two traditions reflects her and other teachers' commitments to liberal Judaism. Almost all Jewish meditation teachers affiliate with the liberal branches of American Jewish life, identifying as Reform, Reconstructionist, Renewal, Conservative, or nondenominational/postdenominational Jews. Common across these different liberal movements is the belief that Judaism should change and adapt to meet the needs of the Jewish people in the contemporary moment.[18] This commitment to a continually evolving Judaism allows these teachers license to incorporate Buddhist practices and techniques into Judaism.

Some of the Jewish meditation teachers, however, have openly expressed certain limits on what feels, to them, like permissible Jewish-Buddhist blending. Lew (1996, 49) touched on such limitations in a piece he wrote called "It Doesn't Matter What You Call It: If It Works, It Works." In it, he observed,

> We don't have to *kasher* [to make kosher] meditation. Many forms of meditation do not threaten or oppose Jewish theology. There's no reason why we can't assimilate them into Jewish practice, whether or not there's a Jewish precedent for them. Judaism assimilated aspects of the ancient Near Eastern oral tradition into the Torah, Greek tradition into the Talmud. . . . As a friend once said to me, Judaism seems to have a kind of cell-like mechanism. We seem to know intuitively what it can absorb and what's toxic. To me, meditation that involves visualizing deities or reciting Hindu mantras would be toxic to Judaism. But a simple awareness exercise, a meditation which helps penetrate our experience of reality through becoming more aware of our breath and posture and our thought processes, would not under any circumstances be toxic to Judaism. Therefore, I have no problem adopting such techniques.

Lew made it clear in this passage that Judaism has a long history of cross-fertilization with other religious traditions, yet he felt an intuitive boundary is in place between allowable and forbidden blending. He did not feel that elements from Buddhism (or Hinduism) were acceptable practices to incorporate into Jewish meditation if they opposed Jewish theology. In this passage, Lew exposed the boundaries of his own religious liberalism. Though committed to an evolving Judaism, he was opposed to altering Jewish practice in any way that would violate historic Jewish law (halacha).

The Legitimation of the Jewish Meditation

As Jewish meditation developed into a nationwide movement, its teachers began to make the case for why this new practice belonged in organized Jewish life. In part, these arguments for why Jewish meditation has a place in contemporary Jewish life seemed to be an attempt at warding off potential critics from within the Jewish community who might express a suspicion or disapproval of incorporating a seemingly new and/or foreign practice into Judaism. Partly, too, these arguments served more pragmatic ends. Jewish meditation teachers needed to demonstrate to Jewish organizations (Jewish community centers, synagogues, etc.) that Jewish meditation should be housed in their confines, and they needed to attract members of the Jewish community to attend the classes they were offering. For some teachers, like Laichter and Shy—the JMC cofounders—their funders required them to clearly articulate the value and place for Jewish meditation in Jewish communal life.

In making a case for the place of meditation in Jewish life, Jewish meditation teachers generally drew on three arguments to explain why Jewish meditation was a compelling and legitimate practice for American Jews. First, these teachers frequently emphasized in their classes as well as writings that meditation is therapeutically and psychologically beneficial to the Jewish community, just as it is to all people. Jewish meditation teachers, like many of the Buddhist meditation teachers in the earlier chapters, present meditation as a clear and useful tool that helps people cultivate a range of positive outcomes: increased intentionality, stress reduction, compassion, gratitude, awareness, wisdom, and loving-kindness.

Slater (2004, xx) teaches in *Mindful Jewish Living* that the practice of mindfulness leads people "to wake up to the manifold ways that we also hide from our feelings, project our anxieties onto others, let our fears control us, and otherwise 'miss our lives.'" Similarly, Lew (2005, 112) writes that meditation helps individuals work though arguments that they may have going on in their minds, or antipathy they may feel toward various people or circumstances. In the manual that Weinberg (2008) created for IJS, she explains that the purpose of meditation is "to reveal the unseen and hidden fears, desires, obstacles and barriers to living lives of gratitude, generosity and service." In sum, these teachers delineate to their Jewish audiences the clear psychological and therapeutic benefits that meditation offers its Jewish practitioners.

Second, Jewish meditation teachers convey the message that in addition to its psychological benefits, meditation is spiritually and religiously beneficial to the American Jewish community—a message that will be emphasized in chapter 6. Jewish meditation, they suggest, provides American Jews with a new spiritual means to engage with Judaism. The history of the JMC (n.d.), as found on its website, explains how meditation reconnects many Jewish people to Judaism by providing them with new spiritual opportunities. In its mission statement, the JMC makes it clear that meditation benefits the American Jewish community by supplying it with "deeply authentic versions of spiritual practice." In his book *The Handbook of Jewish Meditation Practices*, David Cooper (2000, 5) also underscores the importance of meditation as a vehicle to connect disaffected Jews to new spiritual and even mystical elements within Judaism:

> The complaint of a large number of people who want to be connected with their Judaism is that individual practices, like prayer or occasional Torah study, a Sabbath morning in a synagogue, or the celebration of a ritual, are primarily devoted to a form but lack spiritual content. . . . On the other hand, many who have been discontented with Judaism have been drawn to simple practices of sitting quietly, chanting a few words of repetition, or singing to God while focused on basic thoughts of lovingkindness, forgiveness, gratitude, generosity and so forth.

In this paragraph, Cooper echoes a claim—one particularly strong among the teachers with ties to the Jewish Renewal movement, but salient in the discourse surrounding Jewish meditation more generally too—that contemporary American Judaism has emerged as spiritually unfulfilling and difficult to access. He offers meditation as a solution to that problem.

Not all Jewish meditation teachers, however, view normative American Judaism as spiritually deficient and meditation as its salve. In his writings, Lew was clear that he viewed normative Judaism as a rich spiritual path. He felt that meditation benefited Conservative Judaism, the wing of Judaism in which he was trained and served as a rabbi, not by filling a spiritual vacancy in the tradition, but by augmenting its existing spirituality. In Lew's (2005, 7–8) book *Be Still and Get Going*, he writes,

> For the past ten years, first at workshops and retreats and then finally in our own meditation center, we have been practicing mindfulness meditation side by side with ordinary Jewish spiritual activities. The members of our formal practice period meditate together early in the morning and then go next door to my synagogue to attend daily minyan. They meditate on Friday nights and Saturday mornings and then go next door to attend Shabbat services. . . . Over the years, in the course of these activities, we have used dozens of classical Jewish texts to support the integration of meditation into Jewish contexts. Laying these texts end to end, we began to see that taken as a whole they delineated a clear spiritual path of their own—a kind of soul within the body of Jewish ritual, a spiritual companion practice standing side by side with normative Judaism and supporting it, helping it to reach its full natural depth.

Lew felt that meditation worked alongside—enhancing—normative Judaism. He viewed meditation as a way for Jewish people to access Judaism's inherent spirituality (see also Lew 1996).

Finally, the last way that Jewish meditation teachers explained that meditation was a legitimate Jewish practice was by historicizing it within the Jewish tradition. Historically, Jewish contemplative practice has consisted of myriad spiritual directives that range from chanting, to candle gazing, visualizations, and fasting, to deep concentration and recitations of names for the Divine Presence. These practices—and their wide variety spanning many centuries—are considered forms of *hitbodedut*, which literally translates to isolation or seclusion. This deep contemplative world of hitbodedut is closely tied to the world of Jewish mysticism and ecstatic Kabbalah.[19]

Aware of this history, Jewish meditation teachers frequently stress in their teachings that meditation has deep roots in Judaism. In doing so, they contextualize the practice of meditation within the larger arc of Jewish history. In the opening vignette, for example, Laichter introduces the meditating practice by explaining to the participants in the beginners' sit at the JMC that "Judaism has a long, historical meditative tradition." She gives the example that the Amidah, a central part of the Jewish synagogue service, is often considered an opportunity for silent prayer or meditation. This statement invites the participants at the JMC to imagine their meditative practices as part of an age-old Jewish tradition. The founding teachers of Jewish meditation understood that sitting on Buddhist cushions while doing Buddhist-inspired breath awareness exercises was not the same practice as hitbodedut taught by Rabbi Nachman of Bratslav. Rather, Jewish meditation teachers tended to historicize the practice of meditation by noting that it is "a new form of an ancient practice."[20]

Conclusion

Through creating a new cultural container for meditation that incorporates elements of both Judaism and Buddhism, Jewish meditation teachers have rendered it both familiar and legitimate, yet different and alluring, to American Jews.[21] Right now, many practitioners of Jewish meditation, like Jacob at the JMC, have only a vague awareness that the practices they do in their Jewish meditation classes have roots in the Buddhist tradition. Many of the Jewish meditators view their syncretic practice just as Jacob does: like therapy with Jewish friends.

That Jacob understands meditation as a uniquely Jewish therapeutic practice is not an accident. Instead, it was the result of both historical and cultural forces working together. First, on the supply side, the 1990s witnessed the presence of a handful of Jewish-born Buddhist teachers interested in teaching meditation. Second, on the demand side, that same time period saw a growing openness among Jews, like Jacob in the opening vignette, to learning about meditation. Third, acting as a bridging force between the teachers and a receptive audience, the funding and support of the Nathan Cummings Foundation and IJS spurred dozens of Jewish-Buddhist collaborations along with the infrastructure and training for new contemplative Jewish organizations to develop. Fourth, as this chapter demonstrated, a prominent group of elite Jewish teachers and leaders performed a significant amount of cultural work that systematically de-emphasized certain Buddhist aspects of meditation while highlighting others, thus effectively remaking the practice of Buddhist meditation for American Jews. All these processes taken together explain the development and configuration of Jewish meditation as well as the syncretism of religious practice.

Although the American Jews in this chapter could be viewed as acting as "Buddhist appropriators"—a label that religious studies scholar Jeff Wilson (2009, 157) coined to describe those who do not necessarily identify as Buddhist but nonetheless borrow Buddhist practices, ideas, or beliefs—what they created with Jewish meditation was not a mere appropriation of Buddhism. Rather, they built an entirely new syncretic religious practice that has roots in both the Jewish and Buddhist traditions. They weeded out elements of Buddhism that did not feel relatable to them as Jews, including reverence to the Buddha, traditional cosmological explanations, and bowing practices. They introduced meditation and mindfulness as psychotherapeutic as opposed to historic religious practices. And importantly, they intentionally recontextualized meditation in Jewish terms by reformulating it within a Jewish idiom using Jewish language, texts, and customs; giving it a Jewish purpose (e.g., to help Jews connect to God or achieve heightened spirituality); and supplying it with a new history by embedding it within the larger arc of the Jewish mystical tradition. These transformative processes were all informed and shaped by the teachers' liberal commitments, including a demand for egalitarianism, an elevation of the moral authority of the individual, and a cosmopolitan appreciation of the value of different religions.

American Jews' distancing of Buddhism from its Asian cultural systems and ethnic identities—and recasting it within a Jewish framework and idiom—is shrouded in questions about power and authority. The rise of Jewish meditation hinged on obscuring the Buddhist context of meditation by reformulating it so successfully that it felt convincingly and authentically Jewish to those who practiced it. The construction of Jewish meditation thus began with a radical detraditionalization and even secularization of Buddhism, and ended with a retraditionalization and sacralization in Jewish forms.

CHAPTER SIX

Mapping Jewish Buddhist Spirituality

BOORSTEIN, the prominent Jewish meditation teacher discussed in the last chapter, wrote the popular book *That's Funny, You Don't Look Buddhist: On Being a Faithful Jew and a Passionate Buddhist.* In it, she tells the story about attending an international interfaith women's conference in Toronto as a Buddhist delegate in the late 1980s. The conference included eight Jewish delegates, and Boorstein worried that they might be thinking, "What's a nice Jewish girl like you doing as a Buddhist delegate?" This worry bothered her throughout the conference up until the end of the weeklong event, when Deborah, one of the Jewish delegates who came from Jerusalem, invited her to have breakfast. Deborah, an Orthodox Jew, told her that the Jewish delegates had been wondering about her background, but had hesitated to speak to her directly. As a woman who came from a similar upbringing—a New Yorker, the child of eastern European immigrant Jews, and a Barnard alum—she felt that she could approach Boorstein to try to understand how her life path led her to Buddhism.

With a sense of relief, Boorstein spoke with Deborah. She explained to her, "I never stopped being a Jew . . . and I have very affectionate feelings for Judaism." But she went on to add that ten years earlier, she had found herself frightened and worried about the fragility of life. It was the 1970s—a time when meditation and Eastern philosophy were becoming popular in the West—and she met some Buddhist teachers who spoke to the very issues that she was frightened about. She explained to Deborah that before meeting these Buddhist teachers, she did not know that it was "spiritual understanding" and "spiritual solace" that she was lacking. Had she known that, she told Deborah, she might have sought out a Jewish spiritual teacher. Deborah listened carefully to Boorstein's story, and the two women forged an understanding with each other. Ultimately, as Boorstein (1997, 6–8) writes a few pages later, what she found in Buddhism was a "great spiritual path" that promised her transformation.

Although Boorstein is a prominent teacher at the intersection of Judaism and Buddhism in the United States, the conversation above highlights an important pattern I observed among the lay Jewish practitioners of meditation: they spoke about and understood Buddhism in terms they defined as spiritual. In this chapter, I shift my analytic focus from the syncretism of religious practice to the syncretism of spiritual discourse, examining how my respondents construct a new form of "Jewish Buddhist spirituality." I narrow in on a specific group of lay practitioners who maintain an active and practicing relationship to both Judaism and Buddhism. I do so because this group of Jews, different from the cultural or secular Jews described in the next chapter, imagine Buddhism as an important means to enhance or enrich their sense of spirituality *and* complement their Judaism and Jewish practice. I ask how these respondents, a group I call the *spiritually enriched*, assign Jewish spiritual meaning to their Buddhist practices, and how that meaning is in turn charged with particular political and religious investments.

Nearly all the spiritually enriched among my respondents belong to and regularly attend a synagogue or other informal Jewish worship groups. About a third of them are Jewish religious leaders, mainly rabbis and cantors, who see themselves as professionally engaged in and committed to spiritual work.[1] And compared to the cultural Jewish respondents, this group tends to have a less significant engagement with Buddhism as a religious community. These respondents often read Buddhist books, maintain a daily meditation practice at home, and attend occasional meditation classes or weeklong retreats, but they maintain little to no organizational affiliation with a Buddhist center.

These spiritually enriched respondents overwhelmingly identify as "spiritual" people, and more generally, spiritual ideas and spiritual talk play a discursively important role in their understandings of themselves along with their relationships to both Judaism and Buddhism.[2] The discursive salience of spirituality among this group of practicing Jews seems to both reflect and emerge from their particular participation in organized Jewish life. In her wide-ranging study of religion and spirituality in American religious life, *Sacred Stories, Spiritual Tribes*, sociologist Nancy Ammerman (2013) demonstrates the link between organized religious involvement (such as involvement in a Jewish congregation) and spiritual engagement. She shows that the spiritually engaged tend to also be religiously active, suggesting that religious communities are crucial vehicles in nurturing and producing spiritual discourse. If these respondents take comfort in spiritual discourse from their Jewish communities, then their particular understanding of spirituality—what it is, and how it should function—was inflected by both the Jewish and Buddhist worlds in which they practice, their liberal politics, and larger American ideas about religious individualism.

By carefully situating spirituality within the historical and contemporary orbits of Judaism, Buddhism, and US religious and political life—that is, giving it a particular social specificity—I contribute to a new and emerging literature that critiques as well as revises deeply entrenched ideas about American spirituality that suggest that it is something that exists within the interior of the individual and outside the world of the social.[3] I also advance that work in two central ways. First, this emerging body of scholarship has largely overlooked how spiritual discourses are shaped by and vary across religious traditions, especially minority religious traditions. In this chapter, I show how Jewish and Buddhist communities produce particular spiritual vocabularies, and how these vocabularies get integrated among people who move between these religious communities over their lifetimes.[4]

Second and related, I deliberately analyze both what Jewish Buddhist spirituality is—its discourses and contours—and what Jewish Buddhist spirituality does—how it sets boundaries around and makes claims about both Judaism and Buddhism. In doing so, I substitute spirituality for religion in the functional question that sociologists of religion commonly ask: What does it do for individuals? I show that the language of spirituality shapes the boundaries that the respondents draw in terms of allowable Jewish-Buddhist blending while also providing them a discursive framework for critiquing Judaism for being too parochial, insufficiently therapeutic, and overly hierarchical.

In what follows, I first describe the background and characteristics of the spiritually enriched. Then I examine the patterns in how they understand and describe the spiritual, in turn constructing a syncretism of spiritual discourse or Jewish Buddhist spirituality. I highlight the four discursive frames of Jewish Buddhist spirituality that emerged from my conversations with these respondents: spirituality as performed, spiritually as universal, spiritually as personally meaningful, and spirituality as chosen. As I do so, I demonstrate how this Jewish Buddhist spirituality is informed by the particular practices, expectations, and histories of Judaism and Buddhism as well as the respondents' social position as liberal Americans.

Locating the Spiritually Enriched

The stories in this chapter come from interviews I conducted with seventeen observant American Jews who also practice Buddhist meditation. These respondents all actively practiced Judaism by observing—to varying degrees—the Jewish religious laws, commandments, and holiday celebrations. Every one of the spiritually enriched people I interviewed identified with a liberal rather than Orthodox wing of Judaism, particularly the Reform, Conservative, or Reconstructionist movements. They all identified Judaism as their primary "religious" tradition or path too. As mentioned earlier, nearly a third of this group were Jewish religious leaders, mainly rabbis and cantors, who were especially committed to Jewish life. This group contained more women than men (by about a margin of 1.5 to 1), and often had well-articulated and formulated responses to questions about their religious practices and beliefs, reflecting their professional work and training.

Two different trajectories led most of the spiritually enriched to Buddhism. The first involves a path from the Judaism of my respondents' childhoods to Buddhism and then back to an active involvement in

Judaism. These respondents typically experienced a period of disconnection from Judaism when they first encountered and studied Buddhism. The respondents who took this trajectory into Buddhism largely followed a path similar to many of the cultural Buddhists of the last chapter. Different from that group, though, they left the Buddhist world and reengaged with Judaism, frequently by enrolling in rabbinical school. Despite their positions of Jewish leadership, many still maintained daily Buddhist meditation and sometimes yearly retreat practices. The story of Rabbi Lew discussed in chapter 4—the well-known leader of Congregation Beth Sholom in San Francisco who practiced Zen Buddhism for nearly a decade before reconnecting with Judaism—perhaps best epitomizes this trajectory.

The second trajectory that led the spiritually enriched to Buddhism involves less circling. For the majority of them, they pursued Buddhism as committed and practicing Jewish adults. This group sought out Buddhism, particularly insight meditation, as a path toward greater well-being, health, and wisdom. The spiritually enriched who took this path to Buddhism, however, were much less organizationally involved in Buddhism than those respondents of the last chapter. They were not actively involved in a Buddhist center, nor did they speak about the importance of the friendships they made through Buddhist connections. Commonly, their only organizational involvement in Buddhism consisted of a week-long Buddhist retreat once or perhaps twice a year.

Few respondents from either trajectory saw themselves as currently connected to communal life at a Buddhist center, and only one identified as Buddhist. Everyone else identified simply as Jewish or, occasionally, a Jewish meditator. Most tried to maintain a daily meditation practice that they then augmented by either a Buddhist retreat practice or occasional visits to local Buddhist meditation centers. Finally, just as the respondents all identified with the liberal wing of Judaism, they all identified as politically and socially liberal. They held a deep cosmopolitan appreciation of religious diversity and pluralism that shaped their understanding of spirituality by way of making it notably democratic as well as universal. They also overwhelmingly felt that all religious traditions offered spiritual truths or practices, and more generally, at their heart, all religions shared a common spirituality. When asked directly, most respondents struggled to define spirituality. It had an ineffable quality, they suggested, and they just knew it when they saw or felt it. Listening to how the respondents talked about ideas of the "spiritual" or "spirituality" extemporaneously in conversation, though, revealed four distinct patterns, as described below.

Spirituality as Performance

When these respondents talked about the spiritual, they emphasized, first and foremost, its performative character. They experienced or achieved spirituality through doing or practice. Sara, a rabbi at a synagogue in New England, underscored this clearly when talking about her relationship with meditation. Sara first attended a meditation retreat the summer after graduating from rabbinical school, and viewed her "meditation career" and rabbinic career as coterminous and inextricably linked.

After this first meditation retreat, Sara attended various other meditation retreats held at Elat Chayyim (the Jewish retreat center in the Catskills mentioned in chapter 4), but then pursued meditation in a Buddhist context in order to learn the practice "straight from the horse's mouth." In 2000, she completed her first weeklong insight meditation retreat at IMS, and has dedicated at least a week every year to retreat practice at IMS. In talking about her relationship to meditation with me, she stressed how she sees it as a form of dedicated and often-difficult spiritual work. "I feel like my work as a human and as a rabbi is to work on my own spirit, and nourish my own spirit, and help nourish the spirits of others," she explained. "When people are going through hard times, I will say to them, 'What do you do to nourish yourself?' And just like we need to nourish our bodies, we need to nourish our spirits." Speaking swiftly, she continued,

> Spiritual practice, I think, are those things that help me be more present and wiser in the world. And so that kind of practice is not easy; that's hard. Spiritual practice is like *going to the gym*; it doesn't feel good to lift—but if I do it, in a mindful way, carefully, I will get

stronger. . . . I mean, there have been [meditation] retreats that are excruciating, either physically excruciating or mentally excruciating, but it's like I'm going to sit here and do this because I know I'm learning something from that. I mean not excruciating, that's a little strong, but hard, painful, boring, whatever, unpleasant—and I'm sitting here doing this, because I know it's of benefit to me and to the world. . . . I would say it's a spiritual practice not because it makes me feel all groovy but because it helps me be a better container of godliness, which to me is the ultimate goal of spiritual practice: to be a vessel of godliness in this world, for my own benefit and the benefit of others.

In portraying what it means to be spiritual, Sara underscored that spirituality can be inwardly or outwardly directed, for her own benefit or that of others, but it was something that was performed; it was achieved through doing. Spirituality was something she learned, cultivated, and refined through practice. By drawing an analogy between spiritual practice and gym workouts, she also emphasized the habitual and everyday nature of spirituality as a type of ritualized performance.[5] For Sara as well as the other spiritually enriched respondents, spirituality was not an inherent property (of the self, religion, environment, etc.) but rather a practice of becoming (better, wiser, and more mindful).

Not all the respondents saw spiritual practice as a form of such hard work, but all highlighted its cultivable quality. The clergy (rabbis and cantors) in this group frequently saw spirituality as a practice toward developing an "awareness of God" or "connection to God," without assigning God a gender or the particular anthropomorphic qualities often attached to a supreme being (i.e., king, supreme ruler, shepherd, healer, etc.).[6] The clergy tended to employ a robust and clearly articulated theistic vocabulary when they spoke about God, describing God in broad terms that associated it with inexplicability, totality, and potentiality (in contrast, many of the nonclergy expressed agnostic or atheistic ideologies). For the lay members of the spiritually enriched, they tended to view spirituality as a practice directed toward connecting them to something beyond or bigger than themselves. They spoke about this as connecting to "something that feels real," the "spirit of the universe," or something that has a greater "energy."

This discourse of spirituality as a form of practice (directed toward theistic or nontheistic ends) bears the imprint of the Jewish and Buddhist worlds that the respondents occupy. Both Judaism and convert Buddhism, as traditions, stress practice as a central obligation or meaning-making activity within the tradition. In a sense, they share a practice-oriented identity, with the observance of Jewish laws as central to the Jewish tradition and the practice of meditation as central to convert Buddhism in the United States. This emphasis on practice within Judaism and Buddhism contrasts with the centrality of belief within Christianity. In her wide-ranging study of how Americans talk about spirituality, Ammerman (2013, 26) found that roughly half of them commonly describe the spiritual in terms of mystery, ritual, awe, and belief—all integral elements of Christianity. These facets of spirituality had little salience in the stories that my respondents told, reflecting their religious orientations and backgrounds.

Other popular and scholarly ideas about spirituality suggest, building on William James's idea of religion as a solitary experience of transcendence, that religion's central modus operandi are mystical or metaphysical *experiences*.[7] Yet the spiritually enriched rarely talked about spirituality as an experience or something that otherwise passively happens to them. They placed their emphasis on spirituality as something that one achieves rather than something that one is, believes in, or experiences. That the respondents' sense of "spirituality as practice" differs from popular American ideas about spirituality reinforces the notion that it has deep roots in the practiced-based repertoires and expectations that they learned from Judaism and Buddhism.

This construction of spirituality as performance also shaped the boundaries that individuals drew in terms of allowable Jewish-Buddhist blending. The respondents embraced those aspects of Buddhism that felt to them like "spiritual practice"—particularly meditation and mindfulness practices—and downplayed or distanced themselves from those aspects of Buddhism that were not practice oriented. This practically translated into their rarely, if at all, taking the Buddhist refuges or vows, believing in Buddhist mythological or cosmological explanations, partaking in holiday celebrations, or claiming a Buddhist identification. Although some of the respondents mentioned in the next chapter embraced these aspects of Buddhism, the spiritually enriched respondents largely viewed them as beyond the pale of what to them felt like spiritual practice and, accordingly, acceptable Jewish-Buddhist mixing. Similarly, the spiritually enriched rarely embraced the communal aspects of Buddhism (i.e., enjoying a sense of belonging from participating in Buddhist communities or pointing to the importance of the friendships they formed at their Buddhist centers), and de-emphasized the significance of communal belonging. Instead, they tended to speak about their synagogue or Jewish group as their primary source of communal life.

Maintaining a practice-oriented relationship to Buddhism allowed the respondents a way around the argument that they were transgressing Jewish law by committing *avodah zarah* (foreign worship) because they did not see themselves as adopting a new religious tradition but only some of its practices. They engaged with, borrowed from, and enjoyed certain aspects of Buddhism, but never claimed to affiliate with Buddhism as a religious tradition. It allowed them a language to justify their picking and choosing from—or what others might view as their selective appropriation of—Buddhism.

Spirituality as Universal

The second quality of spirituality that the respondents routinely noted was its universal and perennialist essence. They viewed spirituality as having a universal character that people, from all religious backgrounds including none, could access and from which they could benefit. They also tended to emphasize that spirituality had a shared, underlying core that transverses all religious traditions. For example, Jon, a clinical psychotherapist and insight meditation practitioner in his early sixties, explained that all religions have a "core of mysticism and spirituality" that provide "different ways of understanding the truth." One of the youngest respondents with whom I spoke, David, echoed Jon's view that all religions have a spiritual essence, but thought it was a "disservice to spirituality as a whole to have it be partitioned into different groups." A program manager in his late twenties, David studied contemplative studies in college and described himself as deeply interested in questions about spirituality—a curiosity that has led him to plumb the spiritual depths of insight meditation and Judaism. He characterized spirituality in terms of an inchoate sense of "inner unity," or that which "feels real" and "does not resist life." Although spirituality held a seemingly ineffable quality to Jon, he underscored that "there is nothing exclusive or religious [about spirituality] . . . it's human."

Other respondents drew on elaborate metaphors to capture the universality of spirituality. Jesse, the spiritual leader of an independent Jewish congregation, used the metaphor of mountains, rivers, and wells in explaining his understanding of spirituality. His topographical explanation seemed to be shaped by his own religious journey, which took him from Judaism to Buddhism and then back to Judaism again. He grew up in an active Conservative Jewish household, but after college, started practicing insight meditation in Northern California. He spent considerable time on residential retreats and even committed to monastic life by taking the vows to become a monk while in Asia. He eventually disrobed, returned to the United States, and reengaged with Judaism by studying in Israel and ordaining as a rabbi. Reflecting on this journey, Jesse said,

> I see it [spirituality] as a mountain range, and there are distinctions between the mountains, but that they all have altitude, and when you get to the top they all have a view. And in this teaching that I heard when I was twenty-one or twenty-two, the specific [Buddhist] teacher said something about one spiritual river and many wells down to it. I remember thinking at the time that I thought that was an oversimplification I didn't completely believe in, but that there was something to what was being said, and that I reflected on the well that we grew up with. The well that we come from is usually the one with the most muck on the top, and the most algae and leaves; it's the muckiest. But it's also probably the one that goes the deepest. And so I made somewhat of a conscious young-adult-early-twenties-black-and-white

determination that I would seek what I was finding in Buddhism back in Judaism. If it was here, it must be there as well, even if it's a little more mucked up and harder to find, and that I would consciously make the move not away from Buddhism per se but back into Judaism.

Jesse first imagines spirituality as a mountain range of different paths that all lead to a place of spiritual truth. He proposes that even though religions (the mountains) are distinctive, their spiritual potential (the view) holds the same or similar value. In the other metaphor, Jesse explicitly links spirituality (the river) to religion (the well down to it), showing the interconnection between the two. This metaphor suggests that all religions are paths pointing toward the same consummate reality, with every religion containing ultimate truth(s), and no religion owning them all.

Although Jesse did not recognize it, his universalist view of spirituality has deep roots in American religious history, and specifically, the religious and political discourses of nineteenth-century American liberalism. As religious studies scholar Leigh Schmidt (2005) has provocatively shown, the rise and flourishing of religious liberalism in the nineteenth century gave birth to an ecumenical perspective on spirituality that was couched in a sympathetic appreciation of all religions. Nineteenth-century Americans espoused the same view as Jesse: the conviction that all religions of the world were cut from the same cloth and, at their heart, shared a common spirituality. And this common spirituality was available to all earnest seekers without regard to religion, creed, sex, or race. Religious liberals in the nineteenth century used these universalistic religious sentiments as a language to engage with religious others and seek out shared religious truths. As chapter 2 demonstrated, these universalist and perennialist ideas about spirituality were also imposed on Buddhism during the nineteenth century in order to make it more readily acceptable to as well as accessible for Americans of all religious backgrounds. Jesse's story thus reflects the continuation of an American story about universal spirituality as both an expression of religious liberalism and means to bridge religious differences in a search for a wider, more complex religious world. It simultaneously represents a discursive framework that diminishes the entire religious and cultural universe that is specific to any religious tradition.

Similar to Jesse, Susan, a professor in her early sixties, expressed an idea about the universal accessibility of spirituality, but she embedded this universalistic impulse in the charged politics of the 1960s and 1970s. She spoke about her experience of being "radicalized" in college in the early 1970s. Susan was significantly involved in social justice work in and right after college, fighting against the roots of racism, antisemitism, and sexism. About midway through her story about her consciousness-raising work, she paused, and seemingly parenthetically, noted, "Jews who were politically conscious didn't see any worth in their Jewish identity. They didn't understand that it was connected, actually, to thousands of years of teachings about justice, and thinking about that, the whole Left is still like that pretty much . . . like when you become spiritual it can't be Jewish. When you become political, it has to be anti-Israel in some way, right?"

This observation that spirituality cannot be directly tied to Judaism reflected, according to Susan, a liberal perspective—one that she seemed more attached to during the height of her activist work in the 1970s than she does today—that what made something spiritual was that it was *precisely* not Jewish. This view of spirituality insists that it must have resonance beyond the Jewish community; that it must be a universal rather than a parochial impulse. Susan suggested that this liberal universalistic agenda to which spirituality seems to be tied emerged from the radical Left of the 1960s and 1970s, yet as described above, these universalistic ideas about spirituality have older historical antecedents. Susan's story, however, made plain that particular claims about spiritual universalism are entangled with the respondents' experiences as Jews in the United States. American Jews have historically embraced a liberal universalistic position, which has translated into a specific repudiation of Jewish particularism, often by the adoption and championing of other marginalities or embattled groups.[8] In this way, the respondents' views of spirituality—perhaps their involvement in Buddhism as well—are shaped by the liberal, universalistic positions that Jews have historically held.

As much as these universalistic ideas about spirituality have historical links to American Judaism, they also bear the imprint of Western ideas about pluralism and the coexistence of religious difference. As sociologists Courtney Bender and Omar McRoberts (2012, 17) argue, contemporary American ideas about spirituality frequently "designate the ligaments of a shared humanity spanning deep cultural and political divides."[9] Some respondents used the construction of spirituality as universal to celebrate the similarities between religious traditions and wash away the particular religious (and political, historical, and cultural) differences. Whereas religion divides, spirituality unites faiths and cultures, and erases difference. The metaphor of one spiritual river, for example, occluded how different religious traditions construct and promote different notions of the spiritual.

Finally, it bears highlighting that the respondents' universalistic ideas about spirituality allowed them a language and framework in which to embed as well as legitimize their relationship to Buddhism. By viewing their Buddhist practices as "spiritual," and evoking the universality of spirituality, they could claim that meditation existed as extra-Buddhist or as not in the province of any one religious tradition. It was, rather, a universal spiritual experience, available to anyone and everyone. Paradoxically, the universalistic views of spirituality that were so implicated in the progressive Jewish communities to which these respondents belonged, helped—albeit unwittingly—to pave the way for practicing Jews to also practice Buddhism.

Spirituality as Personally Meaningful

The third characteristic of spirituality that the respondents routinely emphasized was its personal meaningfulness. They frequently asserted that spiritual practice informed, guided, and ultimately enhanced their everyday lives. They demonstrated this by associating spirituality with various adjectives, such as "accessible," "relevant," or "personally meaningful." For example, Maya, a lawyer in her early thirties, shared that during her childhood, she always had a strong, positive connection to Judaism. She loved in particular celebrating Shabbat and holidays with her family.

Despite her fondness for the holiday celebrations, however, she never felt interested in God and Jewish religious services. The Conservative synagogue to which she belonged felt to her "very much in the Conservative mold . . . devoid of energy and heart." It was rich with community and friends, she noted, but "there was no *spirituality*, there was no connection to my heart there." She attended Jewish summer camps and Hebrew school, but never spiritually connected to or found meaning in those activities either.

As Maya narrated her story of her Jewish upbringing, she employed the language of spirituality to critique normative Judaism, especially Conservative Judaism, for lacking relevancy and profundity. The prayer services, practices, and beliefs of the Conservative Jewish world in which she was raised did not feel inspiring or resonant to her. She developed this critique more fully when she described her experiences with Judaism in college. Maya deliberately never set foot in the Jewish center on campus, remarking,

> I remember looking up their [Hillel] program and then just being completely bored by the sound of all of the classes, which were, even when they were trying to make it interesting. . . . Jewish classes that they were trying to sound interesting but had nothing to do with what was really happening in my life, which was a lot of loneliness, feelings of dislocation, trying to figure out who I was. All of my psychological, *spiritual* kind of feeling that really exemplified what college was to me, there was nothing in my college Jewish life that spoke to me at all.

Maya's story about feeling so removed from Judaism during college helps to explain her criticism that her Jewish upbringing felt so devoid of spirituality. To her, Judaism felt disconnected from the central struggles and concerns in her life, and thus was unable—perhaps unequipped—to help her work through feelings of dislocation and upset.[10]

Maya's conception of spirituality revealed an important tie that the respondents drew between the spiritual and therapeutic. What made something feel spiritual, she suggested, was its capacity to provide comfort, healing, and relief. In that sense, Judaism lacked spirituality because it was insufficiently therapeutic in her life. By later noting that "mainstream Judaism, in my experience, deals 80 percent, or 80 to 90 percent, with the head," she also gestured to a larger trend that Jewish studies scholars have acknowledged: the modernization of Judaism, in the United States as in Europe, has led to a form of Judaism that is highly rational and intellectual (Sarna 2004, 345).[11] And what this intellectual and highly rational form of Judaism lacks are practices that allow Jews to better cope with the stresses and demands of everyday life.[12]

In contrast, as an adult, Maya found herself attracted to Zen Buddhism because it felt directly beneficial to her day-to-day life. And in turn, the everyday relevance of Buddhism made it feel spiritual to her. Maya thought about Buddhism as her "spiritual identity" because, as she put it, "I feel like there is endless truth in it [Buddhism], and it completely resonates in my life. The deeper I go with the teachings, the more I come closer and closer to feeling free and happy and like my deepest self." She stated that the "the magic of meditation" comes down "to really being in what is happening now. And then the next now and the next now." From meditation, she felt that her life had become fuller, happier, and more grounded. She explained, "I'm filled with an ability to hold huge ups and down and a flexibility, and I still have huge ups and downs, but I have something to land on." Unlike the rituals and practices of her Conservative Jewish upbringing that felt spiritually empty, meditation resonated deeply with Maya's everyday life; it helped her to feel "so much better, so much happier." The instrumentality—the practical benefits of the practice—imbued it with a sense of spirituality, or a feeling of well-being and nourishment.

Returning to the conversation that I had with Sara, the rabbi of a synagogue in New England, helps further illuminate the connection between spirituality and the therapeutic. Sara noted that meditation allowed her to feel "more grounded, more centered, more aware . . . less reactive." She continued, "I think to me it [meditation] is a spiritual quest as well as a psychological benefit. . . . It feels like mental health, just living more wisely and better in the world." Like Maya, Sara linked the spiritual with the psychological, emphasizing that spiritual practices have the capacity to help improve her life or, as Sara commented earlier, become a better "container of godliness." In describing the practical benefits of meditation,

Sara drew on a story about working through the sadness associated with the death of a close family member:

> And sometime early in that [grieving] process, I don't know, it was in the first week or the first couple of weeks, I remember just sitting, and I was just noticing what was arising in me and noticing the sadness arising. And I suddenly saw very clearly two streams of sadness, and one stream was just sadness, just loss, and it was very pure and simple and not unpleasant. You know, it was just, "All right, someone I love is gone." And the other stream was—it's like the little me or the selfish part, or like the scared part . . . like, "Who's going to take care of me?"

Sara paused briefly and then added,

> I could sort of see that and not be angry, but just be OK. And people will see those two streams and be able to say, "OK, I don't really—like that one, OK, it's arising, but I don't really need to go there. I'm an adult, and I'm OK." . . . And to distinguish that from just the sadness was really important—so that to me, like I could never have done that without this practice, to be able to sit, to actually be aware of what's arising, to see it with that much clarity, and from there to be able to sort of say, OK, you can let go of this one stream. . . . It was enormously helpful in my own mourning. . . . I think it helped me move forward, so I wasn't getting caught up in feelings that were unproductive and could just be present with what was real. And that's what was real, was just the sadness.

Sara expressed that meditation afforded her the tools to work through the sadness and grief associated with the loss of a loved one. The practice of meditation enabled her to be more present and aware of her feelings, and cut loose various nonproductive streams of thought. Meditation offered Sara psychological and therapeutic benefits, making it feel meaningful and relevant, and in turn, spiritually rich.

Just as the construction of spirituality as "performed" reflected the Jewish and Buddhist paths of the respondents, the construction of spirituality as "personally meaningful" reacted to those religious orbits as well. When the respondents claimed that Buddhism felt spiritually meaningful in comparison to Judaism, they evoked the language of spirituality to intentionally distance themselves from a form of inaccessible Judaism that they clearly rejected. Many respondents echoed Maya's sentiments that Judaism felt spiritually unfulfilling or difficult to access, particularly vis-à-vis Buddhism. They struggled to relate to the Torah, or find meaning and guidance within the ancient Jewish texts written in a foreign language about topics meaningful to Jewish life in antiquity.

For example, Rebecca, a cantor at a New England synagogue, reflected, "I wish that the Torah was laid out more like some of the Buddhist teachings, where it was a little more obvious how it can, like, guide your life in certain ways. The Torah talks a lot about mitzvoth [commandments], so that's significant. But what I'm saying is more I wish that, *spiritually*, the Torah was more obvious. I know a lot of people think it's great that's it not because then there are all these different interpretations, but for me, I need things like laid out."[13] Rebecca made the point that in comparison to Judaism, Buddhism felt spiritually fulfilling because it had obvious practical relevance and felt easily accessible. This was because she and other respondents practiced Buddhism in centers that presented highly psychologized versions of the teachings of the Buddha in English, meaning they rarely (if at all) critically engaged with Pali scriptures or sutras, or Buddhism's complex teachings about suffering, cycles of life and death, and liberation. Thus, when the respondents spoke about how Buddhism was easy to access or relate to, they were underscoring that they did not have to work to make the teachings or practices meaningful to their lives. In Buddhism, that interpretative work was done for them by a long line of Buddhist teachers, an important number of whom in the United States were Jews themselves.

This construction of spirituality as meaningful that was explicit in Rebecca's, Sara's, and Maya's stories was, more broadly, a discourse that the respondents employed to simultaneously criticize Judaism and applaud Buddhism for aligning with the particular expectation that religion should serve as a means to better the human condition by making people feel better and healthier. By wishing that "spiritually, the Torah was more obvious" in guiding her life, Rebecca used the language of spirituality to fashion a critique of normative Judaism for feeling inaccessible and distant. And in the reverse, her appreciation of Buddhism as spiritually meaningful to her daily life tacitly celebrated how Buddhism has been "domesticized" in the United States, largely shed of its mythical and traditional elements, and presented as a practice and philosophy of improving the human condition (Wilson 2014).

Although the respondents often spoke about struggling to find spirituality within Judaism, they remarked—ironically—that they were able to better appreciate Judaism as a "spiritual" path—that is, as meaningful and relevant to their everyday lives—after practicing Buddhism. Many respondents reported that Buddhism, or more specifically the framework of mindfulness, allowed them to understand their Jewish practices—prayers, blessings, or wearing tzitzit (ritual fringes)—as spiritual exercises, as practices toward greater intentionality, appreciation, and awareness. Sara, for instance, mentioned that

> there are Jewish practices that are mindfulness practices, like saying a blessing. I say *brachot* [blessings] before I eat and—I eat and do everything quickly. I eat quickly. So that to me is a really nice little Jewish mindfulness exercise. I'm about to put something in my mouth. I have to stop. And actually, the brilliance of the food blessings is you have to know what you're eating to know which blessing to say; it's great, it's brilliant. . . . In some way it helps me appreciate the Jewish practice—to have the language of mindfulness to say, "Oh, that blessing, that's a mindfulness practice." . . . It just gives me a way of understanding it, because the Jewish one [observances], you just do it; I mean, there aren't—there's not a theory behind it. So to bring another [theory]—from a different cultural perspective, it's like, "Oh, that's what that's doing." You know, that's actually a mindfulness practice. And to bring that into the language of Judaism; it just talks about it in a different way, so it's like a frame.

Sara, like other respondents, explained that reframing her Jewish observances as practices in mindfulness elevated them from obligatory or even senseless performances to spiritual worship. It was not the substance of Jewish prayers that mattered, nor was it the fulfillment of an obligation to perform them, but instead it was the repetitive and habitual nature of the *practice* that gave Jewish prayers their meaning. By transforming an otherwise rote Jewish ritual into a version of Buddhist practice, the respondents were able to elevate Jewish worship into a spiritual exercise in mindfulness and awareness. Framing their Jewish practices as mindfulness practices also allowed respondents a means to circumvent the language, idioms, gender politics, and narratives they often found troubling in Jewish liturgy. They no longer had to struggle with the literal meaning of Jewish prayers when it was the act of saying the prayer rather than the content of the worship that carried spiritual weight. Buddhism, in this sense, strengthened the respondents' connections to and appreciation of Judaism.

Spiritually as Individual Choice

The final characteristic of spirituality that the respondents highlighted was its volitional character. The story that Katie, a government planner in her early thirties, shared about her Jewish upbringing demonstrated the importance of choice to her understanding of spirituality. Although Katie had many warm memories of Judaism during her childhood, she underscored that Judaism never felt to her like a meaningful spiritual path, recalling,

> I liked the [Jewish] holidays. . . . I've always loved the Kabbalat Shabbat service. I like singing, and even though in the Conservative synagogue I grew up in, it was like stand up when they say to stand up, sit down when they say to sit down. There wasn't much feeling in it. . . . We kept kosher growing up, but that was just another, like, rule. It didn't mean anything. . . . I felt like I learned all the rituals, and I learned, like, all the motions, and I had no idea what most of them meant. Like I bow on this word in this prayer, I don't know why. And then I guess when I was a teenager and I got more into Buddhism, it felt so *spiritually meaningful*. . . . And I also felt like I was doing all this out of, like, guilt and obligation.

Echoing the sentiments of the respondents in the section above, Katie suggested that Judaism did not feel spiritually meaningful, particularly in comparison to meditation, because it did not connect or seem relevant to her everyday life. But she *also* emphasized that the Judaism of her childhood lacked spiritual meaning because it felt forced, regulated, and overly authoritative. The Jewish practices felt empty because she never experienced them as linked to a greater source of meaning. Judaism insisted that she "stand up," "sit down," and keep kosher, dictating gratuitously, and perhaps even paternalistically, what she and others should be doing.

In contrast, Buddhism and meditation more generally felt spiritually meaningful to Katie because she experienced them as voluntary rather than obligatory. Katie practiced meditation in a range of different contexts—writing meditation, Jewish meditation, and even toothbrushing as meditation. She explained, "I have different core practices. . . . For many months, I would go walk to a pier, and just sit, and just regulate my breath to the waves, because that felt comforting, and that's all I wanted, comfort. But for years before that I would do, like, loving-kindness practices, like blessing practices; blessing people who I loved, people who I didn't love, myself." As Katie described her various meditation practices, she intimated that an important part of what made meditation feel spiritual to her was the fact that she had control over when, how, and where to meditate, and that these practices were inwardly rather than outwardly directed. As she noted, they began from within her. In contrast, a crucial part of what made Judaism feel so spiritually unfulfilling was that Jewish practices, especially Jewish prayer, were largely compulsory, formulaic, and outwardly directed (particularly toward God). For Katie as well as others, spirituality was linked to a sense of individual choice and expression.

Several of my other respondents made explicit these ties between spirituality and individual choice by juxtaposing spirituality with halacha (Jewish law). When Jon, the clinical psychotherapist and insight meditation practitioner described earlier, recounted his Shabbat rituals, he stressed the connection between spirituality and free choice: "We do Friday night [Shabbat] at home. We do a Friday night ritual. I see myself as observing Shabbat, more spiritually than halachically; like I don't really stick to a lot of rules about it. It's more like certain things I don't do. I see it as a day of rest for myself, a day of renewal for myself. . . . I might just spend the day by myself." In comparing spirituality with halacha, Jon—who felt deeply connected to both his synagogue and Judaism—suggests that spirituality has an improvised quality that makes it personally meaningful. Unlike Jewish law, spirituality is not beholden to regulation and codification, nor is it faithfully passed down from generation to generation. It is instead chosen, self-constructed, and flexible. When Rebecca spoke about the strengths and limitations of Judaism as a religion, she too juxtaposed spirituality with halacha:

> I feel like a lot of times people get so caught up in what are the rules to follow that they don't look at what's beneath it. And I always struggle between feeling kind of a guilt for not doing more halachically, but at the same time, just feeling kind of not as motivated halachically as I am spiritually, you know. . . . I feel a little bit lonely in that. I feel like there are not a lot of people who I can talk to about that, although there probably are a lot more than I realize.

Rebecca, like Jon, made the point that spirituality has a chosen and self-constructed quality that made it different from prescribed religious law. Even though Rebecca was a cantor, a member of the Jewish clergy, she struggled with the obligatory nature of Jewish law as well.

Different from Rebecca, Shelly, a writer with no professional obligation to maintaining or promoting Jewish laws, vociferously rejected the compulsory nature of Judaism. In her early sixties, Shelly had been practicing meditation at Spirit Rock for over twenty years. She saw herself drawn to meditation much more strongly than Jewish prayer, observing,

> I'm not a big lover of prescribed spirituality, and this is why I don't keep kosher, because I always say what I eat doesn't seem to inform my spirituality. And I like to have a very particular kind of spiritual life that's based a lot on intuition and dreams, and kind of this general belief that there are many worlds, and meditation really supports all of that, and seems to provide, kind of I want to say a foundation, but I'm not sure if that's the right word.

As Shelly mentioned, her sense of spirituality was directly linked to her own intuition and extemporaneous expression. She did not keep kosher or pray because those practices felt scripted and forced on her; they were not acts she experienced as volitional.

In emphasizing the volitional nature of Buddhism, the respondents commonly told me that the message they heard at their Buddhist centers was "take what you want from Buddha's teachings and leave the rest"—an interpretation of the Buddha's message to "come and see," to try out the path he described and judge its value for oneself. This message gave my respondents license to choose freely among various different elements of Buddhism, and adopt only those they found personally meaningful and not in contradiction with the Jewish tradition. The respondents tended to "take" from Buddhism the practice of meditation and various teachings of the Buddha that they found beneficial to their lives (particularly various interpretations of the Buddha's teachings about mindfulness, loving-kindness, freedom, and equanimity), and discard the traditional elements of Buddhism associated with the historical religious tradition.

The frame of spirituality as choice reflects various concerns that the respondents had with issues of religious power and control. The American Buddhist traditions in which these respondents participate have been deliberately created to be self-consciously voluntary and antihierarchical. The stress on personal choice and self-direction within these traditions has imbued them with what the respondents experience as a deep sense of spirituality. Although the liberal wings of American Judaism have witnessed a move toward more individualized and "empowered" religiosity since the 1970s, the respondents expressed that they still experienced a Judaism that seems constrained by historic religious laws, theological positions, and hierarchical religious structures, all of which has detracted from what the respondents viewed as Judaism's spiritual promise.[14]

The respondents' ideas about spirituality as choice bear the mark of deep-seated American ideas about religious individualism. Scholars have demonstrated that whereas religion in premodern societies was largely an ascribed and immutable identity, it is increasingly now experienced—and indeed celebrated—as a matter of personal choice and religious achievement in the West (see Berger 1967; Bellah et al. 1985; Warner 1993; Madsen 2009; Putnam and Campbell 2010). The deeply held premise of religious individualism has led to a great deal of shifting within America's religious culture, exemplified by these respondents' fluid movement between Jewish and Buddhist practices. The spiritual premium that the respondents placed on religious individualism and choice affirms the importance they put on crafting a sense of themselves as self-sufficient, creative, and independent actors.

Conclusion

The sections above show how the respondents construct a Jewish Buddhist spirituality or syncretism of spiritual discourse built on four specific frames: spirituality as performance, spirituality as universal, spirituality as personally meaningful, and spirituality as individual choice. Different respondents placed different emphases on each of these frames, but generally when they spoke about spirituality, they did it in the context of one of these four frames. Reflected in these four frames of spirituality are the celebration of various values associated with religious liberalism—individualism, voluntarism, egalitarianism, pragmatism, an appreciation of both religious variety and the unity in diversity, and an aspiration for the therapeutic.

These four frames also bear the imprint of the Jewish and Buddhist religious worlds to which the respondents belong. The respondents' understanding of spirituality as performance resulted from the emphasis on practice as the central obligation or meaning-making activity within their Jewish and Buddhist communities. This stress on practice differs from popular American ideas about spirituality that commonly associate it with belief, awe, or metaphysical experience, underscoring how religious communities nurture and produce spiritual discourse (Ammerman 2013).

The respondents' universalist ideas about spirituality also have deep historical ties to discourses of American religious liberalism as well as frames of "pluralism" embedded in Western ideas about the coexistence of religious difference (Bender and McRoberts 2012). The respondents perceived Buddhist meditation, especially when removed from its traditional Asian historical and cultural context, as universalist—and thus spiritual—rather than particularist, minimizing the historical, cultural, and religious distinctiveness of the tradition. And in the reverse, the respondents critiqued Judaism for feeling insufficiently spiritual because it lacked the universality they associated with Buddhism. This universalist frame of spirituality exposes a deep tension within liberal Jewish communities about balancing a commitment to the particulars of Jewish peoplehood with a concern for a universal, shared humanity.

The construction of spirituality as "personally meaningful" and "chosen" were reactions—in a different way—to Judaism and Buddhism as well. When the respondents claimed that Buddhism felt spiritually meaningful in comparison to Judaism, they evoked the language of spirituality to intentionally distance themselves from a form of inaccessible and prescribed Judaism that they clearly rejected (i.e., a Judaism beset by rabbinic authority, religious obligations, ancient texts, and foreign languages). And they employed spiritual discourse to tacitly celebrate how Buddhism has been reformulated and modernized in the West, largely shed of many mythical and hierarchical elements, and presented as a practice and philosophy of improving the human condition. Not only did these four frames of spirituality develop in response to Buddhism and Judaism, but they set boundaries around those traditions in terms of allowable religious mixing. Respondents embraced meditation and mindfulness practices—elements of Buddhism that felt to them like "spiritual practice"—while discarding the elements of Buddhism commonly associated with the historical religious tradition, such as Buddhist devotional rites, beliefs in mythological or cosmological perspectives, or holiday celebrations.

Relating to Buddhism as a form of "spiritual practice" allowed the respondents to engage with, borrow from, and enjoy certain aspects of Buddhism while not affiliating with Buddhism as a religious tradition. It allowed them a way around the argument that they were transgressing Jewish law by committing avodah zarah (foreign worship) since they did not see themselves as adopting a new religious tradition, only some of its practices. Because Buddhism was a spiritual practice, the respondents felt free to selectively appropriate from Buddhism, adopting the practices that they found most meaningful and not in contradiction with their understandings of Jewish tradition. These respondents thus borrowed from Buddhism the practice of meditation and various teachings of the Buddha that they found helpful to their lives (particularly various interpretations of the Buddha's teachings about mindfulness, loving-kindness, freedom, and equanimity) and abandoned various other aspects of Buddhism that did not feel as relevant, such as Buddhist devotional rites, beliefs in mythological or cosmological perspectives, or holiday celebrations.

Finally, relating to Buddhism and Judaism in spiritual terms did more than establish boundaries; it also built bridges between the two traditions and served a means to strengthen the respondents' connections to the latter. Through Buddhism, a number of the respondents reconnected with Judaism and began to view their Jewish observances as spiritual practices in mindfulness. The framework of mindfulness offered them new perspectives on how to approach and interpret ritual. These respondents found that it was not the specific content of the Jewish prayer that mattered to its spiritual quality, nor the fulfillment of a commandment (mitzvah), but rather its habitual recitation and ritual performance. Practicing meditation and mindfulness made these respondents feel more alive as Jews.

The emphasis on how individuals relate to Judaism and Buddhism continues in the next chapter, though the focus shifts from an analysis of syncretic discourse to the construction of syncretic identities. The next chapter considers how a different group of Jewish Buddhists—those Jews who maintain a cultural rather than a practicing relationship to Judaism—situate themselves among as well as construct relationships with Judaism and Buddhism.

CHAPTER SEVEN

Constructing a Jewish Buddhist Identity

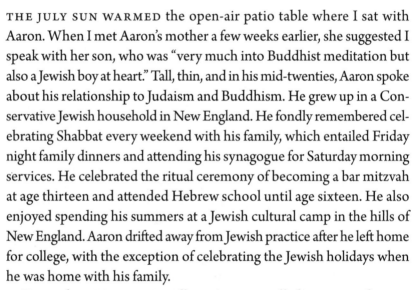

THE JULY SUN WARMED the open-air patio table where I sat with Aaron. When I met Aaron's mother a few weeks earlier, she suggested I speak with her son, who was "very much into Buddhist meditation but also a Jewish boy at heart." Tall, thin, and in his mid-twenties, Aaron spoke about his relationship to Judaism and Buddhism. He grew up in a Conservative Jewish household in New England. He fondly remembered celebrating Shabbat every weekend with his family, which entailed Friday night family dinners and attending his synagogue for Saturday morning services. He celebrated the ritual ceremony of becoming a bar mitzvah at age thirteen and attended Hebrew school until age sixteen. He also enjoyed spending his summers at a Jewish cultural camp in the hills of New England. Aaron drifted away from Jewish practice after he left home for college, with the exception of celebrating the Jewish holidays when he was home with his family.

During his junior year in college, Aaron enrolled in an introductory course in Buddhism. The Tibetan teacher who led the class presented a basic mindfulness meditation that emphasized "stability and clarity of mind, and just a focus on the breath." Enamored by this course, Aaron continued to take classes with other teachers in the Zen, Tibetan, and insight meditation traditions, both in college and after graduating. Eventually he developed a daily meditation practice largely focused on vipassana.

Currently he has a "meditation space" in his bedroom—an area cleared of miscellaneous objects, save for two meditation cushions (a zafu and zabutan) and a small table draped in a tapestry of earth-toned colors on which he has placed a stone Thai Buddha. Shortly after waking each morning, he sits on his cushions on his hardwood floor, closes his eyes, and meditates, using a process he describes as "gathering my body and my mind, my thoughts, kind of a grounding exercise." He focuses on his breath, and pays attention to the sensations in his body and mind, not in an attempt to control or alter his feelings but to just be present with his thoughts. In addition to this daily practice, Aaron participates in a small vipassana meditation group that meets twice a month in the nearby meditation center. He also attends a silent weeklong retreat at IMS two to three times a year.

Aaron's turn from an involvement in Judaism during his childhood to participation in Buddhism in his adulthood raises questions about how he understands himself in relation to both traditions in contemporary American society. Conventional theories about religious shifting or conversion suggest that when individuals change religions, they abjure identification with their former religious group in favor of their new chosen group, often through a radical "rupture with a former identity" (see, for example, Travisano 1970). Yet Aaron did not shed his identification with Judaism when he entered into a new relationship with Buddhism. To the contrary, he maintained and valued a relationship with both traditions; he constructed a syncretism of religious identity. He held an almost-instinctive connection to Judaism. Being Jewish, he told me, was "not a choice"; it was his religious history and people—the culture from which he came. His Buddhist identity, in contrast, felt chosen or even optional. Sometimes he identified as a Buddhist, and at other times he did not. Mostly, he explained, his Buddhist identity was about what he does; he imagines himself as someone who practices meditation and learns from the Buddhist path.

Aaron's experience points to the way that Americans are forging meaningful relationships and identifications with more than one religious tradition. Most American Buddhists, Jewish or otherwise, are not particularly troubled by issues of identity (Cadge 2005; Coleman 2001). Often they interpret the Buddha's teaching about nonattachment, or the view that attachments and cravings are the principal sources of suffering, to mean that they should not cling tightly to or put great stock in a specific identity. Jewish Buddhists, however, also recognize that other people, especially members of the Jewish community, frequently view Judaism and Buddhism as mutually incompatible. When faced with the need to justify themselves to others, they have created explanations for who they are and what they do.

This chapter examines those explanations by probing the syncretism of religious and cultural identities, asking how individuals view themselves in relationship to Judaism and Buddhism. I focus on a new group of lay practitioners: those Jewish Buddhists who do not maintain a practicing relationship to Judaism and instead view themselves as "culturally Jewish." I draw on an analysis of thirty-two interviews with Jewish-born individuals like Aaron who have turned their hearts and minds toward the teachings as well as practices of the Buddha. I label these individuals "converts," even though Buddhism does not have a formal conversion process.[1] Despite their relationships to Buddhism, all these respondents also identify as Jews, even if they do not practice Judaism as a religious tradition. I explore how these respondents identify differently with Judaism than they do with Buddhism, demonstrating how they view their Jewish identities as ascribed and culturally inherited and their Buddhist identities as achieved and enacted. I then describe four approaches that these respondents take to integrating their two identities into one syncretic Jewish Buddhist identity. As fluidity and mixing play increasingly important roles in contemporary American religion, these approaches offer an analytic framework for understanding how people connect to and identify with more than one religious tradition.

Religious Identification in the United States

In the West, religious identities are widely imagined as bounded, stable, and unitary.[2] The Western idea that each individual has one religious affiliation has deep roots in the Abrahamic notion that a person must have fidelity to and faith in one religious tradition to the exclusion of all others. When an individual changes religious traditions, scholars thus argue that it requires a total and wholesale adoption of the new religious tradition along with an abjuration of the former one. Conversion has traditionally been understood to be powerful precisely because it forces people to make a radical, sharp distinction between past and present identities.[3]

Over the past few decades, though, a growing body of research has challenged these ideas about bounded identities and total conversions. Both ethnographic research and survey data have demonstrated that religious identities are growing increasingly elastic and fluid in the United States, and that conversion often has a partial, segmented nature.[4] Individuals do not necessarily shed an identification with their past religious identity when they begin practicing a new religious tradition. Rather, they more freely and fluidly mix religious practices and beliefs, forming both-and as opposed to either-or religious connections.

In addition to recognizing the role that fluidity and blending play within American religion, scholars of religion have begun to broaden their understandings of how people connect to it more generally. Scholars have long viewed religious identities as sustained by beliefs that relate the individual to the supernatural.[5] New scholarship, however, particularly from research on western Europe, has shown that many people have religious identities that are rooted not in ideology and supernatural belief but rather family memories, ethnic pride, and cultural heritage.[6] The sociologist N. J. Demerath III (2000) coined the term "cultural religion" to describe this connection between a collective religious identity and historical past, absent a commitment to the core practices and beliefs around which the religious community originally formed.

Similarly, scholars of Buddhism have demonstrated that supernatural commitments are not central to the way that many convert Buddhists, like Jewish Buddhists, identify with the tradition. As described in chapter 3, many convert Buddhist communities, especially those affiliated with the insight meditation tradition, have placed the practice of meditation at the center of the movement, and minimized the framework of Buddhist cosmological ideas about renunciation and detachment that have historically supported this practice (Wilson 2014). In consequence, practice, most often in the form of seated meditation, fundamentally sustains American Jews' relationship to Buddhism, with "doing" rather than "believing" forming the core of their Buddhist identities.

A connection to Judaism as a cultural religion and commitment to Buddhism as "a way of practice" are woven into the narratives that Jewish Buddhists tell about their syncretic identities. Jewish Buddhists view being Jewish as an inherent part of who they are and where they came from. Analytically, I use the concept of "ascription" to refer to how people construct their culturally Jewish identities. Ascribed characteristics are those that people believe to be fixed and immutable, frequently starting at birth; they are qualities that are *inherited, essential,* and *unchangeable*.

In contrast, Jewish Buddhists view Buddhism as something that they *do* to create a sense of identity. They "practice" Buddhism more than they "are" Buddhist.[7] I use the term "achievement" to categorize how the respondents explain their Buddhist identities. Achieved characteristics are the conscious choices that people make through the practices they perform or enact.[8] They are *chosen, optional,* and *performed*. Jewish Buddhists understand their relationships to these traditions through the narratives they tell about being and performing these two identities.

Constructing a Jewish Cultural Identity: An Ascribed Identity

The Pew Research Center's (2013) "A Portrait of Jewish Americans" revealed that Jewish identity has undergone a significant transformation over the past quarter century. The study showed a decline in Jews who identify Judaism as their religion and an uptick in Jews who describe themselves as having no religion. The Pew researchers labeled the former group "Jews by religion" and the latter "Jews of no religion." Although Jews have a long history of secularism, this shift in Jewish self-identification seemed to reflect a broader trend among Americans to increasingly eschew any religious affiliation.[9] Rather than identifying with Judaism as their religion, "Jews of no religion" identified as Jewish on the basis of ancestry, ethnicity, or culture, and compared to "Jews by religion," were much less connected to Jewish organizations (both religious and cultural), less likely to observe Jewish law and traditions, and less engaged in the Jewish community.

If the Pew researchers had interviewed the Jewish Buddhists in this chapter, they would have found that they resemble the "Jews of no religion." They identify as Jewish on the basis of heritage and ethnicity rather than religion. Few respondents believed in a single, all-powerful God who created the world or any Jewish eschatological ideas, and nearly all described themselves as atheistic, nontheistic, or agnostic. They also observed few, if any, Jewish laws and traditions and rarely participated in Jewish communal life. Judaism did not serve as an ethical guidepost or a meaning-making system in these respondents' lives. Yet these respondents did not imagine themselves as "Jews of no religion"; instead, they viewed themselves as "culturally Jewish," and used this term to describe and talk about their Jewish identities. "Culturally Jewish," in the way that these Jewish Buddhists used it, refers to how they orient themselves toward and embody a set of dispositions generated from the social, religious, and historical experience of American Jews.

I view these culturally Jewish identities as ascribed identities because the Jewish Buddhists emphasized their choiceless and unchangeable aspects, and in doing so, the respondents often blurred the analytic distinction that scholars make between cultural inheritance (e.g., rituals, beliefs, ancestry, etc.) and biological inheritance (e.g., genetic code, physical characteristics, hereditary traits, etc.). Frequently, Jewish Buddhists stressed that being Jewish was an internal, essential part of their cultural identity, so much so that it was ingrained in their genetics or biology. In this way, they subsumed biology and genetics under their conception of culture.

For example, Jaime, a therapist in her early thirties, explained that she thinks about Judaism as her "culture" because "it's just in my blood. . . . It's very interesting, isn't it? Because that's blood. I was taught by my parents to hold on dearly to it. People have died for it [Judaism]. I'm proud of it and—I don't have to do anything to be Jewish. I just have to breathe." Other respondents underscored how Jewishness was "in their genes"—a cultural identity with which they were born or seemed to inherit biologically.[10] Recent research has revealed that many contemporary Jews essentialize their Jewish identities by emphasizing their biological, genetic basis, even though racially and biologically determined concepts of Jewish identity have been debunked (see Tenenbaum and Davidman 2007).[11] Jewish Buddhists adopt this genetic essentialism to underscore the ascribed and choiceless aspect of their Jewish identities.

The culturally Jewish identity of my respondents closely relates to what scholars might label a Jewish ethnic identity. Typically, scholars refer to Jewish ethnic identities as a shared or collective identity that includes an attachment to Jewish peoplehood, identification with the long and bitter history of antisemitism, and pride or celebration in Jewish culture.[12] The rise of Jewish ethnic identification in the United States occurred in tandem in the late twentieth century with ethnic revivalism, which produced a heightened awareness and celebration of ethnic origins as well as differences among diverse ethnic groups.[13] That Jewish Buddhists understand their attachment to Jewish heritage and peoplehood as cultural rather than ethnic suggests that culture has come to replace ethnicity as the salient category of Jewish self-identification. In what follows, I trace the three defining characteristics of a culturally Jewish identity.

A Liberal Social Ethic

A deep-seated appreciation of a sense of Jewish social distinctiveness lay at the center of these respondents' culturally Jewish identity. In terms of residential patterns, class, education, and occupation, these Jewish Buddhists, like other American Jews, occupied a distinctive position in the US social amalgam (Smith 2005).[14] All but a handful grew up in or around an urban area, and came from middle- to upper-middle-class families, with most continuing to live a middle- to upper-middle-class lifestyle. As a group, they had exceptionally high levels of educational attainment. All but one of the respondents had at least a bachelor's degree, over 90 percent had an advanced degree (MA level or higher), and a third earned the terminal degree in their field (MD, PhD, JD, etc.). Politically, these respondents overwhelmingly described themselves as liberal or left leaning, often radically so. Among those respondents of the baby boomer generation, most had been active in the countercultural movements of the 1960s and 1970s, including social movements in support of a more radically democratic society (like the Students for a Democratic Society) along with women's rights, gay rights, and antiwar movements.

These respondents spoke about their educated, liberal, and socially active dispositions as rooted in their Jewish upbringings and internalized in their sense of themselves as cultural Jews. Jonathan, a teacher in the insight meditation tradition, explained this well. He grew up in the 1950s and 1960s in New York City, where his family belonged to a Conservative Jewish synagogue. Despite observing the Jewish holidays at home, attending Hebrew school, and becoming a bar mitzvah, he never felt like Judaism was a religious way of life. Rather, it was part of his cultural identity that shaped the way he understood and acted in the world. As he put it, "Judaism was definitely a major part of my cultural heritage, and identification. . . . There's a—it's not quite pride; there's an appreciation; there's a deep appreciation for everything in the Jewish culture that is wonderful, like the emphasis on education, learning, fairness, justice, mitzvoth, and doing good." Jonathan continued, observing,

> It's not an accident that our culture has produced some of the greatest minds that have ever lived on the planet, and there's a pride with that, and a deep appreciation of that. We were just so fortunate that education was our root. . . . There's such an emphasis on education, we've developed ourselves in that way, and I've been the beneficiary of that, absolutely, and I have a deep appreciation for that. And the values— it's not an accident that Jews tend to be more liberal, progressive, compassionate, understanding of what the underdog is. In general, the culture that I grew up in was progressive, and liberal, and Democrat, and seemed to side with inclusiveness, and caring for those less fortunate. Those things are fabulous, and I really value them.

Jonathan deeply appreciated the emphasis on education, justice, and doing good deeds that he saw as rooted in his Jewish upbringing. These values were ingrained within him and shaped his value system. Like Jonathan, many other respondents understood their liberal politics, commitment to social justice, and intellectualism as a central component of their culturally Jewish identity.

A Chain of Memory

Also at the heart of my respondents culturally Jewish identity rested a set of dispositions produced by their relationship with Judaism as a historical religious tradition. These dispositions were not founded on a belief in Jewish scriptures, observance of Jewish laws, or belonging to Jewish organizations. They were instead an orientation toward Judaism that emphasized the importance of locating oneself within the context of Jewish history and heritage. This orientation bears resemblance to what French sociologist Danièle Hervieu-Léger (2000, 81) labels "religion as a chain of memory," or when individuals see themselves as part of a "chain" that gathers together past, present, and future memories. Hervieu-Léger understands this chain of memory to occur through anamnesis, or when a group demonstrates publicly and visibly that they belong to a distinctive religion by recalling the past to memory through rites.

The Jewish Buddhists' chain of memory, however, did not occur through public rituals. Rather, they drew on and identified with the well of their Jewish past privately and especially narratively. They told cherished stories that located themselves and their families within the arc of Jewish history. These stories and memories varied by the number of generations that their families had been in the United States. Those respondents who were first- or second-generation Americans frequently highlighted the importance of their family's Jewish immigration story to their culturally Jewish identity. They told tales about the different European cities (or as was the case for a few respondents, Middle Eastern ones) that their families came from, routes they took to the United States, languages their families spoke, hardships they faced, and sorts of Jewish immigrant food their families cooked and ate during their childhoods.

For the respondents who were third- and fourth-generation Americans, the chain of memories that connected them to Judaism was tied less to the particulars of their family's immigration story and more to a shared, if undefined, sense of belonging to the Jewish people. These largely younger respondents struggled to precisely articulate with what aspects of their cultural heritage they specifically identified. Some spoke about feeling connected to the tradition of Jewish humor or American Jewish immigrant success story. Others talked about feeling connected to pastrami sandwiches, gefilte fish, or New York deli food.

Across the different generations, however, the Holocaust factored centrally into the respondents' Jewish identities. Deborah, a forty-six-year-old psychologist and social activist, was especially articulate about the significance of the Holocaust to her identity as a cultural Jew. We sat together in the living room of her house, and she shared with me stories about the experiences of her French Jewish mother during World War II. She showed me pictures of her mother's family and the refugee boat called the *Serpa Pinto* that they took to escape France in 1942. She also shared with me a newspaper clipping documenting the story of the landing of the *Serpa Pinto* at Staten Island. Reflecting on this, she explained, "This is the story of my mother's family. A Jewish family living in Paris and then hiding out in the South of France for two years, and then taking the last ship over from Casablanca to the United States as French Jews is—it's a powerful history and a powerful story, and I identify very strongly with it. So certainly I identify with being Jewish very strongly, and I think that history has always affected me." Deborah captured in this story the intergenerational effects and legacy of the Holocaust, or what sociologist Janet Jacobs (2010, 157) calls "social inheritance of genocidal histories." In her book *Memorializing the Holocaust: Gender, Genocide, and Collective Memory*, Jacobs demonstrated that the descendants of Holocaust survivors have a remarkably mature capacity to contextualize and understand their families' traumatic experiences, and what they had to do in order to survive. In explaining this inheritance, Deborah continued,

> So some people actually would call me a Holocaust survivor, although I didn't directly survive the Holocaust. But I think my family escaping from France, I remember as a child having fantasies, sort of Anne Frank fantasies of it. The Nazis came, hiding in the attic, pulling down this sort of ladder thing and hiding in the attic from the Nazis. And I grew up in a home, where I realize now it's not normal, but to me it was just normal: all the windows were nailed shut, and they still are. . . . So

clearly it [being Jewish] had an impact, but not so much the religious aspect of it, just more being Jewish culturally.

Deborah emphasized the importance of her mother's escaping the Nazis during World War II to her sense of herself as a cultural Jew. She saw herself as a descendant of a Holocaust survivor and located herself within this larger arc of Jewish history. She also felt like her liberal politics and commitment to social activism connected specifically to the cultural narrative of "never again," which meant to her never again to any people.[15] This relates to how recent scholarship has demonstrated that the Holocaust has become a cultural frame embedded in various social movements as a call for action (on both the right and left of the political spectrum) (Stein 1998).[16]

Although the story about the *Serpa Pinto* is uniquely Deborah's, most of the other respondents also identified strongly, if not as specifically, with the Holocaust. Indeed, research has shown that identifying with and remembering the Holocaust is central to what it means to be Jewish in the United States today.[17] Many respondents who were not direct descendants of Holocaust survivors and for whom the Holocaust was largely a historical event also viewed it as an important signifier of their Jewish identity. They too linked their identity politics and social activism to the legacy of the Holocaust. Identification with the Holocaust was not based on a perceived or real sense of Jewish victimhood but rather the translation of history into a concern about the victimization and oppression of others.

Not Being Christian

The third component of my respondents' culturally Jewish identity relates to their position as a Jewish minority living in a largely Christian society. If the Jewish Buddhists struggled at times to define what being Jewish meant to them, they had an easier time making clear what they were not: Christian. Some respondents spoke about direct experiences with antisemitism that shored up their own sense of themselves as Jews. For example, during my conversation with Barry, a clinical psychologist in his early sixties, he explained that the reasons he had joined a Jewish fraternity largely had to do with an implicit form of antisemitism he experienced in college. He remembered, "I went to Cornell. Jews went to Jewish fraternities. And the term at the time was 'whites' for the other fraternities. Christians joined white fraternities. And Jews did not join white fraternities; whites did not join Jewish fraternities."

Barry continued, "And in the cafeterias, student cafeterias, there was an invisible—but very well-known—line down the center, down this cafeteria where the whites sat on one side and Jews sat on the other side. And you didn't cross it. And if you did, I mean, nobody would attack you or even say anything to you if you crossed it, but it was known. It would be known that we would be violating the strong social borders of the school." Barry expressed how these experiences with antisemitism shaped his Jewish identity by reinforcing boundaries between Jews and Christians. He perceived himself as a Jew because he was perceived as one; his Jewish identity was a reflexive response to feeling like a religious minority.

Later in our conversation, Barry mentioned that his Buddhist meditation group frequently meets in a Unitarian Universalist church. I asked him if he had any affiliation with the church, and he replied, "It's hard for me to sit in a Buddhist mediation group in a Unitarian Universalist church. . . . Even though I appreciate it, and its philosophy is that all religions are fundamentally at some level the same, the word 'church' has been contaminated for me [from my Jewish upbringing]." Feeling unwelcome or uncomfortable in Christian settings was part of what it meant to him to be a Jew in the United States.

Beyond the direct experiences with antisemitism, though, the majority of the Jewish Buddhists seemed to hold a quiet uneasiness about Christianity tied to the historical waxing and waning of social discrimination that American Jews have experienced as religious minorities in the United States (see Sarna 2004, 216).[18] During my conversation with twenty-seven-year-old Julie, she made plain that part of her culturally Jewish identity related to the experience of living as a minority religious group in a largely Christian society, noting, "Christianity in particular just gives me the heebie-jeebies because of its unique history of having an ideology that lead to persecuting my family. . . . I've also had a lot of really negative interactions with missionaries. I have a lot of respect for various individual Christian groups and people I know, but I would never feel comfortable actually being part of a Christian group." The historical persecution of the Jewish people by Christians left Julie and other respondents with a wariness of Christianity and Christian settings, shaping and defining their sense of themselves as Jews.

Constructing an American Buddhist Identity: An Achieved Identity

The Jewish Buddhists do not imagine that their Buddhist identities are fixed in their genetic code, as they do with their Jewish identities. Rather, these respondents talk about their Buddhist identities using the language of "choice" and "practice." They held an active engagement with Buddhism, emphasizing how it is something they do, and a perspective or worldview they cultivate through practice. Listening to how these respondents talked about their Buddhist identities led me to conceptualize them as "achieved," or an identity that these respondents created through their actions and volition.

In stressing the achieved character of their Buddhist identities, these respondents frequently distanced themselves from an ethnic or cultural affiliation with Buddhism. They underscored that they were not Buddhist in the way a Japanese, Tibetan, or Chinese person is Buddhist, conveying that they did not view Buddhism as their inherited historic or ethnoreligious tradition. Less than a quarter of these Jewish Buddhists had visited Asia, and few felt connected to Buddhism as it is practiced and institutionalized there.

Rather, these Jewish Buddhists identified with a Buddhism that was constituted in and adapted to the United States. Across the specific lineages with which these respondents affiliated, they saw themselves as practitioners of "American Buddhism."[19] The Jewish Buddhists in my sample all practice Buddhism in organizations affiliated with the Zen, Tibetan, or Theravada traditions—the three traditions from which many convert Buddhists are drawn.[20] On average, the Jewish Buddhists reported affiliating with their Buddhist centers for about seven years, with some affiliations spanning over three decades, and a few hovering around a year. Most respondents reported that they try to regularly take classes and participate in events at their Buddhist centers. Those respondents under the age of thirty were all part of young adult groups at their Buddhist centers, and many of the older practitioners participated in various other affinity groups at their centers (LGBTQ, older practice, or regular sitting groups). Most Jewish Buddhists attended their Buddhist centers weekly or biweekly, and nearly everyone tried to maintain a regular meditation practice at home. Some of the Jewish Buddhists, especially those who practiced in the Tibetan tradition, held traditional beliefs about karmic rebirth, the nature of existence, and enlightenment—all beliefs integral to the Tibetan centers to which those respondents belonged.[21] The majority of Jewish Buddhists, however, did not express a belief in the metaphysical teachings of Buddhism because their teachers, as described in earlier chapters, focused primarily on the practical details of meditation and minimized the framework of the Buddhist cosmology that surrounded that practice. In what follows, I lay out the three defining characteristics of these respondents' American Buddhist identities, demonstrating their achieved nature, and how they are produced by the teachings and practices of their Buddhist organizations.

A Way of Practice

The Jewish Buddhists in my study, like other convert Buddhists, related to Buddhism fundamentally as a way of practice.[22] They frequently told me that the message they heard in their Buddhist centers was "be a Buddha, not a Buddhist." They felt Buddhism was not about "the -ism," or about claiming an institutionalized identity, but rather about a set of practices that are linked to and support a Buddhist worldview. Although the respondents differed in their Buddhist practices, they all placed a central emphasis on the practice of meditation, echoing, as described in earlier chapters, the stress that their own teachers placed on the practice of meditation.

Recent research has demonstrated that American Buddhist centers, especially those that cater to convert practitioners, give prominence to the practice of meditation (Coleman 2001; Cadge 2004; Seager 2012). In James Coleman's (2001, 119) sociological exploration of Buddhist centers in the United States, he found that 92.4 percent of the North American Buddhists in his study ranked meditation as the single most important activity that occurred in their Buddhist communities. As discussed in chapter 3, the emphasis on meditation in the convert Buddhist communities stands in stark contrast to the role of meditation in Buddhism in Asia, where meditation has historically been practiced by ordained monks and nuns, as part of a much larger system of supporting practices and beliefs ordinarily associated with world renunciation as well as the pursuit of nirvana (Wilson 2014).

The respondents' practice-oriented relationships to Buddhism varied by the tradition or lineage with which the individual affiliated. The Jewish Buddhists who affiliated with the Tibetan tradition had a practice-oriented relationship to Buddhism that has closer ties to Buddhism as a historic religious tradition because Tibetan Buddhism has not undergone the same degree of modernization as the Zen and Theravada traditions. More so than the practitioners who affiliate with the insight meditation tradition, these practitioners tended to have taken various Buddhist vows; performed advanced meditation techniques that incorporated visualizations of meditational deities, mantras (sacred syllables or phrases that are chanted), mudras (ritual hand gestures), and mandalas (symbolic representations of enlightened worlds); observed various Buddhist celebrations and/or holidays; and believed in complex Buddhist cosmological explanations. In the Tibetan tradition, these aspects of Buddhism are integral components of the teachings and practices of its meditation centers.

Different from the Jewish Buddhists who affiliated with the Tibetan tradition, those who affiliated with the insight meditation tradition (or some Zen and/or various nonsectarian groups) had an achieved identity tied much more closely to viewing Buddhism as a psychotherapeutic practice. As outlined in chapter 3, all the first-generation Jewish Buddhist teachers in the insight meditation tradition promoted a distinctive psychologized Buddhist practice. This psychotherapeutic orientation has taken such a hold in the tradition that all the insight meditation practitioners I interviewed saw Buddhism as a set of practices associated with the cultivation of a present and mindful way of life. These respondents learned these perspectives from their Buddhist communities, where their teachers largely viewed and taught meditation outside its historic as well as religious context.[23]

Many of these insight meditation practitioners held deeply entrenched secular worldviews and commitments, and expressed a frequent wariness of organized religion in general (despite their belonging to and participating in their Buddhist centers). They practiced and felt comfortable with Buddhism largely because they viewed it as irreligious and nontheistic. These Jewish Buddhists largely sought out Buddhist techniques, particularly meditation, because they felt they offered both physical and psychological benefits, helping to reduce stress and encourage calmness in their lives.

Like-Minded Fellowship

Although practice rested at the heart of my respondents' Buddhist identities, they also found meaning in belonging to a community of others who thought and cared similarly about the world. Julie told me that she really values belonging to her Tibetan Buddhist community because she feels part of a larger group of people "who are all interested in figuring out how to be better humans." She deeply appreciated the conversations she had with fellow Buddhist practitioners about creating a more democratic, just, environmentally conscious, and equitable society. Although Buddhism as a historical religious tradition has no inherent ties to left-wing or progressive politics, its embrace by and enmeshment with the American counterculture throughout the 1960s and 1970s has left it with a decidedly liberal bent, so much so that to be both Buddhist and conservative seems anathema to the convert American Buddhist community. Most Buddhist centers in the United States support liberal values (racial tolerance, gay rights, feminism, and environmentalism) and attract members who support them as well (Wilson 2014, 387). The

demographic base of the American Buddhist mainstream closely resembles that of American Judaism: most convert American Buddhists
are white, highly educated (usually college or university educated, and
often with advanced degrees), middle- to upper-middle-class Euro-
Americans, and socially and politically liberal (Coleman 2001,
192–93).[24]

Studies have shown that belonging to a community of like-minded
others is important to American Buddhist practitioners generally,
whether they are of Jewish or non-Jewish heritage (Cadge 2005; Coleman 2001). But for these Jewish Buddhist respondents, it seemed that
they found in Buddhism a community where their deeply (and Jewishly)
ingrained sense of themselves as educated, liberal, and politically progressive could thrive. Their Buddhist communities thus served as a universe that welcomed and cultivated the liberal values with which they
were raised. The social resonance of Buddhism felt to many respondents
more than familiar; it was familial. Indeed, over a dozen of my respondents spoke about "feeling at home" quickly after beginning to practice
at their Buddhist centers.

Although nearly all my respondents felt that belonging to a like-
minded community of practitioners was important to their senses of
themselves as Buddhist, those of the baby boomer generation seemed
especially attracted to their Buddhist communities for their social appeal.
These respondents largely came to Buddhism from the counterculture,
and felt a strong attraction to Buddhism's liberal and even radical history
in the United States. The Jewish Buddhists of the baby boomer generation, especially those who were artists, writers, and intellectuals, spoke
about their Buddhist communities as places where their radically left-
wing perspectives were valued and welcomed. Many of these respondents spoke about the importance of forming communities of others who
valued the same antimaterialist, and even sometimes anticapitalist, sensibilities and views that they themselves cherished.

This search for like-minded fellowship within Buddhism parallels the
way others among the baby boomer generation sought out and joined
alternative religious/spiritual communities (or what scholars term "new

religious movements") that functioned as a space of social connection and support as well as a protest against the values of mainstream and frequently conservative religious institutions.[25] The period beginning in 1965 saw exceptional growth in the new religious movements, particularly of groups associated with Asian religious traditions. These groups often began with converts as their primary membership base, attracting alienated, affluent youths who felt spiritually disaffected from established religious life and the materialism of American capitalism. These new religious movement converts saw themselves in search of spiritual enlightenment, personal development, or transcendent connection. They offered their followers a meaningful and compelling moral context, clearing a path for them to get "saved from the sixties" (Tipton 1982).

Cultivating Meaning through Meditation

The last defining aspect of my respondents' American Buddhist identities was the cultivation of a new epistemological view based on the Four Noble Truths, Eightfold Path, and various teachings about mindfulness that supported their meditation practice. Jewish Buddhists, like American Buddhists more generally, found tremendous meaning in various teachings from the dharma, the view of nature based on teachings attributed Siddhārtha Gautama, or the Buddha. The teachings of Buddhism offered the respondents a new epistemological view of human existence that was based on a radically different set of Eastern assumptions than those they heard in their Jewish upbringings. Unlike the Abrahamic religions, the teachings of the Buddha, as conveyed to the respondents in their Buddhist centers, did not emphasize a single powerful God, validity of sacred texts or scriptures, or belief in a larger sacred narrative. The nontheistic character of Buddhism in particular resonated with many Jewish Buddhists who were uncomfortable with Judeo-Christian understandings of a supreme God.

Though different teachings of the Buddha resonated with different people, nearly all the respondents found meaning in the Buddhist perspectives on suffering. For example, Deborah spoke directly about how the teachings of the Buddha with regard to suffering gave her great comfort. The Four Noble Truths, which revolve around the truth, origin, cessation, and path of cessation of suffering, contain the essence of the Buddha's teachings. The first noble truth is the truth of suffering (*Dukkha*). The second is the truth of the origin of suffering (*Samudāya*). The third is the truth of the cessation of suffering (*Nirodha*). The fourth is the truth of the path to the cessation of suffering (*Magga*). The attention that Buddhism pays to suffering, and the way it universalizes and accepts it as a human experience, resonated deeply with Deborah.

Deborah suffers from multiple sclerosis, a chronic and often debilitating autoimmune disorder that affects the central nervous system. The disease came on suddenly. She remembered that one day she was riding bikes and climbing mountains; the next day, she sighed, "it was all done, forever." For nearly three years after the onset of her first symptoms, she had to lie down flat on her couch for most of the day, barely leaving her apartment. She became severely depressed, noting that "at first I was like, poor me, poor me, poor me. 'This is happening to me. It doesn't happen to other people.' And then . . . I read widely about Buddhism. I had bought into society's view that the most important thing is being healthy, and that the way you're healthy is if you exercise and you eat right." Deborah continued,

> So suddenly I found out that I have MS. I'm not particularly healthy, and I can't exercise. It doesn't matter how many vitamins I take. It's not going to change it. So I had to come to terms with the fact that what society was teaching me and telling me was not the truth, and Buddhism and the teachings of Buddhism actually gave me great comfort, because the teachings about change, illness, suffering, . . . to me they rang so true, and I felt like I understood what really reality is about, as opposed to what the culture tells you. . . . I learned, oh this [suffering] happens to everybody. This is normal. This is life, and it's not poor you. . . . You see that suffering is universal and it allows you—it increases your compassion for others and therefore, your suffering is alleviated by that, because you realize that it ties you into everybody else, and it allows you to care for others in a better way, because you've been there.

In this story, Deborah explained that the teachings of the Buddha that normalize the experience, interconnectedness, and prevalence of suffering counter deep-seated American ideas that suggest that if an individual behaves responsibly and prudently, then good things will befall them. These messages brought Deborah meaning and comfort during some of the hardest moments of her life. They provided a new way of seeing and making sense of the world, cultivated through the practices of Buddhism.

Combining Ascribed and Achieved Identities: Four Discourses of Integration

Jewish Buddhists integrated their achieved Buddhist identities with their ascribed Jewish identities into the accounts they told about their syncretic Jewish Buddhist identity. They did so through four primary discursive approaches: foregrounding ascription and backgrounding achievement, foregrounding achievement and backgrounding ascription, compartmentalizing ascription and achievement, and drawing parallels between ascription and achievement.

Foregrounding Ascription and Backgrounding Achievement

One way that Jewish Buddhists accounted for their syncretic identities was to give prominence to their ascribed identities over their achieved ones. These respondents emphasized that "who they are" as a Jew was more central to their identity than "what they do" as a Buddhist. The common way that the respondents explained this was by imagining themselves as "a Jew who practices Buddhism or Buddhist meditation." At the heart of this approach is the view that cultural Judaism functions as an individual's primary interpretative filter, despite one's involvement in and connection to Buddhism. This approach was especially common among those Jewish Buddhists who practice in the insight meditation tradition, and relate to Buddhism more as a tool kit of psychotherapeutic practices and teachings than a historical religious tradition.

Donna, for example, a forty-two-year-old social worker, identifies as a Jewish person who practices Buddhism. She was born and raised in the Jewish tradition. Her family belonged to a Conservative synagogue, and she felt that she had a positive and joyful Jewish upbringing. Donna had some exposure to meditation during her childhood, but only took a serious interest in Buddhism in college. She practiced in various different Buddhist communities throughout her young adulthood. Now she mostly participates in a Buddhist community in the tradition of Thich Nhat Hanh. She currently maintains no active Jewish observances, and does not belong to a synagogue or other Jewish organization.

When Donna explained how she understands her relationships to Judaism and Buddhism, she said, "I have put my allegiance with Judaism. I think I feel like I have to choose, and I'm a Jewish person who meditates, who adopted a Buddhist meditation practice. Actually the meditation practice is more important to me than anything in Judaism, but I'm Jewish and not Buddhist. That seems so strange, but it is likely how I'm going to have to divide it up a lot. I don't right now identify as Buddhist." Donna understood her relationships to Judaism and Buddhism by emphasizing that she was first and foremost a Jewish person, and second a Buddhist meditator.

Sensing a certain hesitation about her relationship to Buddhism, I asked her why she does not identify as a Buddhist, particularly given that meditation practice is more important to her than any Jewish practice or belief. She responded,

> There are a lot of things I haven't figured out. Like how would I behave? I'm all over the map. I think if I were to identify as Buddhist I would have to be on a path toward being vegetarian. And I would have to be on a path toward being stolid and a pacifist. It might help if I called myself a Buddhist, like it might help me stay on my practice. It might help me be more reflective. I just do not identify as Buddhist. . . . I think I swear too much; I'm too sarcastic; I'm flip. I don't want to be calm all the time, I don't. It's all those things. . . . I'm already bad at being Jewish, why take on another one [identity] and be bad at it too?

Donna felt that in order to take on a Buddhist identity, she would need to adhere more closely to the principle ethical and moral teachings associated with Buddhism. In another way, as Donna joked with me later, she felt almost "too Jewish" to be Buddhist. Donna saw herself as "a 100 percent New York Jewish," even if she currently does not practice Judaism as a religious tradition. She was raised doing walkathons, and as she put it, "always think about and care about all people in the world." She worked as a clinical social worker and felt committed to helping better the world. Donna valued her wry sense of humor and sarcastic edge, both of which she saw as closely tied to her New York City Jewish background. These culturally Jewish pieces that prioritized social and worldly engagement felt to her like they were in direct contradiction to the ethical teachings of the Buddha.[26] She appreciated that Buddhist meditation allowed her means to navigate various relational situations and her strong emotions, especially the negative ones. But fundamentally, she understood that "her way of looking at things," or her primary interpretative lens, was Jewish, or at least Jewishly informed. She approaches the world as a culturally Jewish person who has adopted a new set of Buddhist practices.

Foregrounding Achievement and Backgrounding Ascription

The second approach that some Jewish Buddhists take to explaining their syncretic identities is to foreground their chosen Buddhist identity and shift their ascribed Jewish identity to the background. These Jewish Buddhists give prominence to what they "do" as Buddhists and minimize "where they came from" as Jews. The common way that the respondents foregrounded their achieved identities and backgrounded their ascribed ones was by imagining themselves as Buddhists who are of Jewish heritage. This identity was primarily associated with people who had been active in Buddhism for many years and related to it as their principle meaning-making system. Judaism, in contrast, lay dormant in the background as a matter of ethnic or cultural heritage. Practitioners in the Tibetan tradition were particularly notable for adopting this discursive approach.

For example, Michael, a fifty-eight-year-old student of Tibetan Buddhism who had been practicing for over two decades, underscored the importance of his achieved Buddhist identity: "I identify as being Buddhist, because that's what I do. That's the tradition that I'm in." He imagines Buddhism as a compelling approach to realization, a "view of suffering, impermanence, and nonself as marks of the human experience." Michael cultivates this view by performing often complex *vajrayana* (Tibetan Buddhist) practices (including deity visualizations, aspirations, Buddhist practices similar to prayer, and devotional rites). For decades, Michael has been involved in his Tibetan Buddhist center and, to some degree, the vajrayana community more globally. He participates in his community's organized celebrations, especially their sacramental meals and festivities (*ganachakra*). He has taken various Buddhist vows (refuges) and has two root teachers whose lineage he honors through acts of devotion. The teachings of his Tibetan Buddhist tradition inform his understandings of birth, death, suffering, and human existence. He views the universe working as a closed system of karma and rebirth, and understands the world and his place in it through a Tibetan Buddhist lens.

Despite the integral role that Buddhism plays in Michael's life, he also identifies with Judaism. When I asked Michael if he thought of himself as Jewish, he answered, "Yes. Well, that's where I came from. There's little sense in denying that or trying to discard that. . . . I am of Jewish extraction. I have that kind of cultural background." Michael grew up in a Jewish family in upstate New York. Although his family affiliated with an Orthodox synagogue, where he attended religious school, they did not keep Jewish laws or customs in the home beyond holiday observances. Michael enjoyed studying Jewish history in religious school and learned some Hebrew, but his relationship to Judaism, he told me, felt confused. After he left home for college, he disconnected completely from Judaism as a religious tradition.

When I asked Michael what aspects of his Jewish background he identified with, he explained, "I appreciate some of the basic community values, the notion of history, and maybe a sense of tradition." Our exchange continued when I asked him what community values he appreciated.

MICHAEL: Well, in most cultures, you go and, as a rite of passage, you go and kill a deer, or kill a person. In the Hebraic tradition, you demonstrate that you know how to read.

ME: Anything else?

MICHAEL: Well, you know, that, I think, says a lot.

He later admitted—proudly—that he "likes pastrami sandwiches more than the average person" and sees himself as a "Jewish comic wiseass." Ultimately, he summed up his relationship to Judaism by saying, "I'm a Yid [Jewish ethnonym]. I have no problem with that."[27] That Michael retained aspects of a Jewish cultural identity does not negate or even lessen the significance of his achieved Buddhist identity. Michael has a deep and committed relationship to Buddhism. He did not withdraw his Jewishness, however; he backgrounded it as a cultural identifier.

Compartmentalizing Ascription and Achievement

The third approach that Jewish Buddhists take to explaining their syncretic identities is to emphasize the differences between their ascribed and achieved elements. These Jewish Buddhists do not imagine themselves as valuing one identity over another; rather, they see the two identities filling fundamentally different roles in their lives. Similar to the way that one might maintain and value both a professional identity (i.e., as a doctor, teacher, or therapist) and personal identity (as a parent, partner, or even friend), these respondents saw themselves as equally valuing both their Jewish and Buddhist identities. The common way that respondents expressed this was by compartmentalizing their relationships to both traditions, highlighting how their two identities functioned differently in their lives.

Younger Jewish Buddhists were especially likely to adopt this approach. Most of the Jewish Buddhists under thirty years old had only been practicing Buddhism a few years or less, and many spoke about possibly returning to Jewish practice and belonging to a synagogue, if and when they had families of their own. Because American Judaism has developed as a tradition oriented around families (i.e., educating children, supporting families, celebrating life cycle moments, etc.), many of these younger Jewish Buddhists felt that American Judaism had little to offer them at their stage in life, even if they appreciated it as a religious tradition. Nearly all the younger Jewish Buddhists with whom I spoke were members of and felt connected to the young adult groups (often called the "under-thirty group") at their Buddhist center. Buddhism provided these young adults with social support and like-minded community that was specifically tailored to their situation in life.

Julie made it clear that Buddhism and Judaism filled different roles in her life. When I asked her how she thought about both traditions, she stressed the differences between them, explaining,

> Buddhism is really a very different way of thinking about things than what I'm used to. Christianity and Islam are not exactly that different in terms of the way you see the world. . . . And the pieces that they cover are the same. I mean they're closely related things, they all have the community ritual piece, the calendar piece, the individual prayer piece, the text piece. All those pieces correlate with something in Judaism, something [in Judaism] that makes more sense to me. Buddhism *covers pieces that are different* than in Judaism, that just don't overlap. There's nothing like meditation. . . . There is no idea of having a practice that's about learning how to be a better human. That's a really different thing. I don't see needing to replace anything with Judaism.

Julie understood Judaism and Buddhism as "covering different pieces" in her life. She imagined that Judaism was similar to the other Abrahamic religions because it had religious rituals, a Hebrew calendar, codified prayers, and sacred texts, but that Buddhism was different from these traditions because it was centrally focused on the practice of meditation and human betterment. Julie looked to Judaism for the sacred texts, holidays, and prayer, and to Buddhism for the techniques or practices to live a better, happier life.

In pointing to the centrality of meditation to Buddhism, Julie demonstrated a deeply Western understanding of the tradition. Throughout

Asian history, Buddhism has operated within a traditional religious worldview that included complex and rich mythological as well as cosmological teachings. It has also included sacred scriptures, established institutions (often monastic ones), and even a set of (lunisolar) calendars—characteristics similar to the Abrahamic religions. Yet Julie largely viewed, and was taught to view, Buddhism outside its historical religious context. This allowed her to imagine that Buddhism existed not as religious tradition but rather, as she later noted, a "set of tools or a path that teaches us how to be a better human." And importantly, this set of tools felt decidedly non-Christian, and by extension, not threatening to her. Her involvement in Buddhism was not a rejection of Judaism; instead, it was an appreciation of the new and different practices as well as meaning-making system that Buddhism offered her.

Julie does not label herself a Buddhist, but does see herself as a practitioner of Buddhism and someone who benefits from the teachings of the Buddha. In contrast with this Buddhist identification, she identifies firmly as Jewish, even if she does not currently practice the tradition. She said that Judaism is "where I come from, and it's also where I am." When I asked her what that meant exactly, she replied, "That is really tough, because it is like, 'What is it to be a woman?' That's what it is like to be Jewish." For Julie, being Jewish was just part of the essence of who she was as a person.

Julie's relationship with Judaism has waxed and waned over her lifetime. She was largely disconnected from the tradition during childhood, but became connected to Judaism through her youth group in high school. She was involved in Jewish life in college, but then drifted away from Jewish observance as a young adult. She explained that Buddhism "fills a very different place" in her life than Judaism does. She imagined that "Judaism points me in the direction of wanting to be certain ways, and then Buddhism has some ideas about how to get there." When I asked her if she could describe those specific direction(s), she observed that Judaism taught her to want to be loving, kind, and appreciative, and Buddhism gave her the tools, specifically the practice of meditation, that allowed her to cultivate those desirable qualities.

Drawing Parallels between Ascription and Achievement

The fourth approach that Jewish Buddhists take to negotiating their syncretic identities is to underscore the similarities between the ascribed and achieved elements of them. The common way that the respondents drew bridges between their identities was by explaining how "being Jewish" and "practicing Buddhism" complemented each other—how they were synonymous approaches to understanding the world. Specifically, the respondents viewed both these identities as paths to improving and bettering the world refracted through a prism of liberal, progressive values.

This bridging approach is what Jaime, the therapist described earlier who imagined that Judaism was "in her blood," took to uniting her Jewish and Buddhist identities. She felt that these two identities reinforced each other because they shared a set of "ethical, moral ground rules." When I asked her what ground rules both traditions specifically shared, she explained, "Be good to people. Put your intentions into doing good deeds and taking care of people. . . . With my temple, . . . it was like, 'Do good. Just do good.'"

Comparing these Jewish messages to those she heard in Buddhism, Jaime continued, "In Buddhism, I think it's the same thing. It's like, 'Well the Buddha learned this, so just be good.' . . . It's all very upbeat. . . . It's a very optimistic, positive frame, which I feel, for me, Judaism and Buddhism both have in common." Raised in a Jewish home that loosely identified with Reform Judaism, Jaime heard messages in her childhood that being Jewish was about doing good deeds. The ethical rules she heard in Hebrew school stressed doing acts of kindness and compassion—or what Reform communities often discuss as performing mitzvoth and/or *tikkun olam* (repairing the world). Later in our conversation, Jaime talked about how these acts of doing good were tied to the socially progressive nature of her Jewish community, which was largely liberal and democratic. She noted that she was reared with messages that everyone deserved access to health care and people should work to help the poor.

Similarly, Jaime saw Buddhism as emphasizing a similar set of values. When she spoke about the importance of "doing good" within a

Buddhist context, she referred to learning how to be more compassionate and mindful about herself, others, and the world in which she lived— perspectives centrally stressed in her Zen center. Her Zen center under-scored the importance of being inclusive of all types of people, and sup-ported the messages of nonviolence, environmental awareness, and the creation of an equitable society. Jaime was active in her Zen center, par-ticipating in meditation sits and communal meals every day. She also did considerable volunteer work for her Buddhist community.

Despite her involvement in her Buddhist center and commitment to practice, she did not identify as a Buddhist. She felt she would need to be a "better person" to imagine herself as Buddhist, indicating that she would need to be calmer, more serene, and perhaps even enlightened. About her identification with Buddhism, she remarked, "If I say I'm a Buddhist, somehow I feel like I'm saying I'm better than others, or I know something more, or I'm identifying with something. Buddhism is about nonattachment, and not getting stuck in language or the mind. Half the time I'm being a total jerk. So I just say I practice Buddhism. I practice the Buddhist philosophy, and I try, try, and try." Jaime imagined that Ju-daism was simply present in her blood while Buddhism was cultivated through practice, and what united them was their common set of ethical values about trying to do good and right in the world.

Conclusion

Jewish Buddhists draw on ideas about ascription and achievement in the narratives that they tell about being and performing their syncretic identi-ties in the contemporary United States. They relate to Judaism as a cultural identity, emphasizing its essential and unchangeable aspects. In contrast, they stress the chosen and performed character of their Buddhist identi-ties, distancing themselves from a cultural identification with the Buddhist tradition. Intertwining ideas about ascription and achievement, they con-struct a syncretic Jewish Buddhist identity.

As Americans increasingly forge more multidimensional religious and cultural paths than the ones they inherited, the four approaches that Jew-ish Buddhists take to integrating their identities reveal patterns in how individuals combine commitments to more than one religious tradition. The relationships that Jewish Buddhists have to both traditions are not predicated on claims to efficacy and truth, or absolute and exclusive religious beliefs. Such relationships would have made problematic the possibility of a Jewish Buddhist identity. Rather, for these Jewish Buddhists, their largely cultural relationship to Judaism facilitated an easy shift into—and arguably an ideal fit with—their practicing relationship with Buddhism.

The transformation of both Judaism and Buddhism in the United States, and the way that both traditions have adapted to the American cultural context, enabled the development of these syncretic Jewish Buddhist identities. Judaism has a long history of secularism—of a tradition of "Jewishness without Judaism"—that dates back to the premodern era (see Biale 2010). As mentioned earlier, beginning in the 1990s, the number of Jews who identified as secular or as having no religion began to rise significantly in the United States, reflecting the broader trend among Americans in the last decade of the twentieth century to eschew a religious affiliation (Pew Research Center 2013). This American trend toward secularism helped to facilitate the rise of this cultural Jewish identification. Similarly, as a result of the historical processes explained in chapter 3, many convert Buddhist communities emphasize the practice of mindfulness meditation, and minimize the importance of the wider historical and religious Asian contexts in which that practice was derived. This reconfiguring of Buddhism enabled the respondents to hold a practice-orientated identification with Buddhism.

In addition, the organizational rules of the Jewish and Buddhist communities in the United States facilitated individuals' seemingly smooth shift in identification between Judaism and Buddhism. According to the halacha (Jewish law) that guides most traditional Jewish communities, Jewish descent is passed down through the mother, granting anyone born to a Jewish mother status as a Jew. Jewish Buddhists did not explicitly associate their cultural Jewish identity with the tenets of Jewish legal prescription; nevertheless, that they were all born to Jewish mothers implicitly assured them a sense of irrevocable Jewishness.

In a different way, the organizational rules of many Buddhist medita-tion centers in the United States also helped enable the possibility of multiple religious identities. Jewish Buddhists experienced a great deal of institutional latitude mixing Judaism and Buddhism in their lives. This was mostly due to the "loosely bound" nature (i.e., nonstrict) of the Bud-dhist meditation centers with which they affiliated (Cadge 2004). Bud-dhist meditation centers, particularly those that cater to converts, have few organizational rules around who can and cannot become members, and what members can and cannot do. While people are proud of their particular meditation centers, they rarely identify in terms of them. The communities generally do not speak about membership as having any special significance, and there is no formal ceremony when people join as members.

The Jewish Buddhists frequently spoke about how the permissiveness or loosely bound nature of their American Buddhist organizations en-abled their Jewish Buddhist identities to flourish. They felt comfortable attending Buddhist retreats or participating in their Buddhist centers because, as one respondent explained, "Buddhism does not ask you to give up who you are." Buddhist centers do not require individuals to take any formal oaths (although some respondents did take vows), undergo a conversion, commit to raising their children Buddhist, or express theo-logical beliefs in order to benefit from the wisdom of the Buddha's teachings. Rather, these centers encourage people to "come and see," taking what they like and leaving the rest. This allows them to keep their Jewish roots and—to borrow the metaphor from one of my respondents—let Buddhism rain down on them.

Conclusion

AFTER *THE JEW IN THE LOTUS*

IN 1994, Kamenetz published the best-selling book *The Jew in the Lotus*, which chronicled the meeting between eight Jewish delegates—a group of progressive rabbis and scholars from across various wings of American Jewish life—and the Dalai Lama in Dharamsala four years earlier. If the Dalai Lama were to invite a group of American Jewish delegates to meet him in Dharamsala today, the dialogue would look far different. For example, one of the pressing questions at the 1990 meeting was how the lack of spiritual and contemplative practices within American Judaism effectively propelled Jews to Buddhism. Changes in the American Jewish community over the past few decades, including the development of the movement for Jewish meditation discussed in chapter 7, have rendered this question considerably less significant now.

Today, American Jews who seek practice-based models of spirituality—including meditation, yoga, or contemplative worship—do not have to go outside their tradition to find teachers and training. Emphasizing this point in looking back on his Jewish Buddhist trajectory, Fischer told me that had Jewish meditation been available when he was coming of age, he would likely have chosen that path rather than the Zen one. He reminisced, "My path was completely conditioned by the time and what was there. . . . If I was a young person and had met Rabbi Lew, I would probably have been his disciple instead." The contemplative and spiritual practices created by Lew and other Jewish meditation teachers have broadened as well as enriched the spiritual opportunities available to younger generations of Jews.

In these concluding pages, I want to gather and tie together some central threads that have been woven into the chapters. In doing so, I review the overarching argument set forth in *American JewBu*: that the distinctive social position of American Jews shaped the encounter between Judaism and Buddhism. I also return to the question of why Jews seem disproportionately attracted to Buddhism and offer some final thoughts based on the lived experiences of my respondents. I then revisit the issues of boundaries, power, and authority that have cropped up throughout this book, and close by discussing three distinct patterns to how people blend Buddhism and Judaism into their daily lives in the twenty-first century.

Syncretism and Four Periods of Jewish-Buddhist Engagement

At its most general, this book is an examination of religious syncretism in the United States along with the history that produced it and ways individuals experience it in their daily lives. In the first section (chapters 1–4), I explained the broad social and political forces that brought Jews in contact with Buddhism, and then later Buddhism in contact with Judaism in the United States. These chapters provided the historical context to the emergence of Jewish-Buddhist syncretism—the central topic I explored in the second section (chapters 5–7). The book's second section looked at how the encounter between Judaism and Buddhism led to the syncretism of religious practices, spiritual discourses, and identities.

Conceptualizing the Jewish-Buddhist encounter using the framework of syncretism helps to move beyond the various metaphors—bricolage, salad bar religion, and so on—that many sociologists and scholars of religion use to explain (and often dismiss) religious mixing in the United States. These metaphors connote the idea that individuals pick and choose among religious options in highly individualistic and idiosyncratic ways. This study has demonstrated that distinct historical and social conditions shape religious mixing in the United States, from modernization to anticapitalism to counterculturalism. I also draw on the framework of syncretism to challenge the dominant paradigm within sociology that suggests that religions adapt and change in this country by assimilating into the majority, and taking on the characteristics and organizational forms of liberal Protestantism (see, for example, Ammerman 1997; Madsen 2009; Chaves 2004; Warner 1993). Minority religious traditions *also* change by borrowing and integrating elements from each other through a process shaped by their specific social locations in society.

Over the course of the four periods of Jewish-Buddhist engagement in the United States, the distinctive social position of Jewish Buddhists, or what I call the "Jewish social location"—the set of orientations produced by the position of American Jews as a distinctively left-liberal, urban, secular, and upper-middle-class religious minority in the United States—led American Jews to their engagement with Buddhism and fundamentally shaped the character of it. The Jewish social location influenced the encounter between the traditions from the nineteenth century to today. As highlighted in earlier chapters, not all Jews occupy this distinctive social position in the United States at present, nor have they across the centuries of American Jewish history. Yet for those Jews for whom their social distinctiveness was and is an integral aspect of their self-definition as a Jew and American, their social location propelled them into their encounter with Buddhism across all four time periods.

Strauss's intellectual conversion to Buddhism emblematizes the first period of Jewish Buddhist engagement (roughly from 1875 to 1923). In this time period, American Jews were attracted to the rational, romantic, and intellectual aspects of American Buddhism, particularly as they resonated with the values of nineteenth-century American Jewish liberalism. The social position of liberal German Jews like Strauss—financially successful, urban, and well established in the American social order—enabled their encounter with Buddhism in the late nineteenth century and shaped the modernizing influence that they had on it. Strauss's de-emphasizing of Buddhist metaphysics, folk beliefs, and image worship—and stressing instead Buddhism's ethical and scientific nature—places him among the ranks of the earliest Buddhist modernizers in the United States.

Beginning in the 1920s, the intellectual engagement between Judaism and Buddhism persisted, but it became augmented by a growing

appearance of solo American Jews—largely from wealthy and prominent families—who received training by Asian teachers and pursued
Buddhist practices in Asian-founded Buddhist groups. Goldwater, Lewis,
and Segal are exemplars of this period. The social position and material
success of these Jewish Buddhists provided them with the time as well
as means to study and practice Buddhism; it also motivated them to
search for human meaning beyond what could be found in material
comfort.

The third period of Jewish-Buddhist engagement occurred fundamentally in and around the counterculture of the 1960s and 1970s. During
this period, Jews founded and led prominent convert Buddhist groups
and institutions, particularly in the Zen and insight meditation traditions.
In doing so, they helped to create a large-scale infrastructure for convert
Buddhism. The Jewish Buddhists of the 1960s and 1970s were not necessarily, or even largely, from prominent Jewish families (though some
still were). Rather, they drew widely from the left-leaning sector of American society—and especially from the countercultural scene—where
Jews were distinctively overrepresented. The Buddhist teachers of Jewish heritage in this period left a notable historical mark on the tradition
by elevating the practice of meditation, instilling within it an activist ethic,
and increasing its psychotherapeutic orientation.

Finally, the fourth period of Jewish-Buddhist activity began in the early
1990s, when the mainstreaming and medicalizing of meditation in the
United States sparked a Jewish interest in Buddhist that culminated in
the development of a series of new Jewish-Buddhist dialogues along with
the creation of new contemplative Jewish practices, organizations, and
communities. As it did so, the encounter between Judaism and Buddhism
in the United States moved from the left periphery to the center of American Jewish life, sowing the seeds for the syncretism of religious practices, discourses, and identities to take shape. The Nathan Cummings
Foundation in particular played a pivotal role in facilitating this encounter
in the last decade of the twentieth century. As a result of the meeting and
mixing of these two traditions, Buddhism infused American Jewish life
with a new practice-based, contemplative spirit.

Why Was Sheldon on the Top of the Mountain?

This book opened with the humorous story about Sheldon on the mountain—a joke that poked fun at the widespread perception that American Jews have a particular affection for Buddhism. Scholars have offered various reasons for the affinity between the two traditions, but most of the past explanations do not account for why Buddhism appeals especially to Jews rather than other Americans.[1] Past scholarship has suggested, for example, that American Jews are attracted to Buddhism because it offers body-based spiritual practices. My research suggests that this is indeed true, specifically for observant or practicing Jews. But other traditions also offer body-based spiritual practices, so this explanation cannot answer why (or even if) Jews prefer Buddhist practices over those from other religious traditions. I want to be clear that I cannot definitively answer the question of why Buddhism appeals to Jews more than other religious or ethnic groups in the United States (or even verify that this claim is itself true). Proving this assertion is beyond the scope of an ethnographic study. I can offer five explanations, however, for why Buddhism appeals to American Jews—generated from the experiences and perspectives of the respondents in my study, and the unique historical characteristics of the Jewish-Buddhist encounter.[2]

Building on the key argument in this book, the first and most central explanation for the appeal of Buddhism to American Jews is that American Jews and convert Buddhists share a remarkably similar sociodemographic location in society, thus facilitating the mixing of the two groups. The sociodemographic profile of both groups tends to be urban, educated, upper middle class, and liberal (as I described in chapter 7). These two groups flock together, socially speaking. And sharing a social location provided opportunities for syncretism to take place.[3]

Shared occupational space seems to particularly matter to the Jewish-Buddhist relationship. Among my respondents, approximately 20 percent worked in the field of psychotherapy, including those who worked as clinical psychologists, psychiatrists, mental health counselors, or social workers. Although we do not have good data regarding the number of American Jews who currently work in the field of psychotherapy, research does suggest that psychotherapy is a relatively common professional career for American Jews, especially for Jewish women.[4] Similarly, there is a notable concentration of practicing psychologists in the Buddhist convert community, particularly in the insight meditation tradition (Seager 2012, 68–69). Overlapping occupational space served as an important gateway to and site of Jewish-Buddhist interaction.

Second, as highlighted in the last chapter, Judaism and Buddhism do not have a fraught history with each other, especially in comparison to the historical tensions that Jews have had with the other Abrahamic traditions. Beyond the direct experiences with antisemitism, many respondents held a quiet uneasiness about Christianity that seemed tied to the historical waxing and waning of social discrimination that American Jews have experienced as religious minorities. Many respondents explained that they felt comfortable with Buddhism precisely because, as a historical religious tradition, it did not have a legacy of persecuting Jews. Buddhism felt decidedly not Christian—and by extension, not threatening and even welcoming to them.

Third, as described at the end of chapter 7, the organizational rules of the American Buddhist community have also facilitated Jewish-Buddhist mixing. The loosely bound nature of the Buddhist meditation centers with which the respondents affiliated had few organizational rules, including around who can and cannot become members, and what members can and cannot do (Cadge 2005). Many respondents explained that the flexibility and permissiveness of their Buddhist centers enabled them to maintain and preserve their inherited religion, and take from Buddhism the practices and wisdom that support it. For respondents who belonged to a synagogue, the flexibility of the Buddhist centers allowed them to be involved in a range of ways that did not compete or conflict with their temple's rules. And for those respondents who identified more as secular or cultural Jews, their involvement in Buddhism lived harmoniously alongside their cultural Judaism.

Fourth, the appeal of Buddhism to American Jews was directly influenced and enabled by the modernizing efforts of the Jewish Buddhist teachers chronicled in the first section of this book. American Jews played an important role in interpreting Buddhism for an American audience, including for other American Jews. From Strauss to Goldwater to Fischer and Goldstein, all these teachers recast Buddhism in modernist terms that made Buddhism compatible with American expectations and norms, increasing its attractiveness to American Jews.

Fifth, for contemporary Jewish Buddhist practitioners, having a Buddhist teacher of Jewish heritage helped to make American Buddhism feel like familiar territory to the next generation of Jewish practitioners. For example, in my conversation with James Baraz, a teacher in the insight meditation tradition, he emphasized the significance of the Jewish background of Goldstein, his teacher. That he and Goldstein shared a similar background made Buddhism feel immediately comfortable and allowable to him. Baraz explained his first experience with Buddhism this way:

> It was 1974.... I went to Joseph's Essentials of Buddhism class, and that was it. I was there for ten minutes, as I often tell the story, saying, "So this is the great meditation teacher?" He sounded like he was from Brooklyn; I was from Queens, and he was just a couple of years older than me, and I said, "This is it?" And then after ten minutes of that, I heard what he was saying. And realized that he knew something that I wanted to know, and was saying it's possible to not be run by your neurotic thought patterns, which had never crossed my mind before, and I was hooked; summer of '74, no turning back after that.

I asked Baraz if the fact that he and Goldstein were both from New York City was important to his Buddhist path. He answered,

> Well, at first it was a kind of cause for resistance. He was so much like me, so is this any different? But then actually realizing he was so much like me in some ways, but so different in what his inner world seemed like, I said, "If he can do it, I can do it. Maybe I could do it." So there was that resonance, and the fact that he was Jewish, and his name was Joseph Goldstein, and it gave me maybe even a little bit more hope; he's not so different from me.

That Baraz and his teacher came from similar Jewish backgrounds rendered Buddhism permissible to explore. In this way, the first generation of Jewish Buddhist teachers paved the way and actively shaped the possibilities for future Jews to come.

Three Different Types of Jewish Buddhists

I found three distinct patterns emerge in how individuals blend Buddhism and Judaism into their daily lives in the twenty-first century (see table C.1). Taken as a whole, these three groups demonstrate that Jewish Buddhists are not a monolithic group, cut from the same cloth. Rather, there exists important variation in the types of twenty-first-century Jewish Buddhists.

One group of respondents, which I label in chapter 7 as Buddhist converts, view Buddhism as their primary meaning-making system, set of practices, and community. These Buddhist converts, however, also maintain a cultural identification with Judaism, even if they maintain no Jewish observances or organizational commitments. The Buddhist converts background Judaism as a matter of familial or cultural heritage. For them, religious affiliation is not a zero-sum game; taking on a new identity does not necessitate the shedding of their inherited one. Instead, they see themselves as Jewish and Buddhist, with separate and distinct relationships to both traditions.

A second group of respondents, which I call the spiritually enriched in chapter 6, overlay Buddhism on the surface of their Judaism, and use Buddhist meditation and mindfulness techniques to spiritually enhance their active and committed religious relationship to Judaism. Spiritually enriched people connect to Judaism as their primary meaning-making system, identity, and community. They have also adopted some of the

TABLE C.1. Typology of Jewish Buddhist Religious Belonging

	Beliefs		Practice		Identity		Community	
	J	B	J	B	J	B	J	B
Buddhist converts	N	Y	N	Y	Y	Y	N	Y
Dual belongers	Y	Y	Y	Y	Y	Y	Y	Y
Spiritually enriched	Y	N	Y	Y	Y	N	Y	N

* J/B indicates Jewish or Buddhist; Y/N indicates yes or no.

practices and teachings of the Buddha, and in particular the practice of mindfulness, as exercises of awareness and interconnectedness of mind, body, and environment. Despite the important role that Buddhist teachings and practices play in their lives, though, they do not identify as Buddhists. Rather, they view the teachings and practices of Buddhism as techniques to enhance and enliven their connection to Judaism, and cultivate a sense of peace, kindness, and compassion. For these respondents, the process of combining Judaism and Buddhism involves an incorporation of Buddhist practices into their primarily Jewish core.

Finally, a third group of respondents, which consists of only a handful of those respondents I interviewed, seemed to relate to Buddhism and Judaism with equal emphasis, often translating between the traditions' different meaning-making systems. I think of these respondents as *dual belongers* because they see themselves as religious "boths." Perhaps the most famous example of a dual belonger is Boorstein, the prominent insight meditation teacher, observant Jew, and author of the book *That's Funny, You Don't Look Buddhist*. As a practicing Jew and Buddhist, she moves between both traditions' modes of thinking and expression as if she were speaking two languages. When Boorstein and I spoke, she explained that she feels "completely part of the synagogue community," and when she goes to an international Buddhist teachers' conference, for instance, she feels completely part of that community as well. She told me, "I don't feel like a Buddhist who came to teach, or a Jew who came to teach. I feel like me. I always feel like I belong. . . . I just do not have any disjuncture about who I am." She identifies as a Jew and a Buddhist, and sees herself as inextricably both.

Boorstein and other Buddhist teachers of Jewish heritage who maintain a practicing commitment to both religious traditions were able to draw on as well as translate between the communities, practices, and meaning-making systems of both Judaism and Buddhism. These teachers are illustrations of "multiple religious belonging," the label that theologians use to account for the experiences of people who adopt and live the beliefs, rituals, practices, and identities of multiple religious traditions—in this case, Judaism and Buddhism (see Cornille 2002; Knitter 2009; Phan 2003). Maintaining a practicing and committed relationship to more than one religious tradition demands considerable time, which is why I suspect that I only found a handful of people who, like Boorstein, were actively and seemingly equally connected to both Judaism and Buddhism. And for those in this group, they were largely religious professionals whose careers were dedicated to religious pursuits.

It seems worth pausing for a moment to reflect on what the pattern of self-identification among my respondents suggests about nature of Judaism and Buddhism in the United States. Every respondent whom I interviewed as part of this project identified as Jewish, including famous Buddhist leaders like Fischer, Goldstein, and Surya Das. Yet less than half of my respondents identified as Buddhist. That all of my respondents identified as Jews seems to be a reflection of a new pattern in the way that Jews are regarded in the contemporary United States. A recent study by the Pew Research Center (2013) demonstrated that Jews are the most warmly regarded religious group in the United States today. This pattern seems to have led even the most strongly committed Buddhists to feel happy and proud to be (and be known as) Jews. That less than half of my respondents identified as Buddhists likely results from the way that many American Buddhist communities de-emphasize the importance of identity. It is more important to practice and uphold the teachings of the Buddha than it is to identify with the tradition.

Additionally, a pattern emerged around which respondents did or did not embrace the identity of a JewBu. Many of the first-generation Jewish Buddhists, or those who came to Buddhism through their involvement in the 1960s' and 1970s' counterculture, recoiled from that label. They largely viewed the term pejoratively, as a reduction of their serious relationships to Judaism and Buddhism to a playful portmanteau.

Young Jewish adults involved with Buddhism, however, particularly those under thirty, nearly all embraced and claimed a JewBu identity. Many of these young adults had been practicing Buddhism for less than a year, in stark comparison to some of the baby boomers who had been practicing Buddhism for decades. These young adults claim this identity as a way of staking out a progressive and sometimes even radical social position further to the left of the mainstream American Jewish community. To these respondents, the JewBu identity signaled that they were critical of consumerism, and cared more than the average Jewish American about such things as the environment, queer rights, pacifism (especially in respect to their views on Israel), social equality, and other issues of social justice. Their JewBu identity acted as a discursive strategy to locate themselves politically in the United States.

It is important to note that I caught each of the respondents at a particular point in their religious journeys.[5] Had I interviewed the respondents a decade earlier or again a decade from now, I would likely have heard or would hear different stories about their relationships to Judaism and Buddhism than I did between 2011 and 2014, when I conducted my interviews. I write this to note that in some sense, the relationships that individuals have with Judaism and Buddhism represent specific frames in time rather than fixed accounts.

Boundaries, Power, and Authority: A Revisit

Judaism and Buddhism, like all religions, adapt and change. They are living, moving traditions that undergo transformations from their contact and exchange with each other. Flux and mixing, not stasis or uniformity, have been the norms in Jewish and Buddhist history.[6] That these two traditions have been altered and reconfigured as a result of their encounter is inevitable and unavoidable. And it is not my charge as a scholar to make a normative judgment about the new reconfigurations, thus assigning them a certain worth, good or bad. Rather, throughout these chapters, I aimed to call attention to the rise of new religious (and cultural) configurations and provide an explanation for how and why they developed.

In particular, I highlighted through the pages of this book the role that American Jews played in the project of Buddhist modernism. In the late nineteenth century, Strauss's efforts to transform—and even reinvent— Buddhism by emphasizing its compatibility with Western notions of science, activism, democracy, and individualism while minimizing Buddhist metaphysics emblematized the spirit of Buddhist modernism. A quarter century later, Goldwater, Lewis, and Segal also proffered modernized versions of Buddhism that sought to reconcile it with three of the central liberal religious perspectives of their time: universalism, perennialism, and romanticism. Finally, in the second half of the twentieth century, American Jews—including Goldstein, Kornfield, Fischer, Glassman, and many others—participated in the modernization of Buddhism by elevating the practice of meditation, instilling within it an activist ethic, and increasing its psychotherapeutic orientation.

Throughout this book, I have called attention to a broad range of Jewish engagements and identities, amplifying the stories of those Jews who identify proudly and publicly as Jewish *and* those who see their Jewishness as seemingly irrelevant in their lives. In doing so, this book adopts a dispersionist approach to American Jewish history that broadens its scope to include the stories of those who have little to no involvement in communal life (Hollinger 2009). I demonstrate how, in certain instances, respondents' Buddhist trajectories were shaped much more formatively by their social location than by their Jewish beliefs or practices. Upbringing and inheritance are impossible to entirely cast off; the social locations of our past give shape to the religious possibilities of our future.

As a scholar, it remains my responsibility to critically question who (or what) benefited from these religious transformations, and who or what was harmed or lost in the process. American Jewish Buddhists are overwhelmingly racially, linguistically, and class privileged, and thus have the relative power to assert a strong claim about the character and content of Buddhism in this country. Often acting as leading interpreters of Buddhism in the United States—as prolific writers, prominent teachers, scholars, and public figureheads—they wielded tremendous power to speak for Buddhism. Many of the first generation of Jewish Buddhist teachers, including Goldstein, Kornfield, Salzberg, Fischer, and others, rejected or ignored various traditional or historical aspects of Buddhism, inscribing new boundaries around what is and is not Buddhist. Similarly, American Jews have instilled within Buddhism a socially active and psychotherapeutic ethic, altering both the spirit and ultimate mission of the tradition. While I do not think that American Jews intend(ed) to exploit Buddhism, their distancing of Buddhism from its Asian cultural systems and ethnic identities—and recasting it in a socially active and psychotherapeutic framework—effectively "whitened" it in order to make it more appealing to a broad American audience (see Wilson 2014). And their appropriation of Buddhism, and reformulating it to serve the American middle and upper classes, is a quintessential tactic of colonization.

Similarly, in chapter 5, I described the rise of Jewish meditation in the contemporary United States as a process of reformulating Buddhism within a Jewish framework. This process hinged on obscuring the Buddhist roots of meditation by recasting it so convincingly in a Jewish framework that it felt authentically Jewish to those who practiced it. It was also made possible through the Jewish adoption of particular modernist constructions of Buddhism as a "universal technique" or "way of life," detached from dogmas or beliefs, and available for all to experience. The construction of Jewish meditation thus began with a radical secularization of Buddhism and ended with a resacralization in Jewish forms. One could argue that this was a Jewish appropriation of the cornerstone practice of the Buddhist tradition.

Even though the relationship between Judaism and Buddhism was marked by significant power differentials, I largely view the processes of religious adaption and change in this book along with the eventual syncretism of religious forms as an inevitable outcome of sustained religious contact. Religions continually remake themselves in response to changing historical as well as social conditions and interaction with other traditions, adopting elements from each other that enhance their durability, and shedding those that no longer remain compelling or resonant. This process of religious reconfiguration allows religions to survive and carry forward into the future, remaining relevant to future generations.

A Look Ahead: Twenty-First-Century JewBus

The story of the Jewish-Buddhist encounter in the United States is fundamentally a tale about how American Jews have taken an interest in, practiced, and (at various points) served as teachers of Buddhism. One lingering question moving into the twenty-first century is whether Buddhists might begin to take a similar interest in Judaism. Will Buddhists begin to convert to Judaism, just as Strauss famously converted to Buddhism? Will they rise through the ranks to become important Jewish leaders and interpreters? And will Buddhist communities start to incorporate Jewish observances or customs into their practices?

Although these futuristic questions are impossible to definitively answer, recent scholarship about the intermarriage between Jews and Buddhist Asians suggests that the Jewish-Buddhist encounter might be entering a new era. Over the past two decades, Jewish-Asian marriages have grown increasingly common and have captured considerable media attention.[7] Just as American Jews who began practicing Buddhism brought their liberal sensibilities into the tradition, it seems fair to assume that the children of Buddhist-Jewish marriages will bring their Buddhist (and Asian) heritage into Judaism in unanticipated ways in the future. Perhaps the next period of the Jewish-Buddhist encounter in the United States will be one in which Jews take an interest in Buddhism and Buddhists take an interest in Judaism, and the result of these crossovers are new creative Jewish Buddhist and Buddhist Jewish outcomes.

APPENDIX A

RESEARCH METHODS

AS I NOTED in the acknowledgments in this book, the inspiration for this research emerged from a conversation that I had with Wendy Cadge in 2009. I began this project curious as to why so many American Jews seemed to be attracted to Buddhism and/or Buddhist meditation. As this project developed, and as I developed as a scholar of the Jewish-Buddhist encounter, my questions enlarged. I learned that these traditions had a long history with each other, and I wanted to know what social and historical factors shaped that history. I also learned that there was no one "type" of Jewish Buddhist in the United States, thus prompting me to explore the variation in multireligious identities, practices, and spiritualities.

I approached the research in this book using the method of grounded theory as modified by Adele Clarke (2005) to account for the complex situational realities of fieldwork. Grounded theory, pioneered by Barney Glaser and Anselm Strauss (1967), offers an interpretative and reflexive approach to qualitative research. Throughout the research, I was simultaneously involved in data collection and analysis. I constructed analytic codes and categories from the data, developing and modifying theory throughout the research process. I wrote extensive memos about emerging themes and categories, and revised my sampling design throughout the research to ensure that I spoke to the necessary informants. The research for this project developed in four stages spanning nearly six years, as I describe below.

Phase I: Research Pilot

The first phase began during summer 2009, when I conducted some exploratory work with Cadge and Sara Shostak. With the support of the

Theodore and Jane Norman Fund for Faculty Research at Brandeis University, we embarked on a pilot study to identify the organizations, teachers, and lineages at the contemporary intersections of Judaism and Buddhism in the United States, and the relationships that existed among them. We were curious what these intersections were and how they came to be. Mostly, we wanted to create a map of the Jewish-Buddhist landscape that could serve as a starting place for further empirical and historical work.

To make this manageable, I began with the teachers and leaders in the Jewish and Buddhist worlds that had "national" profiles, or those who had taught and given retreats across the country, and had written articles and/or books about their teachings and so on. I started with researching Sylvia Boorstein, Joseph Goldstein, Jack Kornfield, Sharon Salzberg, Jacqueline Mandell-Schwartz, Norman Fischer, Alan Senauke, Rabbi Jeff Roth, and Rabbi Sheila Weinberg. I spent the summer poring over their individual web pages and those of the organizations with which they were affiliated, trying to understand (as best I could) the differences among the people and places. I read all the primary and secondary literature written about Jewish Buddhists that I could find through a combination of general "google" searching as well as targeted academic searching. For example, I entered "Judaism and Buddhism" in LexisNexis searching for newspaper articles, the Library of Congress for books, WorldCat for journals, and Rambi for Jewish sources. I also searched through Jewish periodicals like the *Jewish Daily Forward* as well as Buddhist periodicals like *Tricycle*. I began to visit various different Jewish and Buddhist meditation centers on the East Coast, including the Cambridge Insight Meditation Center, Cambridge Zen Center, Nishmat Hayyim, Shambhala Meditation Center of Boston, Makom, and the Brooklyn Zen Center. At the end of the summer, I had a rough map of the main teachers at the intersections of the two traditions, clearer sense of the kinds of organizations they started and how those organizations related to each other. I had also created a bibliography about Jewish-Buddhist encounters in the United States and had read much of the literature written by prominent Jewish Buddhists.

The following summer, Cadge, Shostak, and I submitted a grant application to the E. Rhodes and Leona B. Carpenter Foundation for funding that would allow us to build on the work we began the summer before. I wanted to meet with and talk to the teachers I identified the summer before (and whose books I had read) and spend time in their organizations. The Carpenter Foundation ultimately awarded us $40,000 in late 2010, which allowed me to start the second phase of this project by funding travel across the country to conduct this ethnographic fieldwork (interviews and participant observation) with teachers central to the intersections of Judaism and Buddhism in the United States.

Phase II: Research on Elite Jewish-Buddhist Encounters

I spent almost three months making contact with the relevant individuals and organizations, arranging interviews and site visits, and organizing the logistics for travel to the different meditation centers. I was able to gain access to these teachers and organizations through existing contacts that Cadge and Shostak had in the Jewish and Buddhist worlds. Cadge (2005) met several of the teachers in Buddhist organizations while writing her book *Heartwood: The First Generation of Theravada Buddhism in America*. Shostak developed relationships with many people in the Jewish Buddhist community during her graduate and postgraduate training in San Francisco and New York City, respectively, and maintained relationships with teachers and practitioners on both coasts.

From early 2011 to the end of 2012, with the generous support of the Carpenter Foundation, I traveled throughout New York, New England, and California to conduct in-depth interviews with thirty-five leading teachers at the intersections of Judaism and Buddhism, and visit nineteen related Jewish and Buddhist organizations. Nearly all the interviews with the teachers were on the record. The interviews took place in people's homes, meditation centers, coffee shops, synagogues, and libraries. Interviewees included prominent teachers like Fischer, Boorstein, Mandell-Schwartz, Goldstein, Senauke, Weinberg, and Roth, all mentioned above, along with David Cooper, Shoshanna Cooper, Seth Castleman, Blanche Hartman, Sheila Katz, Tara Brach, Avram Davis, Zalman Schachter-Shalomi, Rachel Cowan, James Baraz, Wes Nisker, Bernie Glassman, Jonathan Slater, Sherril Lew (on behalf of Alan Lew), Teah Strozer, Gil Fronsdal, Thubten Chodron, Alison Laichter, Yael Shy, Surya Das, Jonathan Omer-Man, Mel Weitsman, and five others who were off the record. After each of the interviews, I would ask the teacher if there was someone else I should speak with. In doing so, the sample of teachers grew through a snowball sampling design. I conducted the majority of the interviews in person, and only a handful over the phone. The interviews were based on a guide, included in appendix B.

Although the teachers were all national figures in the American Buddhist and Jewish worlds, they were all extremely generous in their willingness to talk with me. All the interviews were audio recorded and then transcribed. They lasted from thirty minutes to nearly all evening. I also informally spoke to nearly a dozen other people who were involved in the Jewish and Buddhists worlds in different ways, including people like Rodger Kamenetz and Charlie Halpern. I visited eighteen different meditation centers. Some of them were small centers associated primarily with the Zen and insight meditation traditions. Other organizations I visited were large and prominent Buddhist and Jewish meditation centers across the country. Some of the most prominent centers I visited were the Insight Meditation Society (Barre, Massachusetts), Spirit Rock Meditation Center (Woodacre, California), Berkeley Zen Center, San Francisco Zen Center, Makor Or (San Francisco), Brooklyn Zen Center, Jewish Meditation Center of Brooklyn (JMC), Cambridge Insight Meditation Center, Cambridge Zen Center, Nishmat Hayyim (Brookline, Massachusetts), Shambhala Meditation Center of Boston, and Makom (New York City). I toured most of the organizations that I visited and participated in a sitting meditation session (or sometimes many sessions) in each as well. I wrote up extensive field notes after each visit (following Emerson, Fretz, and Shaw 2011).

Although all the organizations generously and kindly opened their doors to me, the JMC especially welcomed me. I traveled from Boston to New York City four times to visit the JMC in late 2011 through winter

2012, and Laichter, the cofounder of the center, made me feel part of the group. In February 2012, I even participated in a one-day Jewish meditation teacher-training program that Laichter led. After all my site visits, I wrote up detailed field notes as soon as possible. To the extent it was possible, I also went to the archives and libraries of the organizations that I visited. The Barre Center for Buddhist Studies in particular contained valuable documentary materials about Jewish-Buddhist intersections: talks, articles, interviews, and photographs. I had all the interviews and materials that I gathered imported into the software program Atlas.ti. to analyze. Cadge and I also created a series of teaching guides based on these data, which we made publicly available at www.jewbu.net.

All the research that I conducted about the teachers and organizations that they founded gave me a clear sense of the "elite" Jewish Buddhist story—that is, the story of how prominent teachers at the intersections of Judaism and Buddhism came to their paths, began new organizations, and blended, or not, the two traditions. From there, I started the third phase of my research, which focused centrally on the lived experience of nonexpert Jewish Buddhists.

Phase III: Research on Everyday Jewish-Buddhist Encounters

I wanted to know how everyday people of Jewish heritage practiced Buddhism, how they understood their relationships to both traditions, and what organizations and structures supported their relationships to both traditions. I thought about this third phase of the project as a Massachusetts-based case study of Jewish-Buddhist intersections. I conducted approximately seven months of participant observation and interviews in and around the Boston area in 2012 with lay practitioners rather than prominent Jewish Buddhist teachers. I continued to visit and participate in meditation classes at the three largest Buddhist centers in the Boston area that attract a Euro-American participant base: the Cambridge Insight Meditation Center, Cambridge Zen Center, and Shambhala Meditation Center of Boston. I also joined the Nishmat Hayyim's listserv in order to receive announcements about all the Jewish meditation offerings happening in New England. For those seven months (and even for several months afterward), I tried to attend all the different Jewish meditation classes, events, workshops, and sits that came through the listserv. During this third phase of the research, I conducted an additional sixteen different site visits. I participated in meditation sits in living rooms in people's homes as well as the sanctuaries of various synagogues in Newton, Framingham, and Wellesley, Massachusetts, and even the historic Vilna Shul.

I also conducted forty-seven interviews with people of Jewish heritage who had a meditative practice in the Boston area. I was able to find these lay practitioners largely by casting a call for interviewees at the Cambridge Zen Center, Cambridge Insight Meditation Center, Shambhala Center, and Nishmat Hayyim. Some of the centers allowed me to send an email through their organizational listservs. In addition, I posted a sign on the bulletin boards of all the centers introducing myself and asking whether people would be willing to speak with me. In the emails and signs, I specifically asked to talk with "people of Jewish heritage who have a meditative practice." I deliberately asked to speak with people who fit the broad description of having a "meditative practice" in order to capture a range of people with different meditative practices and religious identities. Within a few days of sending out the emails or posting the signs, I had people contacting me, often eagerly, or sometimes just curiously wanting to talk about their relationships to Judaism and Buddhism. I continued to develop my sample through snowball sampling, asking the respondents if there were other Jewish meditators that they thought I should speak with. I continued my interviews until I reached data saturation—the point at which I was no longer gathering fresh insights or developing new analytic categories (Charmaz 2006, 113).

I aimed to interview both women and men, people of different ages and Jewish backgrounds, and people who had been involved in Buddhism for varying lengths of time. Many of the people I interviewed recommended that I also speak to their friends or people that they knew, which I frequently did. Each interview lasted between thirty minutes and two hours, and took place in restaurants, hospitals, coffee shops, and people's homes and workplaces. All the interviews were audio recorded and later transcribed. The interviews were based on a guide, included in appendix C. I asked the participants a series of questions that related to their personal and religious backgrounds, current meditative practice, religious identification, and religious beliefs and ideas.

Phase IV: Historical and Archival Research

Finally, the last phase of the research, which I began in 2011, but amped up toward the end of my fieldwork, was a historical analysis of Jewish-Buddhist intersections in the United States. In order to obtain primary sources for the historical information about the relationship between Judaism and Buddhism in the United States prior to 1950, I examined the following databases: ProQuest's American Jewish Newspapers (including the *American Hebrew*, *American Israelite*, and *Jewish Exponent*), Pittsburgh Jewish Newspaper Project, Jewish South Archive, Southern Israelite Archive, Library of Congress's Historic American Newspapers, Brandeis University's Historical Newspapers and Magazines, Jewish Telegraphic Agency's Archive, Berman Jewish Policy Archive, American Jewish Year Book, and US Census Records. I searched for "Judaism and Buddhism," "Jew and Buddhism," "Jewish and Buddhist," "Jewish and Buddha," "Jew and Buddha," and other terms. I scoured as many Jewish and US historical newspapers as I could in order to better understand the historical relationship between Judaism and Buddhism in the United States. I also searched through the government and census data from Ancestry.com to find more information about Charles T. Strauss and his family.

I began writing my dissertation in 2013, and continued to revisit and analyze these data as the chapters took shape. I reached out to six different people whom I interviewed for clarification about questions or more information during the writing of the dissertation to make sure that my analysis felt resonant to them. I presented on my findings at various academic conferences, and the feedback I received from copanelists and the audience sharpened my arguments and thinking.

Insider-Outsider Positionality and Pregnancy in the Field

Important to my research was my position as both an insider and out-sider in my data collection process. Prior to 2009, I had never meditated nor had I visited a meditation center. I also knew little about Buddhism as a historical religious tradition. I came to this project as a complete Bud-dhist outsider. Differently, I came to this project conspicuously as a Jew-ish insider. I was raised Jewish, and I identify with Judaism as my religion, heritage, and culture. I also have a strong training in Jewish studies. At the time of the interviews, I held a master's degree in Jewish history from Ben-Gurion University of the Negev, and was enrolled in a doctoral pro-gram at Brandeis University that was joint between the departments of sociology and Near Eastern and Judaic studies. At each interview, I would introduce myself as a graduate student at Brandeis in this particular doc-toral program. Immediately the respondents knew that I was Jewish. It just went without saying. They did not know, however, if I was a Buddhist practitioner. Many of them asked me if I meditated or what my "practice" (code for Buddhist practice) entailed. I told them that I was new to Bud-dhism and meditation, and was learning. Nearly all of them encouraged me to cultivate a meditation practice.

My position as a Buddhist outsider had its advantages and disadvan-tages. I often had to ask the respondents to stop and explain various Buddhist language, idioms, practices, and teachings because I was not familiar with them. While I am sure that was tiring (if not annoying) for my respondents, they all remained kind and patient. I worried that I wouldn't be able to understand the depth of the practices and meaning that the respondents derived from them because the practices were mostly foreign to me. I solved this as best I could by including a wide range of Jewish Buddhists in my sample so that I could hear many sto-ries and accounts of Buddhist meaning making. My position as a Bud-dhist outsider had certain advantages too. My respondents genuinely wanted me to understand their Buddhist practices so they took great pains to explain and translate them for me. They frequently offered to accompany me to their meditation centers or lead a short meditation for me, to which I almost always agreed. I am deeply grateful for their efforts to make the unfamiliar familiar to me.

My position as a Jewish insider similarly had its benefits and drawbacks. Having a shared Jewish heritage with my respondents allowed me to build an easy rapport with many of them. My respondents seemed to freely share with me the details of their Jewish upbringings, both good and bad. They didn't feel the need to hide any of the proverbial dirty laundry because they viewed me as an insider, a member of the tribe. I also felt as if I understood my respondents' families through their stories, as often their families and histories resembled my own. I worried, of course, that because their stories and backgrounds felt familiar and expected, I might have missed moments of deeper probing.

Finally, I want to offer an insight about my experience with having two children during the course of this book's fieldwork. In many ways, pregnancy and fieldwork seem coterminous to me; they occupy the same collective set of memories, emotions, and experiences. These pregnancies acted simultaneously as gateways and barriers to my ethnographic fieldwork, as sources of both connection to and disconnection from my research. In this sense, I think about pregnancy as a soft gatekeeper to field research. A gatekeeper is typically imagined as the person who has the power to open up or block access to a field site, as someone who considers themselves and who others consider as having the authority to grant access to a site. My pregnant body did not give me any formal authority to grant myself access to my field sites (nor did it give me authority to grant others access), but what it did do was more informally open doors—and sometimes close doors—to accessing and generating a relationship with my respondents, especially with women. Women who were themselves mothers would read my pregnant body as an invitation to talk about their own experiences of pregnancy and/or motherhood. Even before I could turn on my recording device, these women would tell me about themselves, their children, and their biographies.

I was probably about eight- to ten-weeks pregnant with my first child when I first practiced meditation. And I hated it. Not only did I have what Buddhist teachers call a monkey mind—a mind that was racing all over the place and wouldn't stay focused on my breathe—but I also seemed to have monkey arms and legs. As soon as a silent meditation sit began, my legs would feel restless. My arms would itch. I'd get this tingle in my nose that I would just want to scratch. Meditating was extremely agitating—and even painful—for me. And while I theoretically understood that people experienced benefits from this practice, to me it felt like a version of benign torture.

But then when I was about eighteen-weeks pregnant with my first baby, I found out that she had a rare congenital anomaly. The doctors were quick to remind my partner and me that often anomalies happen in constellations—that is, as part of a larger syndrome—rather than in isolation. They wanted us to come in for ultrasounds every two weeks for the remainder of the pregnancy so they could assess if any other anomalies were developing. Needless to say, my anxiety ran high throughout this pregnancy.

I remember the day that I went to my mediate at the Cambridge Insight Meditation Center shortly after I received the terrible news about my baby. I had barely managed to get through the day. And then I sat down on the meditation cushion and closed my eyes. I focused on my breath, to each inhale and each exhale. I had no monkey mind, arms, or legs that day. I just sat and breathed. And I turned my mind to concentrating on the little kicks of this fetus inside me, to this little one who had no idea that anything was at all wrong with her little body. I closed my eyes, and tried to meditate on her movements and flutters, and on this experience of gestating a baby. All the anxiety, fear, and sadness that I had been trying to suppress just washed over me. As my teachers were instructing, I tried to just be present with my feelings—to acknowledge, accept, and sit with them. That sit began a journey toward an acceptance of the path that life would inevitably have in store for the baby and a greater sense of equanimity in the face of what had previously felt like unbearable uncertainty. For that acceptance and equanimity, I was intensely grateful. That day, I began to gain insight into why and how this practice held meaning for all the respondents in this book.

APPENDIX B

TEACHER INTERVIEW GUIDE

INTRODUCTION: I want to talk with you today about your experiences with Judaism and Buddhism. Before we talk about the intersection between the two traditions, it would be helpful for me to know a bit more about your background and then about your experiences with each tradition.

A. Life History

Childhood

1. I'd like to ask you to tell me the story of your upbringing—not everything, of course, but I'd like to hear about your childhood, where you were living, what you were doing, and who was important to you in that chapter of your life. But mostly I just want you to tell me about where you came from.

Probes:

Describe the characteristics of your family. Professions of your parents?

How would you describe your parents' openness to new ideas, experiences, and people? Would you consider them socially liberal?

What area of the country did you grow up in? What was your exposure to meditation/Eastern religions?

Any important friendships?

Any biographical disruptions?

Is there a story or anecdote that you might be willing to share with me that you think captures the important essence of your childhood?

Young Adulthood

2. Now I'd like to move a step forward and ask you to tell me the story of your young adulthood—again, not everything, of course, but I'd like to hear about where, if applicable, you went to college, where you were living, any important travels, what you were doing, and who was important to you in that chapter of your life. But mostly I just want to better understand your young adult years.

> Probes:
> What did you study in college and where (if you attended)?
> Have you been involved in any cultural movements (antiwar, civil
>   rights, or women's movement; New Left, etc.)?
> Any important travels or experiences abroad?
> Any biographical disruptions?
> Any important friends?
> Any exposure to Eastern ideas?
> Is there a story or anecdote that you might be willing to share with
>   me that you think captures the important essence of your young
>   adult life?

B. Judaism

1. I'd like to ask you now about the Judaism that you were born into. Can you help me understand how Judaism was practiced, talked about, and understood in your family?

> Probes:
> What wing of Judaism did your family affiliate with?
> What wing of Judaism did you grow up in?
> Any special family rituals? Or holiday celebrations?
> What languages were spoken (Yiddish)?
> What, if anything, about Judaism growing up was special to you?
> What, if anything, about Judaism growing up was troubling to you?
> How did your family understand Judaism? Religion? Culture?
> Any important institutions? Important people? Texts?

2. Can you help me understand your particular experiences with Judaism in childhood? I'm just looking to understand what, if any, people, institutions, or experiences in your Jewish background were important.

Probes:

Did you attend Hebrew school? Engage in Jewish learning of any sort? Have a bar/bat mitzvah? Go to a youth group, camp, or Jewish clubs? Attend synagogue?

Did you mark holidays?

Were you involved with other institutions or people?

Did you have Jewish friends?

Can you help me understand how you thought about Judaism growing up? Is there a story that you sometimes tell about your Jewish upbringing?

Did you identify as Jewish growing up? What did that mean to you?

3. Can you help me understand your experiences with Judaism in adulthood?

Probes:

How have any of your practices changed?

How has your involvement with Jewish organizations changed?

Were there key events or moments in your life that caused or marked important changes with Judaism?

If partnered, is your partner Jewish? Are you raising Jewish children?

What is your current Jewish practice, if you have one? Do you observe Jewish holidays? Do you participate in any rituals?

4. Do you personally identify as Jewish?

Probes:

Can you help me understand what that means to you?

Do you consider yourself a spiritual person? Can you explain that for me?

How do you understand Judaism? As a religion, culture, or something else?

C. Buddhism

1. How did you first learn about, or what was your first exposure to, Buddhism or Buddhist practice?

>Probes:
>
>Who was the first Buddhist person you met? What were your impressions of them?
>
>Who was the first person you met who meditates? What was your impression?
>
>Do you have a primary teacher? How did that person come to be your teacher?
>
>When you first began learning about Buddhism, did you think at all about its relationship to Judaism or your Jewish past?
>
>Can you help me understand what it was about Buddhism/Buddhist practice that spoke to you?
>
>How did you first practice Buddhism? How did you first mark holidays or celebrate rituals?
>
>Did you have friends, at that time, who were also exploring Buddhism?
>
>How did your family and other friends react to your Buddhist practice?
>
>How did you respond to those reactions?

2. Can you help me understand how your particular experiences with Buddhism/Buddhist meditation have changed throughout your adulthood? I'm just looking to understand, again, the people, institutions, or experiences, if any, that were important on your Buddhist path.

>Probes:
>
>Any other important teachers to your learning?
>
>Any important institutions?
>
>Were there any students of yours who have gone on to become meditation teachers? Could you briefly give me some of their names?
>
>Any changes in Buddhist practice over time?

Do you personally identify as Buddhist? What does this mean to you, and how has it changed over time?

Do you currently mark Buddhist holidays or participate in Buddhist rituals?

3. If relevant, when you opened X center, or began your teaching, how did you decide what elements of the Buddhist tradition to practice and highlight in your teachings?

Probes:

How is the Buddhism you practice different from the Buddhism practiced in Asia (or among Asian Americans)?

Are there any particular Buddhist beliefs, rituals, or practices that are really special to you?

Are there any that are troubling to you?

What are your views on monastic life?

D. Judaism and Buddhism

Personally

1. How, if at all, was your approach to Buddhism informed by your Jewish background?

2. What sorts of tensions, if any, have you experienced between the teachings, traditions, and practices?

Probes:

In what situations? At a synagogue? Meditation center? Among family? At a meditation retreat?

3. Are there times when you feel more Jewish and/or more Buddhist? Please explain those times and how you felt about them.

4. If you have children, what do you hope they have learned from you about Judaism and/or Buddhism?

5. How do you explain to people the kind of practice you do?

Professionally

1. How do you respond when people ask you why so many Jews are involved with Buddhist meditation?
2. How do you see intersections between Judaism and Buddhism in your daily work with students?
3. Are meditation teachers with Jewish backgrounds different from others in some way?
4. Can you tell me about your interactions with other meditation teachers who were born Jewish?

Probes:

Are you a part of any formal groups or organizations?

Have you had interactions with other meditation teachers with Jewish backgrounds who have been particularly significant to your thinking about the relationship between Buddhism and Judaism? Please elaborate.

E. Demographics

Gender

Age

Marital status

Number of children

Education

How long you have been teaching

Where you teach

What kinds of classes and retreats you teach

LAY PRACTITIONER INTERVIEW GUIDE

INTRODUCTION: I want to talk with you today about your experiences with meditation. I am going to ask you questions about your current practice, and then will ask you more general questions about your life history and experiences with Judaism, and if relevant, Buddhism.

A. Current Practice

1. I'd like to start by asking you to tell me about your current meditative practice. Could you help me understand what your current practice looks like? I'd like to know when (and how often) you meditate, where this happens, who are the community of people who meditate with you, and what the space in which you meditate looks like. The more details you can provide me with, the better.

Probes:

How frequently do you meditate?

Do you meditate in a primarily Jewish or Buddhist (or mixed) context?

What does the space look like? Are there cushions (zafus), Buddha imagery, alters, Jewish ritual objects, and so on?

Who are the teachers and institutions?

How, if at all, is your current practice informed by your Jewish heritage?

Do you have friends who also meditate? Does that help (or hinder) your practice?

When you meditate, do you feel a sense of community? Why do you choose to meditate in a group, if you do, rather than alone? What do you gain from this?

What does meditation feel like to you? Why do you do it?

2. Can you help me understand the trajectory that led you to this practice? That is, can you walk me through your first exposure to meditation and how your meditative practice has evolved since then?

Probes:

Who were your primary teachers? Who were the influential people (friends/family) in this process?

What institutions played a role in your development of a meditative tradition?

What was it about the experience of meditation that first appealed to you?

What sorts of retreats and/or formal seminars have you attended?

Have you experienced any tensions between your meditative practice and Jewish heritage?

How have your family and friends reacted to your practice?

3. Is there anything else about your current practice that I didn't ask you that you think I should know?

B. Life History

1. I'd like to ask you to tell me the story of your life—not everything, of course, but think about the major chapters in your life, and for each, tell me about the important things that were happening then, where you were living, what you were doing, and who was important to you. But mostly I just want you to tell me about who you are.

Probes (make sure to gently probe any biographical disruptions that the respondent mentions):

How would you describe your parents' openness to new ideas, experiences, and people? Would you consider them socially liberal?

What area of the country did you grow up in? What was your exposure to meditation/Eastern religions?

What did you study in college, if you attended, and where?

Have you been involved in any cultural movements (antiwar, civil
rights, or women's movements; New Left, etc.)?

Any important travels or experiences abroad?

What was your formal and informal religious education like (i.e.,
did you attend Hebrew school and/or supplemental Jewish
school? Go to a youth group, camp, or Jewish day school?

What was your parents' religious upbringing like?

How did you feel about Judaism while you were growing up?

What were your family's religious rituals or Jewish holidays?

Is there a story that you sometimes tell about your Jewish
upbringing?

If currently married and/or if you have kids, are they in the same
religious tradition?

What wing of Judaism, if any, were you raised in? What were your
parents' religious affiliations like?

2. Outside Judaism and/or Buddhism, were there other religious traditions or spiritual practices that you've explored? If yes, can you describe
this in more detail?

Probes:

In what contexts do you practice these traditions?

In what ways do you find these practices meaningful?

Who do you do them with?

How did you learn about them?

C. Jewish Practice and Identity

I'd now like to ask you a bit more about your current relationship with
Judaism.

1. Could you tell me a bit about how you practice Judaism, if you do?

Probes:

What holidays do you celebrate? Are there any particular holidays
that are special to you?

What rituals or customs do you observe? Can you help me understand why you observe these rituals—that is, in what ways do
you find them meaningful?

Have your Jewish practices or involvement in institutions changed
over time? Can you describe those changes for me?

Were there key events or moments in your life that caused important changes in your relationship with Judaism?

Are there any particular Jewish beliefs or texts that are really special
to you?

Are there any particular Jewish beliefs or rituals that are bothersome to you?

Are there any holidays or practices that you deliberately choose not
to mark or observe?

2. Could you tell me what being Jewish means to you and how you think
about Judaism?

Probes:

Do you personally identify as Jewish? What does that mean to
you?

Do you consider yourself to be a spiritual person? Can you explain
what that means?

Do you think of Judaism as a religion, culture, or something else?

Are most of your friends Jewish? Does this matter to you?

Have you ever been embarrassed or ashamed of being Jewish? Can
you explain this to me?

Do you wear any special clothing or jewelry that says something
about who you are?

D. Buddhist Practice and Identity

I'd now like to ask you a bit about your current relationship with Buddhism, if you have one. If not, how do you see your meditative practice
as informed by Buddhism?

1. Could you tell me a bit about how you practice Buddhism?

Probes:

What holidays do you celebrate? Are there any particular holidays that are special to you?

What rituals or customs do you observe? Can you help me understand why you observe these rituals—that is, in what ways do you find them meaningful?

Have your Buddhist practices or involvement in institutions changed over time? Can you describe those changes for me?

Were there key events or moments in your life that caused important changes in your relationship with Buddhism?

Are there any particular Buddhist beliefs or texts that are really special to you?

Are there any particular Buddhist beliefs or rituals that are bothersome to you?

Are there any holidays or practices that you deliberately choose not to mark or observe?

2. Could you tell me what being Buddhist means to you and how you think about Buddhism?

Probes:

Do you personally identify as Buddhist? What does that mean to you?

Do you think of Buddhism as a religion, culture, or something else?

Have you experienced any tensions between your Buddhist and Jewish practices?

How, if at all, do you see your Buddhism informed by your Jewish heritage?

Are most of your friends Buddhist? Does this matter to you?

Have you ever been embarrassed or ashamed of being Buddhist? Can you explain this to me?

E. Jewish Buddhist Identity

1. If you have both a Jewish and Buddhist identity, can you explain to me how you describe your dual identity as Jewish and Buddhist to your

friends? To your family? To a rabbi or member of the Jewish community? Are there different strategies that you use to help people understand your experiences?

Probes:
Are there certain times or contexts when you feel more Jewish and/or more Buddhist? Please explain what those times are and how you feel during them.
Are there situations in which you emphasize one identity over the other? Can you describe those situations?

F. Scenarios

I really appreciate your bearing with me. We're almost through the interview. This is the final and most open-ended section. It deals with big life questions and issues. There are no right or wrong answers here; mostly I am just interested in what you think and care about.

1. I know this is a hard question, but can you explain to me how you understand God or the Divine?

Probes:
Are there things that you routinely see or hear that remind you of God (spirituality, etc.)?
Do you experience God directly?

2. Have you ever faced a particularly difficult time, like the death of someone close to you, or an illness or financial crisis? Have you thought about why you think it happened? How have you tried to make sense of this and other sorts of suffering?

Probe:
Do you think that everything happens for a reason? Do you imagine some larger plan for all of us?

3. Do you typically pray? Can you explain how you understand prayer and its place in your life?

4. How would you answer a person who claims that any one religion has a monopoly on universal truth?

Probes:
Can you talk about how you see religions existing alongside each other?
How do you understand the belief that the Jews are the chosen people?

5. Can you describe what you imagine might happen after a person dies?
6. What religious books or sources do you turn to for authority or wisdom?

Probe:
How do you understand these books/teachings (literal, etc.)?

7. If you're under a lot of stress, or in a particularly difficult patch in life, what sorts of things do you do to make yourself feel better?
8. Have you had an important spiritual or mystical experience that you would feel comfortable telling me about?

H. Demographics

Gender
Age
Occupation
Marital status
Education

NOTES

Introduction: Sheldon on the Mountain

1. Unfortunately, Kamenetz does not provide any source for his statistic.

2. For some books on the topic, see Fischer 1995, 2003; Shoshanna 2008; Heiftetz 1978; Kasimow, Keenan, and Keenan 2003; Weinberg 2010. For some popular articles written about the Jewish-Buddhist relationship, see Silvia Boorstein, "Is Meditation a Mitzvah?," *Schmooze*, http://www.schmoozemag.com/?p=1167; "Another Queer Jewish Buddhist," http://anotherqueerjubu.com/; "Thoughts of a Jewish Buddhist," Utterly Boring, January 27, 2004, http://utterlyboring.com/archives/2004/01/27/thoughts_of_a_jewish_buddhist.php; "Jewish Buddhists," *New Buddhist*, January 2010, http://newbuddhist.com/discussion/4564/jewish-buddhists/p1; Angela Himsel, "Come Home," *Huffington Post*, September 2, 2010, http://www.huffingtonpost.com/angela-himsel/come-home_b_702841.html; Ira Rifkin, "The Jewish-Buddhist Encounter," My Jewish Learning, http://www.myjewishlearning.com/history/Jewish_World_Today/Jews_and_Non-Jews/Jewish-Buddhist_Relations.shtml; Louis Sahagun, "At One with Dual Devotion," *Los Angeles Times*, May 2, 2006, http://articles.latimes.com/2006/may/02/local/me-jubus2; Bill Redeker, "JuBus—Embracing Judaism and Buddhism," ABC News, " http://abcnews.go.com/US/Beliefs/story?id=1914402&page=1#.URARluhhXpI.email; Bill Chayes and Isaac Solotaroff, dirs., 1999, *Jews and Buddhism: Belief Amended, Faith Revealed* (Berkeley, CA: Judah L. Magnes Museum), http://www.chayesproductions.com/buddhism.html; Jay Michaelson, "No Crystals Needed," *Jewish Daily Forward*, May 4, 2007, http://www.forward.com/articles/10634/; Allison Gaudet Yarrow, "When Yoga and Mindfulness Meet Torah," *Jewish Daily Forward*, March 3, 2010, http://www.forward.com/articles/126436/; Holly Lebowitz Rossi, "Making Judaism New, Minus the New Age," *Jewish Daily Forward*, September 26, 2003, http://www.forward.com/articles/8225/; Allison Gaudet Yarrow, "Yid Lit: Sharon Salzberg," *Jewish Daily Forward*, February 24, 2011, http://www.forward.com/articles/135681/; Nadine Brozan, "Breaking Down the Barriers between Religion and Medicine," *New York Times*, July 18, 1998, http://www.nytimes.com/1998/07/18/nyregion/breaking-down-the-barriers-between-religion-and-medicine.html?scp=55&sq=Jewish%20Buddhist&st=cse; "Community Discussion: JuBus and Christian Buddhists," *Tricycle*, August 15, 2011, https://tricycle.org/trikedaily/community-discussion-jubus-and-christian-buddhists/.

3. A number of relatively recent dissertations and master's theses also call attention to the historical relationship between Judaism and Buddhism, drawing primarily from Kamenetz's (1994) arguments. See, for example, Libin 2010; Brodey 1997; Rosenberg 2003.

4. Certainly not all Jews occupy this particular social position in the United States today, nor have they done so across the centuries of American Jewish history. It is absolutely the case that there are and have historically been many Jews (like those from all other religious and

ethnic groups) who are wealthy and poor, liberal and conservative, urban and rural, observant and secular. Importantly for the Jews in this book, however, their social distinctiveness was and is an integral aspect of their self-definition as a Jew and American. For more information about the contemporary Jewish distinctiveness, drawing on the General Social Surveys (GSS) conducted by the National Opinion Research Center that compares Jews to other ethnic and religious groups in the United States, see Smith 2005. See also Rebhun 2016; Pew Religious Landscape Study 2013.

5. None of these arguments, however, derive from a methodological approach that would be necessary to make causal claims.

6. Most of the scholarship about the appeal of Buddhism to Jews has been published either in Jewish academic journals or books, or religious studies journals. I examined two of the leading Buddhist studies journals—*Contemporary Buddhism* and the *Journal of Global Buddhism*—as well as the leading religious studies journal—the *Journal of the American Academy of Religion*—to see if Buddhist scholars have written about the appeal of Judaism to Buddhists. I searched the terms "Jews," "Jewish," and "Judaism," and found only one hit. It was an article written by Asaf Federman (2009) about David Ben-Gurion's correspondence with a Buddhist monk.

7. For an expansion on the sociological application of syncretism at the level of individual religious mixing, see Sigalow 2016.

8. For a history of the term, see Leopold and Jensen 2004. See also Greenfield and Droogers 2001.

9. For a summary of that argument, see Stewart and Shaw 1994.

10. While most recent work on syncretism comes out of the field of anthropology, some sociologists have also taken an interest in the blending and synthesis of religions forms. See, for example, Jacobs 2002.

11. This definition follows Stewart and Shaw's (1994, i) use of the term, which they refer to as the "synthesis of different religious forms."

12. For a critique of this, see McGuire 2008, 193–99; Bender 2010, 11–12. For work about spiritual seekers, see Roof 1993, 1999.

13. In *American Grace*, Robert Putnam and David Campbell (2010) demonstrate the important role that fluidity and volition play in contemporary American religion. They show how religious identity in the United States has become less inherited and fixed, and more chosen and changeable. For virtually all American religious traditions, the rate of religious inheritance has declined over the course of the twentieth century, so much so that individual choice has become nearly as important as inheritance in explaining Americans' religious affiliations. A recent poll conducted by the Pew Forum on Religion and Public Life in 2009 called "Many Americans Mix Multiple Faiths" emphasizes these same trends toward religious switching and mixing. The Pew researchers found that large numbers of Americans engage in multiple religious practices and mix elements of diverse traditions in their daily lives. The study concludes, "Religious beliefs and practices of Americans do not fit neatly into conventional categories."

14. For historical studies that have had a particular emphasis on religious contact and exchange, see Albanese 2008; Tweed 1997, 2008; Prothero 2010.

15. For more work on new religious pluralism, see Banchoff 2007; Bender and Klassen 2010. See also Roof and McKinney 1985.

16. For sociological studies, see, for example, Ammerman 1997; Madsen 2009; Chaves 2004; Warner 1993.

17. David Hollinger (2009) argues for the need for a "dispersionist" approach to American Jewish history that would take account of all Jews regardless of their level of observance, identification, membership of Jewish organizations, or involvement in Jewish communal life.

18. Even the term "Buddhism" is fraught with misconceptions. David McMahan (2008, 5) argues that Buddhism, as it is known in the West, has roots just as much in the teachings of the Buddha as it does in the European Enlightenment as well as in romanticism, transcendentalism, and the Pali canon, and the meeting and clash of Asian cultures and colonial powers.

19. Some scholars divide American Buddhists into three or more categories to account for Buddhists who are neither recent immigrants nor converts. For a review of these various typologies, and an insightful analysis of how racism and white privilege operate in the construction of these categories, see Hickey 2015.

20. In doing so, I think about convert Buddhists similar to Thomas Tweed (2000). He establishes a typology of cradle, convert, and Buddhist sympathizers.

21. The early relationship between Buddhism and Christianity, unlike the relationship between Buddhism and Judaism, was tied up with colonialism and missionization. Christian missionaries entered various Asian countries/lands under the auspices of European colonizers. The colonizers converted many Asians to Christianity in order to tame and reform them. See McMahan 2008, 69–70.

22. For more information about the research design and methodology, see the appendixes to this book.

23. By the last two decades of the twentieth century, the leadership of the Theravada-inspired insight meditation community and various Soto Zen communities was passed to a generation of native-born teachers, of which a significant and visible number were Jewish Americans. The insight meditation movement traces its roots to the Southeast Asian Theravada Buddhist religious context, but has emerged in the United States as a new tradition taking shape around the particular meditation practice of vipassana.

Chapter One: Breaking down the Barriers

1. A number of US periodicals described Strauss's "conversion" ceremony. See, for example, *Sun* 1893; *New-York Tribune* 1893; *Atlanta Constitution* 1893; *Galveston Daily News* 1893; *Chicago Daily Tribune* 1893. See also Sangharakshita 1983; Fields 1981, 129; Seager 2012, 257–58.

2. *New-York Tribune* 1893.

3. Dharmapala was an important Ceylonese Buddhism reformer and one of the creators of the Theosophical Society. Southern Buddhism represents Buddhism as practiced in Southeast Asia and Sri Lanka, now considered Theravada Buddhism.

4. *Atlanta Constitution* 1893.

5. *Galveston Daily News* 1893; *Chicago Daily Tribune* 1893.

6. For information about Strauss's family life, see *New York Times* 1879; *Chicago Daily Tribune* 1893; *New York Times, Obituaries and Marriage Notices* 1981.

7. I use the word "conversion" here in the original sense of the term: as someone who turned their heart and mind toward the teachings of a new religious tradition—in this case, Buddhism. This usage follows how Richard Seager (2012, 15) conceptualizes American converts to Buddhism in his book *Buddhism in America*.

8. I examined all the Jewish newspapers in the ProQuest Historical Newspapers™—American Jewish Newspapers database for writings about Buddhism, Buddha, Buddhist, and meditation as well as the Pittsburgh Jewish Newspaper Project. I also searched all digitized newspapers in the Library of Congress from 1850 to 1930 for various combinations of these terms: Jewish, Jews, Judaism, Buddhist, Buddha, Buddhism, and meditation.

9. I use 1923 as the end date for this period because it is the year that Strauss publishes *The Buddha and His Doctrine*.

10. For a spectrum of ways that nineteenth-century Americans identified with Buddhism, see Tweed 2000, 42–77. Thomas Tweed refers to Buddhist sympathizers as those who felt an attraction to Buddhism, attended lectures, or read books on the topic, even if they were not interested in affiliating with the Buddhist tradition. He found that late nineteenth-century American Buddhist sympathizers and adherents broadly fell into three types: esoterics, rationalists, and romantics.

11. Strauss could have read about Buddhism through Edwin Arnold's poetic *The Light of Asia* (published in 1879) or theosophist Henry Steel Olcott's *Buddhist Catechism* (published in 1881). Arnold's *Light of Asia* sold between five hundred thousand and one million copies in the nineteenth century, and was regarded as a book that "had done more than any other book to popularize the story of the Buddha's life in the West" (Fields 1981, 115). Strauss could also have learned about Buddhism from the English-language *Maha Bodhi Journal*, which was edited by Dharmapala and first published in May 1892. Various US newspapers reprinted stories from the *Maha Bodhi*, helping to nurture and spread an American interest in Buddhism.

12. In this sense, Strauss can be understood within the context of what Catherine Albanese (2008) calls "Metaphysical Asia," or the processes and results of how Americans reinvent South and East Asia in their own metaphysical categories and understandings. It is important to note that this reinventing of South and East Asia was happening simultaneously in Europe as it was in the United States. In Germany, for example, Theodor Schultze (1824–98) and Karl Seidenstücker (1876–1936) published critiques of a "decadent Christianity," and celebrated Buddhism as the rational religion of modern times.

13. Nearly every time Dharmapala traveled to New York he mentions his visits with "dear brother Strauss." See, for example, Valisinha 1956a, 1956b, 1958a. See also Guruge 1965, 708; Sangharakshita 1983, 98.

14. Although Strauss studied Pali, in his book, he relied on translations from Thomas W. Rhys Davids and others who made the texts available in English. See Strauss 1923, vi. The *Journal of the Pali Text Society* lists Strauss as a subscriber and donor. See, for example, Davids 1893, 122.

15. Department Passport Application, Charles Theodore Strauss, 1906. The spelling of Strauss's middle name varies across sources. The documents in German, or translated from German, have his name spelled Theodor, while the English documents spell it Theodore.

16. For information about Strauss's work in Europe and Asia, see Muermel, n.d.

17. Following Leigh Eric Schmidt (2005, 11–12), I take religious liberalism to mean the diffuse religious movement that began in the nineteenth century, and was predicated on a variety of precepts and practices, including a contempt of creed and uncritical submission to authority, an emphasis on individual aspirations, the valuing of silence and meditation, the recognition of the immanence of the transcendent, a cosmopolitan appreciation of religious diversity, an ethical earnestness in the pursuit of justice, and a stress on creative self-expression.

18. Strauss's fierce advocacy of Buddhism as an ethical, rational, and scientific tradition makes him a case, par excellence, of those whom Tweed (2000) calls "Rationalists," or nineteenth-century Buddhist adherents and sympathizers who emphasize a rational means of attaining religious truth and meaning, and reject revelational or experiential means, and who place the authority of the individual in religious matters over that of creeds, texts, officials, or institutions.

19. *New-York Tribune* 1893.

20. Strauss was not the first American to "convert" to Buddhism. Olcott, the cofounder of the Theosophical Society and Dharmapala's Theosophical teacher, converted to Buddhism in 1880 in Sri Lanka with H. P. Blavatsky. For more information about Olcott, see Prothero 2010.

21. For a discussion of the limits to Adler's Buddhist sympathy, see Tweed 2000, 19.

22. Again, the Jewish presentation of Buddhism as scientific was not uniquely Jewish. It instead mirrored one strand of the nineteenth-century American conversation about Buddhism that portrayed Buddhism as scientific and rational. See Tweed 2000, 48–78.

23. The romanticizing of Buddhism was ubiquitous in nineteenth-century America and not a uniquely Jewish perception of Buddhism.

24. Officially, Isaac Mayer Wise was the editor of the *American Israelite*, but by 1893, most of the editorials were written by his son, Leo.

25. For the limits of dissent, see Tweed 2000, 133–64.

26. For example, many Jews also began exploring Christian Science at this time (see Umansky 2005). This trend toward religious experimentation was not specific to Jews. A larger "spiritual crisis" was part of a larger pattern of unrest and disquietude, making Americans more open to alternatives in general and Buddhism in particular. See Tweed 2000, 92.

27. The *Chicago Daily Tribune* reported that Strauss was related in marriage to the Stern family, the wealthy merchandising family in New York City. Strauss's wife was the daughter of Isaac Stern, one of the owners of Stern Brothers department stores. See *Chicago Daily Tribune* 1893.

28. This same threat participated in bringing about the Chinese Exclusion Act in 1882. It was one of the most significant restrictions on free immigration in US history, prohibiting all immigration of Chinese laborers. The act was initially intended to last for ten years, but was renewed in 1892 and made permanent in 1902.

29. Ellen Eisenberg (2008) demonstrates how the strength of anti-Asian sentiment and centrality of Asian otherness to white self-definition in the West discouraged Jews from identifying with or publicly supporting Asians.

30. After the World's Parliament of Religions concluded in 1893, Dharmapala traveled across the United States giving lectures about Buddhism from one religious liberal setting to another. He spoke to Unitarian and Universalist congregations, Theosophists and Spiritualist gatherings, and various liberal Jewish clubs and synagogues across the country. See, for example, Valisinha 1955, 1958b.

31. Four years later, the same rabbi at the Huron Street Temple, Rabbi Hahn, gave another lecture titled "Buddha and His Religion, the Great Light of Asia." See *American Israelite* 1890.

32. On Jones's sympathies for Buddhism, see *Chorus of Faith as Heard in Parliament of Religions* 1893. On his life, see *New York Times* 1918.

33. Umansky explains that the former figure assumes that the number of Jews who became Christian Scientists did not exceed 1 percent of the American Jewish population, yet grew beyond 0.25 percent, and perhaps 0.1 percent, out of a population that had grown by 1926 to about four million.

34. The documentary by Hellmuth Hecker in his groundbreaking two volumes *Lebensbilder deutscher Buddhisten* (published in 1996 and 1997) and the analysis of these by Martin Baumann in his 1995 dissertation "Deutsche Buddhisten" evidence that up to a third of those German-speaking Buddhists portrayed in Hecker's *Lebensbilder* had been Jews turned to Buddhism. In this regard, liberal, urban Judaism seems to have had this broad and even international resonance with the teachings and ethics of Buddhism.

35. For more information about the role of the World's Parliament of Religions in bringing Buddhism into conversation with the West, see Seager 1995, 143–62.

36. For more information about the history of Reform Judaism, see Meyer 1995.

37. For a careful study of late nineteenth-century religious liberalism and its birth of "seeker spirituality," see Schmidt 2005. For more information about the rise of nineteenth-century religious liberalism, see Hutchison 2003. For a thorough assessment of late nineteenth-century liberal religious traditions, see Albanese 2008, 257–329.

38. For more discussion of this deracialization of Buddhism, see Wilson 2014, especially 43–74.

39. For an earlier version of this chapter, see Sigalow 2018a.

Chapter Two: Buddhist Paths to Self-Discovery in the Early Twentieth Century

1. The last article I found that positively spoke of Buddhism was in the *American Hebrew* in 1920.

2. For example, Stephen Prothero (2010) demonstrates how Olcott assimilated Buddhism into Protestant categories, assumptions, and vocabularies through a process of "creolization."

3. My use of the term "modernized Buddhism" or "modernized version of Buddhism" is informed by David McMahan's (2008) provocative work on Buddhist modernism, or Buddhism's engagement with the dominant cultural and intellectual forces of modernity.

4. I published some of this material about Julius Goldwater in Sigalow 2018b.

5. Rayette Goldwater, 2006, Ancestry.com; Prothero 1997. Prothero based the story of this article on an interview with Julius Goldwater that took place just a few years before his death.

6. The person most credited with establishing Buddhism on the island is Bishop Emyo Imamura.

7. Goldwater attended the class with Carl Scheid, a German American student of Buddhism who had moved to Hawaii after his wife's death. See Ama 2011, 76.

8. On July 8, 1928, Imamura and Hunt "initiated" nine members of the forum.

9. Prothero (1997, 46) suggests that Goldwater was the only Caucasian member of the temple, but Bishop Masuyama, who assumed the Buddhist Mission of North America office in July 1930, started "initiating" Caucasians into the Nishi Hongwanji in 1933, including Robert S. Clifton. See Ama 2011, 73–74.

10. The date is uncertain, but an article in the *China Press* (1937) describes his trip to Hang Chaw as taking place in 1937.

11. The court ended up ruling in Goldwater's favor, arguing that he only used those funds to the benefit of the Buddhist community. Although Goldwater kept close ties with the Buddhist movement after this lawsuit, he stopped actively participating in the ministerial ranks of the Buddhist Churches of America. See Prothero 1997; Kashima 1977.

12. For an earlier discussion of "strategic occidentalism," see chapter 1.

13. Although he displayed no interest in Judaism as a religion, he still worked on behalf of the Jewish community during World War II. In addition, he had been decorated for work done with army intelligence during World War II and had helped resettle Jewish refugees during the War. See Lewis 2013.

14. Per an email exchange on April 2, 2018, with Wali Ali Meyer, the head of the esoteric school of the Sufi Ruhaniat International and previously Lewis's esoteric secretary, Lewis's family were social rather than religious Jews. Lewis's participation in Jewish ritual and ceremonies was minimal, although he did briefly attend religious school at a synagogue in San Francisco.

15. Later in his life, Lewis was initiated into other Buddhist lineages as well. In 1956, he was recognized by Zen masters of Japan and was initiated into Shingon Buddhism. In 1967, he was ordained a Zen master by Korean Zen master Kyung-Bo Seo.

16. Lewis's various writings are housed in the Sufi Ruhaniat International's online archive. See http://murshidsam.org/Papers1.html. For a sense of how Lewis viewed religion and Buddhism, see his papers "How to Be Buddhist," "The Lotus and Universe," and "This Is the New Age, in Person."

17. For more information about the history of perennialism and its role in Buddhist modernism, see McMahan 2008, 69–87.

18. There is a notable absence of any discussion of Segal's Jewish upbringing in his biographical and autobiographical works.

19. Segal was a longtime member of the Gurdjieff Foundation in New York City.

20. In a personal communication with scholar Jeff Wilson in August 2015, I first learned about the importance of Jews practicing outside the United States during this time period. Most famously, there was the German Jew Nyanaponika Thera (born Siegmund Feniger), who was ordained as a Buddhist monk in 1936. He was a leading Buddhist scholar and translator, and the founder of the Buddhist Publication Society in Sri Lanka. He mastered Pali and translated select teachings of the Buddha into English (a process that started the Buddhist Publication Society). He was also a major promoter of lay meditation in the twentieth century, and his book, *Heart of Buddhist Meditation*, achieved virtual canonical status among Americans interested in Buddhism. Similarly, several other German Jews were ordained and trained with Nyanaponika in Asia.

Chapter Three: Jews and the Liberalization of American Buddhism

1. For in-depth works on Buddhism's explosion in popularity in the United States during these years, see Seager 2012, 39–53; Prebish 1999; Prebish and Tanaka 1998; Coleman 2001. For a narrative account of Buddhism's spread in the United States, see Fields 1981. For an account of how these factors sowed the seeds for the mindfulness movement in the United States, see Wilson 2014, 28–31.

2. Beginning with the founding of the Jewish labor movement in the 1880s, Jews remained consistently the most politically liberal of all white ethnic groups in the United States. See Staub 2004; Michels 2012.

3. We do not have statistics about the number of Jews in convert versus Asian-founded communities, but anecdotally it seems that most American Jewish Buddhists, like most Americans of European heritage, practiced in convert communities. A number of prominent Jews, however, began practicing in Asian-founded communities in this time period as well, including Mark Blum (the head of Japanese Buddhist studies at the University of California at Berkeley and a longtime Shin practitioner), Lee Rosenthal (a leader in the Buddhist Churches of America, especially in California and Arizona), and Ron Epstein (one of Chinese Buddhist teacher Hsuan Hua's important non-Chinese students in the Dharma Realm Buddhist Association).

4. The post-1965 period witnessed a tremendous growth in the number of Buddhist traditions and groups in the United States. As I mentioned in the introduction to this book, in an effort to categorize these various communities, Buddhist studies scholars tend to sort them into two broadly defined groups: American immigrant Buddhist communities and convert Buddhist communities. Immigrant communities largely consist of immigrant and refugee Buddhists who came to the United States after 1965 from a range of Asian nations, and are in the process of adapting their received traditions to this country. Although imprecise in nomenclature, this immigrant group often also includes Asian Americans, primarily from Chinese and Japanese backgrounds, who have practiced Buddhism in this country for four to five generations (for more information about these three groups, see Seager 2012, 16). In contrast to these immigrant group(s) that have ethnic ties to Asia, a different group of American Buddhists, frequently referred to as convert Buddhists, consists of native-born Americans who have come to embrace the teachings and practices of the Buddha. For a detailed study of this Euro-American community, see Coleman 2001.

5. By the last two decades of the twentieth century, the leadership of the Theravada-inspired insight meditation community and various Soto Zen communities was passed to a generation of native-born teachers, of which a significant and visible number were Jewish Americans. The insight meditation movement traces its roots to the Southeast Asian Theravada Buddhist religious context, but has emerged in the United States as a new tradition taking shape around the particular meditation practice of vipassana.

6. Suzuki was the son of a samurai family, spoke fluent English, wrote prolifically, and dedicated his life to Buddhist scholarship and teaching. For more information about him, see Jackson 2010; Coleman 2001; McMahan 2008; Chadwick 1999.

7. For information about the Jewish involvement in radical politics, see, for example, Michels 2012; Moore 2008; Svonkin 1999.

8. Ginsberg was born in New Jersey to Jewish parents and suffered a turbulent childhood in the shadows of his mother's mental illness. He showed a talent for poetry at an early age and enrolled in Columbia University to study poetry. At Columbia, he was introduced to a number of future Beat poets and eventually emerged as one of the central figures in the Beat movement. Bill Morgan—Ginsberg's archivist and biographer—essentially describes the Beat generation as a group of friends who gathered around and interacted with Ginsberg. For information about Ginsberg's Jewish background, see Morgan 2006, 9–122.

9. For the story of Ginsberg's relationship to Buddhism, and in particular how Buddhism informed his writings and worldview, see Trigilio 2007.

10. After a chance meeting with Trungpa in the 1970s on the streets of New York City when they hailed the same cab, Ginsberg began to take up the practice of Buddhism, which became a major focus of his life and influence on his later poetry. He went on to spend weeks on end in silent meditation, study with Trungpa, and start the Jack Kerouac School of Disembodied Poetics at Trungpa's Naropa Institute in Boulder, Colorado, where Ginsberg taught during summer months. See Morgan 2006, 479–81.

11. For a discussion of establishment versus Beat Zen, see Watts 2011.

12. For a discussion of Zen's introduction to the United States, see Seager 2012.

13. For a personal story of this trajectory, see Nisker 1994.

14. The Sokoji itself has an interesting history of Jewish-Buddhist exchanges. Built in 1895 as the Bush Street Temple, the Sokoji building originally housed a group of disaffected members of San Francisco's Congregation Emanu-El who called their new congregation Ohabai Shalome. In the face of declining membership, the Ohabai Shalome congregation sold the building in November 1934 to the Soto Zen Mission of the Sokoji Buddhist Church. See Chiat 1997, 409.

15. Some of Weitsman's famous Jewish-born dharma heirs include Norman Fischer, Alan Senauke, Steven Weintraub, and Teah Strozer.

16. While Weitsman, Fischer, Hartman, Senauke, and Bernard Glassman are perhaps the most famous Jewish teachers of Japanese Zen Buddhism, there have been many other important Jewish Buddhists who study in the Japanese lineages, including Toni Packer, Strozer, Natalie Goldberg, Tova Green, Shery Chayat, and Laurence Shainberg.

17. Joseph Goldstein, Jacqueline Mandell-Schwartz, Wes Nisker, and Lama Surya Das, interviews with the author, May 2012. Wes Nisker (1994) chronicles his experience on the "hippie travel" in his book *If You Don't Like the News Go Out and Make Some of Your Own.*

18. Joseph Goldstein and Wes Nisker, interviews with the author, May 2012.

19. In my interview with Jacqueline Mandell-Schwartz (January 2012), she told me that Goenka "made it clear that he had no interest in convincing young travelers to be Buddhist; in fact, he taught that Buddhism was nonsectarian, a kind of science of the self or spiritual psychology." For more information about Goenka and his teaching style, see Goenka 2000, 2003.

20. Wes Nisker, interview with the author, March 2012.

21. This American-born movement developed out of the Theravada traditions of Burma, Thailand, and Sri Lanka, and is largely independent of Asian institutional oversight, making it fluid and highly variegated. "Insight" is the English translation of the Pali word vipassana.

22. These names were provided to me in various interviews with Goenka retreat participants and confirmed in conversation with Nisker.

23. Goldstein's teachers included Anagarika Munindra, Goenka, Dipa Ma, and Sayadaw U Pandita. Kornfield studied with Ajahn Chah, and later practiced with Mahasi Sayadaw and Ma. Kornfield went on to ordain as a monk in the Thai forest tradition, and Goldstein studied mindfulness in India with Munindra, a lay teacher trained in Burmese vipassana.

24. Many books and articles tell the story of this meeting. See, for example, Cadge 2004, 28–29; Fields 1981, 9, 304–38; Coleman 2001, 78–79. Goldstein had not had much experience in the way of teaching Buddhist meditation right after his return to the United States, but his friend from his travels, Ram Dass, invited him to teach vipassana meditation as part of his course in Boulder.

25. Salzberg and Mandell-Schwartz shared neighboring huts with Goldstein on the Goenka retreats in India. They all shared a similar style of practice. These teachers incorporated the center on May 19, 1975, but it wasn't until January 1976 that they purchased a building in Barre, Massachusetts, to house the center (Cadge 2005, 29).

26. The cofounders of Spirit Rock include Jewish-born Buddhists Kornfield, James Baraz, and Sylvia Boorstein as well as Presbyterian-born Anna Douglass. Under the leadership of Goldstein and Salzburg, IMS has remained closer to the Burmese retreat model, while Kornfield (who holds a PhD in clinical psychology) led Spirit Rock in the direction of an "integrative East-meets-West" psychologized Buddhist model. Although the two centers have developed distinctive styles of teaching, to suggest a full split between the centers is misleading. Most of the teachers (and many practitioners) move between the two centers, and strong bonds and friendships exist between the East and West Coast communities. For more information about the emergence of an East and West Coast vipassana practice, see Gleig 2012. For more information about the history of Spirit Rock, see Cadge 2004, 42–44; Coleman 2001, 78–79; "History of Spirit Rock," https://www.spiritrock.org/2016/about/history.

27. For example, Bhikkhu Bodhi, born Jeffrey Block in 1944, grew up in Brooklyn in a Jewish family, but traveled to Sri Lanka in his early twenties to study Buddhism. He received novice ordination in 1972 and full ordination in 1973, both under the late Venerable Ananda Maitreya, a leading Sri Lankan scholar-monk in the Theravada tradition. Bodhi was appointed the editor of the Buddhist Publication Society in Sri Lanka and only returned to the United States in 2002. Currently, he resides at Chuang Yen Monastery, and teaches there and at Bodhi Monastery. Similarly, Ayya Khema, born as Ilse Kussel to Jewish parents in Berlin, Germany, in 1923, is the first Western woman to become a Theravadan Buddhist nun. She had a turbulent childhood, escaping the Nazis only to be interned in a Japanese concentration camp. Khema later emigrated to the United States and then pursued Buddhism in her forties. She founded several Buddhist centers around the world, and has written over two dozen books of her transcribed dharma talks in English and German. See Bodhi Monastery 2002; Khema 1998.

28. The four main schools of Tibetan Buddhism are Gelugpa, Kagyu, Nyingma, and Sakya. On the history of the development of the Tibetan tradition in the United States, see Seager 2012, 135–57.

29. Although Trungpa was a tulku of the Trungpa lineage of teachers within the Kagyu school of Tibetan Buddhism, he also received training in the Nyingma tradition. Trungpa was known to have abused his position of power in order to have sexual relationships with his female

students. He was widely known to have abused alcohol, and be drunk and disorderly in public as well.

30. For a more in-depth description of this first summer session at Naropa, see Fields 1981, 317.

31. Trungpa founded Shambhala International, a network of Tibetan Buddhist practice communities that blends both the Kagyu and Nyingma lineages.

32. These teachers' name changes reflect their taking a "dharma name," which is often acquired during a Buddhist initiation ritual or monastic ordination.

33. Following Leigh Eric Schmidt (2005, 11–12), I take liberalism to mean the diffuse religious movement that began in the nineteenth century, and was predicated on a variety of precepts and practices, including a contempt for creed and uncritical submission to authority, stress on the individual and their psychic condition, valuing of silence and meditation, cosmopolitan appreciation of religious diversity, and pursuit of social justice.

34. For a thorough history of the role of meditation in the Asian context (and then how it transformed in the United States), see Wilson 2014.

35. For more information about the role of meditation in Asia, see Wilson 2014.

36. This secularized version of vipassana meditation is not to suggest that ritual, symbol, or tradition play no role in practice communities, just that these roles are minimized and downplayed.

37. Norman Fischer, interview with the author, March 29, 2012. For information about Fischer's views of Buddhism vis-à-vis Judaism, see Fischer 1995; Everyday Zen Foundation, n.d.

38. Norman Fischer, interview with the author, March 29, 2012.

39. Emphasizing just this point, Larry Rosenberg, the founder and a guiding teacher at the Cambridge Insight Meditation Center, explained in an unpublished interview with Wendy Cadge in June 2001 that the monastic tradition felt foreign to him because "on my father's side is fourteen generations of rabbis. The Jewish tradition is the complete reverse of Buddhism. That is, they don't give you the highest teaching until you are at least forty-two, married and have two children. . . . So there is nothing in my blood that says spirituality means not to be with a woman. Spirituality means not to have a family. I never had that."

40. For more information about the history and character of socially engaged Buddhism, see Queen 2000; Queen and King 1996.

41. He went back and forth between California and New York for a decade before committing to Buddhist practice and taking up residency at the Berkeley Zen Center in 1981. He was ordained as a priest and received dharma transmission from Weitsman in 1998. Alan Senauke, interview with the author, March 2012.

42. For more information about the role of the Buddhist Peace Fellowship, see Queen 2000. For more information about Senauke's work with engaged Buddhism, see Senauke 2010.

43. Clear View Project, http://www.clearviewproject.org/home.html.

44. Christopher Queen (2000) spotlights her work in his book *Engaged Buddhism in the West*.

45. Seager (2012, 126) also calls Glassman "one of American Zen's most well known innovators."

46. For an in-depth look at the story of Glassman's trajectory from a Jewish boy from New York to a worldwide Buddhist leader, see Glassman 1997. See also Glassman 1998; 2018.

47. The main components of the Greyston Mandela include the Greyston Bakery, Greyston Family Inn, and Maitri Center and Isaan House. The Greyston Bakery, founded in 1982, provides employment for the needy and unskilled, and trains its employees in bakery skills. The bakery produces some of New York's most expensive, high-end baked goods, sold in many of the city's most exclusive restaurants. The Family Inn, established in 1986, supplies housing and support services (including a large childcare center and after-school program) for people making their way out of unemployment and homelessness. The Maitri Center and Issan House, opened in 1997, offers medical care for people with AIDS-related illnesses.

48. For more information about Jews and their historical as well as contemporary involvement in social justice activism, see Svonkin 1999; Cohen and Fein 2001.

49. In his book about the history of Jewish meditation, Mike Verman (1996) writes that Scholem's article in *Encyclopedia Judaica* is the first published article about Jewish meditation. I have not found an earlier article published about meditation, so this claim seems right.

Chapter Four: Buddhism and the Creation of a Contemplative Judaism

1. The scholar, rabbi, and activist Arthur Waskow founded a magazine called *Menorah*, and it was in this magazine that Waskow coined the term "Jewish Renewal" in 1979. See Sarna 2004, 349–53.

2. For more on the history of the Jewish Renewal movement, see Magid 2005; Kaplan 2009, 266–79.

3. Many famous Jewish Buddhists were students and friends of Schachter-Shalomi, including Glassman, Boorstein, Jeff Roth, Sheila Weinberg, and Rabbi David Cooper.

4. For a comprehensive and nuanced examination of the rise of meditation and mindfulness in the United States, see Wilson 2014. For the story about how an elite movement of contemplative leaders catalyzed this popularization of mindfulness in America, see Kucinskas 2019.

5. Jeff Wilson (2014, 75–103) importantly discusses how the encounter between mindfulness and psychology was already brewing prior to Kabat-Zinn's creation of the Mindfulness-Based Stress Reduction clinics. The 1960s saw a widespread attention to Transcendental Meditation, which gave rise to a variety of psychology-based clinical tests seeking to determine the physiological and psychological effects of meditation. See Metcalf 2002.

6. Kabat-Zinn came from a family of scientists and intellectuals. His father was an internationally renowned immunochemist, and his father-in-law, Howard Zinn, was a famous historian, activist, and author of the well-known book *A People's History of the United States*.

7. MBSR has also given birth to a whole host of therapies for specific applications, including Mindfulness-Based Eating Awareness Therapy, Mindfulness-Based Art Therapy, Mindfulness-Based Relapse Prevention, and Mindfulness-Based Relationship Enhancement. The basic method is to take a preexisting form of therapy and restructure it around the practice of mindfulness, using awareness as the new emphasis for achieving healing results.

8. Other Jewish psychologists of that period interested in bringing meditation into the fields of psychology and medicine include Richard Davidson, Gary Schwartz, and Ronna Kabatznick.

9. For more information about how meditation and the practice of mindfulness became mainstream in the United States, see Wilson 2014. See also Seager 2012, 63–65.

10. Rabbi Rachel Cowan, interview with the author, February 2012.

11. Charlie Halpern, interview with the author, September 2012; Rabbi Rachel Cowan, interview with the author, February 2012.

12. Charlie Halpern, interview with the author, September 2012.

13. Rodger Kamenetz, interview with the author, April 18, 2013. See also Niebuhr 1997; Seager 2012, 260–61; Central Conference of American Rabbis 1998.

14. *Insight* (Insight Meditation Center) newsletters from 1993 to 2002 report stories of the conference continuing between those years. Audio recordings from the 1992, 1993, and 1995 Jewish-Buddhist conferences are in the author's possession.

15. Boorstein 1997; Sylvia Boorstein, interview with the author, March 2012.

16. Sheila Weinberg, interview with the author, February 2012; Sylvia Boorstein, interview with the author, March 2012.

17. Sylvia Boorstein, interview with the author, March 2012.

18. Sylvia Boorstein, interview with the author, March 2012.

19. Norman Fischer, interview with the author, March 2012.

20. Lew never stopped identifying as a Jew. Throughout his time studying Buddhism, he heard what he called "Jewish background music," or a waxing sense of Jewishness that he experienced while sitting Zen. His Zen master kept saying, "Just keep sitting with it, and it will go away," but it never did. See Lew 2001, 2003; Sherril Lew, interview with the author, May 2012.

21. Lew 2001; Norman Fischer, interview with the author, May 2012.

22. This is a process of what Jeff Wilson (2014) calls a "domestication" of Buddhism, or the process by which members of a new culture take from Buddhism what they believe will relieve their culturally specific distresses and concerns, and in the process, spawn new Buddhist forms, teachings, and practices.

23. See http://www.awakenedheartproject.org.

24. Jeff Roth, interview with the author, December 2012. In our conversation, Roth explained that Elat Chayyim deliberately created new spiritual practices as well as blended Jewish and non-Jewish traditions in an attempt to just "make it up from scratch."

25. Jonathan Omer-Man, interview with the author, February 2012.

26. Although Davis did not intend to draw on Buddhist teachings or practice, in her ethnographic exploration of Chochmat HaLev, Cia Sautter (2002) found that the center offered a meditation practice that closely resembled the Buddhist practice of vipassana meditation.

27. A few studies have explored the importance of philanthropy to the American Jewish community. Joel Fleishman (2009) has written about the role of philanthropic foundations in shaping American civic culture, and Eric Fleisch (2014) wrote his doctoral dissertation about the impact of Jewish philanthropies on organized Jewish life. Shaul Kelner (2011) also wrote a piece that looks at the role of foundation funding in the Jewish community.

Chapter Five: Making Meditation Jewish

1. The hamsa is an old Near Eastern symbol imported into Jewish cultures from broader cultural usage.

2. A voluminous number of books and articles have also been written about Jewish meditation and/or Jewish mindfulness. Books about mindful Jewish living, courses on mindful Jewish meditation, blogs about mindful Jewish parenting, and seminars on mindful Jewish eating abound. See, for example, Slater 2004; Corrigan 2013; Silvers 2013.

3. Some Jewish meditation offerings in the United States, including those offered by Davis and Omer-Man, as described in chapter 4, and many Orthodox or ultra-Orthodox Jewish teachers, have no explicit ties to Buddhism. In this chapter, I focus specifically on Jewish meditation as it emerged from the encounter between Judaism and Buddhism in the contemporary United States.

4. For more information about social scientific thinking about diffusion and famous diffusion studies, see Granovetter 1973; DiMaggio and Power 1983; McAdam 1995; Orlando and Patterson 2005; Frickel and Gross 2005.

5. For more information about cultural approaches to diffusion, see Strang and Meyer 1993; Snow and Benford 1992; Kaufman and Patterson 2005.

6. This prominent group of teachers, or founding teachers of Jewish meditation, are the first generation of Jewish meditation teachers in the United States who learned to meditate from teachers in the Buddhist tradition and helped to introduce Buddhist-inspired practices of meditation into the Jewish world. Second-generation teachers, by comparison, are those Jewish meditation teachers who learned to meditate from within the Jewish tradition. Included in this list of first-generation teachers are Boorstein, Lew, Fischer, Weinberg, Roth, the Coopers, Slater, Laichter, Seth Castleman, and others.

7. By "cultural container," I work off the conceptual designation that Wendy Cadge (2004, 84) uses (in her case, an "organizational container") to discuss and compare how the teachings and practices are present in two communities of Theravada Buddhists in the United States.

8. For more information about how meditation and the practice of mindfulness became mainstream in the United States, see Wilson 2014. See also Seager 2012, 63–65.

9. For more information about the rise of Jewish mindfulness in the United States, see Niculescu 2015. Mira Niculescu describes the process by which mindfulness becomes first Western and then reformulated as Jewish.

10. In my conversations with Boorstein, Weinberg, and Laichter, for example, they all spoke about the issue of how to make a Jewish meditation space free of Buddha imagery and comfortable to Jewish meditators who might come from a range of different backgrounds.

11. This quote (Song of Songs 5:2) should be transliterated as *ani yesheinah v'libi eir*.

12. Jeff Roth, interview with the author, December 2012.

13. Roth taught Jewish mysticism for a decade before he met and began studying meditation with Boorstein.

14. For a discussion of why he avoids Jewish mystical approaches to meditation, see Lew 1996.

15. Boorstein (1997) describes a Shabbat meditation retreat where the participants arrive on Thursday, practice mindfulness meditation in silence until Friday evening, and then celebrate Shabbat with ritual, liturgy, Torah reading, and study.

16. The Coopers were students of Buddhist teachers in the Theravada, Zen, and Vajrayana traditions, and have also studied meditative practices from Hinduism and Sufism.

17. Shoshanna Cooper, interview with the author, December 2012.

18. The degree to which these liberal movements embrace change, and the process for instituting that change, varies across the movements.

19. For a history of different Jewish meditative practices, see Verman 1996.

20. I heard this phrase used by numerous teachers during my fieldwork.

21. This point is made in distinction to David Strang and Sarah Soule's argument (1998, 276) that practices diffuse as they are rendered familiar. In this chapter, I show how practices also diffuse when they are made equal parts familiar and different.

Chapter Six: Mapping Jewish Buddhist Spirituality

1. I should note that I did not have any Orthodox-identifying Jews in my sample.

2. A few of the cultural Jews of the last chapter talked about Buddhism as a spiritual practice. In general, however, the respondents who maintain an active Jewish observance related to Buddhism centrally in terms of spirituality, and used spiritual rhetoric more frequently, elaborately, and with greater assuredness than the cultural Jews of the previous chapter.

3. This new scholarship has emerged in reaction to widely held ideas about the individuality and elusiveness of spirituality. For a review, see Bender and McRoberts 2012. See also Bender 2007 and Wuthnow 1998. In attempting to add social specificity to work on spirituality, an emerging and interdisciplinary body of scholarship has begun to investigate the history and genealogy of the discourse as well as forms of the spiritual (Schmidt 2005; Albanese 2008; Bender 2010; Klassen 2011), spirituality in medicine (Cadge 2012), and science (Bender 2010; Taves 2009; Taves and Bender 2012), and how people narrate ideas of the sacred in their everyday lives (Ammerman 2013).

4. Ammerman's (2013) *Sacred Stories, Spiritual Tribes* points to the important role that religious communities play in nurturing and producing spiritual discourse. Her study, however—by virtue of its breadth—could not discern in a nuanced way the discursive differences among the religious traditions in the United States, particularly among the minority religious traditions.

5. Catherine Bell (1992) shows the importance and power of habitual practice in the construction of meaning making and identity.

6. In doing so, they embedded spirituality in what Ammerman (2013) calls "theistic discourse."

7. For work on the intersections of spirituality and experience, see Bender 2013; Schmidt 2005; Albanese 2008.

8. Indeed, observing this very point, Jewish studies scholar Naomi Seidman (1998, 261) writes about the Jewish-Buddhist relationship that "in the absence of a particularist Jewish political affiliation that could also satisfy the progressive universalist agenda with which Jewish politics

has been historically linked, adopting the particularist position of another group paradoxically becomes a distinctively Jewish act."

9. For more discussion about spirituality and pluralism, see Bender and Klassen 2010; Hicks 2010.

10. After telling me about her experiences with Judaism in college, she paused to note, "The one thing that I really did [spiritually] connect to was at my synagogue back in New York, and that was just because the music was so beautiful. . . . They had really, really beautiful music, and so I just connected to that, and I would go to services a lot just for the peace of it, but other than that, really barely had any kind of Jewish community. I continued to do the Shabbat by myself, really." Again, Maya reinforced the idea that spirituality had direct ties to a particular sense of instrumental relevance: that listening to the beautiful Jewish music felt spiritual to her because it brought her repose and comfort.

11. Other respondents made this claim more explicitly. Rebecca noted, "So, but as far as Judaism, like sometimes I feel like we're so intellectual that we're just missing a big part of what the religion can offer. We're just not focusing on the more kind of spiritual side of things and that works for some people."

12. Although the Sex and the Law class deals centrally with sexuality, which is clearly an everyday issue, I think what Maya was saying was that as a woman who does not base her life decisions and behaviors (sexually or otherwise) on Jewish law, this sort of class did not feel meaningful to her life.

13. I heard this same sentiment echoed from Jon, who explained, "I have a hard time with some of the language of the Prayer Book. So sometimes I think the way that I've learned about Buddhism and Buddhist meditation is much easier to relate to for me than Jewish prayer. Jewish prayer I feel like I have to do a lot of translating. I have to spend a lot of time making— figuring out how to make it work, because the way the language just doesn't work for me as it is . . . like just as you read it, it's like I don't relate to this. But you know when I—when I learned about Buddhism, it was like, 'Oh that makes sense.' It is like immediately it makes sense."

14. For the rise of "empowered" or more individualized and self-directed Judaism, see Kaunfer 2010.

Chapter Seven: Constructing a Jewish Buddhist Identity

1. In doing so, I use the same language as Seager (2012, 9) and Tweed (2000).

2. For a critique of this view, see McGuire 2008, 185–213.

3. For a review of this conversion literature, see Gooren 2007. See also Rambo 1995.

4. A variety of ethnographic studies have focused on the fluidity and heterogeneity within American religious life, and the partial nature of religious conversion, including Jacobs 2002; McGuire 2008; Bender 2010; Bender and Klassen 2010. Additionally, a survey conducted by the Pew Forum on Religion and Public Life in 2009 emphasized these same trends toward religious fluidity and mixing. The Pew researchers found that large numbers of Americans engage in multiple religious practices and mix elements of diverse traditions in their daily lives. See Pew Research Center 2019.

5. This is in line with Rodney Stark and Roger Finke's (2000, 89) notion that "religion is concerned with the supernatural, everything else is secondary."

6. See Ecklund and Lee 2011; Hervieu-Léger 2000, 2006; Zuckerman 2008; Kasselstrand 2015.

7. Religious identities are enacted or performed much in the way that Candace West and Don Zimmerman (1987) see gender as a matter of performance, as they argue in their essay "Doing Gender."

8. Sociologists have long recognized that ascription and achievement are two distinct ways of constructing identities or aspects of identities. Sociologists have widely argued that religion in premodern societies was largely an ascribed and immutable identity, while now it is more a matter of personal choice or religious achievement (Berger 1967; Bellah et al. 1985; Warner 1993; Putnam and Campbell 2010). Recent work has begun to critique this dichotomous perspective, showing that individuals often combine ideas about ascription and achievement in the narratives they tell about their identities. In this chapter, I specifically use the same definitions and understandings of ascription and achievement as Cadge and Davidman (2006).

9. The Pew study found that the percentage of US adults who say they are Jewish when asked about their religion has declined by about half since the late 1950s and currently is a little less than 2 percent. And the number of Americans with direct Jewish ancestry or upbringing who consider themselves Jewish, yet describe themselves as atheist, agnostic, or having no particular religion, appears to be rising and is now about 0.5 percent of the US adult population.

10. The stories I heard from the respondents that blur the cultural and biological divide bear a striking similarity to those that sociologists Shelly Tenenbaum and Lynn Davidman heard in their research on contemporary Jews and biological discourse. For example, Tenenbaum and Davidman (2007, 440) describe the story of a man named Hal, a thirty-eight-year-old artist who saw his Jewish identity as more ethnic and cultural, and articulated it in this way: "I'm a Jewish individual who lives my Judaism every day, but not through the outward trappings of the religion itself, but through the religious and ethnic heritage which is ingrained in my family and tradition, and in my genetics." In this case, Hal, like the Jewish Buddhists in this chapter, linked genetics with his ethnic and religious inheritance. Similarly, in their book on moderately affiliated Jews, Steven Cohen and Arnold Eisen (2000) argue that their respondents displayed a keen sense of tribalism built on the notion that Judaism was in their blood.

11. In the United States and Europe during the nineteenth and early twentieth centuries, racial discourse pervaded social and national thought, and groups of people were commonly divided into biologically determined racial types. Adolf Hitler's use of racial pseudoscience during World War II, however, made the application of the term "race" to Jews pejorative and antisemitic. After World War II, white European groups, including Jews, were ethnicities—a postwar social category that emphasized the shared history and culture of these groups. For a discussion about Jews and racial categories, see Goldstein 2006.

12. For more information about how scholars classify Jewish ethnic versus religious identities, see Cohen and Eisen 2000; Jacobs 2002. There is no scholarly consensus, though, on how to analytically distinguish between Jewish "religious" versus "ethnic" identities, so the definitions of these categories often vary from one research study to the next.

13. For an sharp review of ethnic revivalism and how it produced a desire for Jewish identity, see Jacobs 2002.

14. Drawing on the General Social Survey data, Tom Smith shows that more than any other religious or ethnic group in the United States, Jews live in and near the largest cities, exceed all other groups in socioeconomic status, and surpass all other groups in the highest degree attained, mean years of schooling, and high-status occupations.

15. Debra Kaufman (2007) found many Americans draw on the cultural narrative of "never again" to similarly inspire their political activism.

16. In another article, Arlene Stein (2009) makes the argument that the children of Holocaust survivors piece together family histories by searching for a coherent narrative within which to situate their own origin.

17. The Pew Research Center (2013) study found that 73 percent of US Jews say that remembering the Holocaust is central to being Jewish in the United States. See also Jacobs 2014; Kaufman 2007; Williams 2007.

18. Jews have experienced anti-Jewish hatred and discrimination across nearly all time periods and many geographic contexts as well.

19. While I emphasize how my respondents think of themselves as American Buddhists, I also recognize that there is no singular entity called American Buddhism.

20. I only sampled Jewish Buddhists who participated in convert or white-majority Buddhist groups, and do not have data about the participation of Jews in Buddhist groups that are majority Asian American.

21. As described in chapter 3, Tibetan Buddhism arrived in the United States largely untouched by the modernization process that had transformed and Westernized Zen and Theravada Buddhism, and as a result, the Tibetan tradition has preserved more of its historic religious worldview, complex mythological perspectives, and devotional rituals.

22. For a discussion of this practice-oriented identity, see Coleman 2001, 91–139; Cadge 2005, 94–115; Seager 2012, 61.

23. For a study of how American practitioners of insight meditation relate to the tradition, see Cadge 2005.

24. That American Buddhism shares a similar demographic base to American Judaism creates a chicken-and-egg question: Did American Buddhism's demographic distinctiveness proceed the entrance of American Jews into its ranks, or did American Jews, who seem to have a disproportionate presence in American Buddhist centers, help to create this distinctiveness?

25. For more information about those who seek out and join new religious movements, see Lewis and Tøllefsen 2016, 17–116. See also Jacobs 1989; Tipton 1982; Robbins and Anthony 1972.

26. Although Donna felt that Buddhism prioritized introspection and pacifism over worldly engagement, many Buddhist teachers and traditions emphasize the importance and centrality of applying the teachings of the Buddha to alleviating social as well as political injustice—a central goal of the movement for a socially engaged Buddhism described in chapter 3.

27. Although Michael used this descriptor positively, the term "Yid" historically has a pejorative connotation.

Conclusion: After *The Jew in the Lotus*

1. In the introduction, I provide a detailed list of the past explanations that scholars have put forth about the Jewish-Buddhist affinity.

2. For an in-depth description of the factors that structure how individuals pick and choose among religious offerings, see Sigalow 2016.

3. This explanation supports Coleman's (2001) demographic argument that suggests that Jews are overrepresented in the segments of society to which Buddhism appeals most strongly: the highly educated upper middle class, intellectuals, artists, and bohemians.

4. American Jews have historically played a central role in shaping the field of psychoanalysis, and more generally, America's psychological and therapeutic culture (Heinze 2004). See also Fishman 2000, 42–43.

5. Bethamie Horowitz (2000) uses the term "religious journey" to describe how Jewish identities and connections change as well as develop throughout the life course.

6. For a thoughtful analysis of religious flows and movements, see Tweed 2008, 2015.

7. Two sociologists, Helen Kim and Noah Leavitt (2016) from Whitman College, have been leaders in the research on the relationships between Jews and Asian Americans in the United States. They have demonstrated that the children of mixed Asian-Jewish marriages overwhelmingly think of themselves as Jews. The majority of these children grow up going to Hebrew school or Jewish day school, attending synagogue, celebrating the High Holidays, and feeling part of a larger Jewish community. See also Fong and Yung 2000.

REFERENCES

Adler, Felix. 1876. "A Prophet of the People." *Atlantic Monthly* 37 (224): 687–89.

———. 1905a. *The Essentials of Spirituality*. New York: James Pott and Co.

———. 1905b. *The Religion of Duty*. New York: McClure, Phillips, and Co.

Albanese, Catherine. 2008. *A Republic of Mind and Spirit: A Cultural History of American Metaphysical Religion*. New Haven, CT: Yale University Press.

Ama, Michihiro. 2011. *Immigrants to the Pure Land: The Modernization, Acculturation, and Globalization of Shin Buddhism, 1898–1941*. Honolulu: University of Hawaii Press.

American Hebrew. 1895. "The City." February 15, 441.

———. 1896. "Display Ad 7." December 11, 155.

———. 1897. "The Books of the Season." December 10, 171.

American Israelite. 1886. "Cleveland." June 11, 1.

———. 1890. "Cleveland." December 1, 5.

———. 1893a. "Jews' College Literary Society: The Rev. Isidore Harris, M.A. on 'Buddhism.'" May 18, 7.

———. 1893b. "Notes and Comments." October 5, 1.

Ammerman, Nancy Taton. 1997. *Congregation and Community*. New Brunswick, NJ: Rutgers University Press.

———. 2013. *Sacred Stories, Spiritual Tribes: Finding Religion in Everyday Life*. New York: Oxford University Press.

Atlanta Constitution. 1893. "Embraced the Faith of Buddha: Remarkable Religious Researches of J.W. Strauss, of New York." September 28, 3.

Banchoff, Thomas, ed. 2007. *Democracy and the New Religious Pluralism*. New York: Oxford University Press.

Barnes, Bart. 1998. "Barry Goldwater, GOP Hero, Dies." *Washington Post*, May 30, A0.

Bell, Catherine. 1992. *Ritual Theory, Ritual Practice*. New York: Oxford University Press.

Bellah, Robert N., Richard Madsen, William M. Sullivan, Ann Swidler, and Steven M. Tipton. 1985. *Habits of the Heart: Individualism and Commitment in American Life*. Berkeley: University of California Press.

Bender, Courtney. 2007. "Religion and Spirituality: History, Discourse, Measurement." Social Science Research Council. January 24. http://religion.ssrc.org/reforum/Bender .pdf.

———. 2010. *The New Metaphysics: Spirituality and the American Religious Imagination*. Chicago: University of Chicago Press.

Bender, Courtney, and Pamela Klassen, eds. 2010. *After Pluralism: Reimagining Religious Engagement*. New York: Columbia University Press.

Bender, Courtney, and Omar McRoberts. 2012. "Mapping a Field: Why and How to Study Spirituality." Social Science Research Council Working Paper. https://tif.ssrc.org/wp-content/uploads/2010/05/Why-and-How-to-Study-Spirtuality.pdf.

Berger, Peter. 1967. *The Sacred Canopy: Elements of Religion*. Garden City, NY: Doubleday.

Bhabha, Homi K. 1994. *The Location of Culture*. New York: Routledge Press.

Biale, David. 2010. *Not in the Heavens: The Tradition of Jewish Secular Thought*. Princeton, NJ: Princeton University Press.

Bodhi Monastery. 2002. "Ven. Bhikkhu Bodhi." August 8. http://bodhimonastery.org/ven-bhikkhu-bodhi.html.

Boorstein, Sylvia. 1997. *That's Funny, You Don't Look Buddhist: On Being a Faithful Jew and a Passionate Buddhist*. San Francisco: HarperSanFrancisco.

Brill, Alan. 2009. "The Lubavitcher Rebbe on Transcendental Meditation." *Book of Doctrines and Opinions* (blog), November 30. https://kavvanah.wordpress.com/2009/11/30/the-lubavitcher-rebbe-on-transcendental-meditation/.

Brodey, Deborah A. 1997. "From Judaism to Buddhism: Jewish Women's Search for Identity." Master's thesis, University of Toronto.

Cadge, Wendy. 2004. "Gendered Religious Organizations: The Case of Theravada Buddhism in America." *Gender and Society* 18 (6): 777–93.

———. 2005. *Heartwood: The First Generation of Theravada Buddhism in America*. Chicago: University of Chicago Press.

———. 2012. *Paging God: Religion in the Halls of Medicine*. Chicago: University of Chicago Press.

Cadge, Wendy, and Lynn Davidman. 2006. "Ascription, Choice, and the Construction of Religious Identities in the Contemporary United States." *Journal for the Scientific Study of Religion* 45, no. 1 (February): 23–38.

Center for Mindfulness in Medicine, Health Care, and Society. n.d. "Mindfulness-Based Programs." University of Massachusetts Medical School. http://www.umassmed.edu/cfm/mindfulness-based-programs/.

Central Conference of American Rabbis. 1998. "Seders for Tibet." June. https://www.ccarnet.org/ccar-resolutions/seders-for-tibet-1998/.

Chadwick, David. 1999. *Crooked Cucumber: The Life and Zen Teaching of Shunryu Suzuki*. New York: Broadway Books.

Charmaz, Kathy. 2006. *Constructing Grounded Theory*. London: Sage Publications.

Chaves, Mark. 2004. *Congregations in America*. Cambridge, MA: Harvard University Press.

Chayes, Bill, and Isaac Solotaroff. 1999. *Jews and Buddhism: Belief Amended, Faith Revealed*. New York: Filmmakers Library.

Chiat, Marilyn J. 1997. *America's Religious Architecture: Sacred Places for Every Community*. New York: Wiley.

Chicago Daily Tribune. 1893. "Convert to Buddha." September 28, 2.

China Press. 1937. "American Jew Says Buddhism Best Religion." March 4, 9.

A Chorus of Faith as Heard in Parliament of Religions Held in Chicago, 10–27 September 1893. 1893. Chicago.

Clar, Reva. 2002. *The Jews of Los Angeles: Urban Pioneers*. Los Angeles: Jewish Historical Society of Southern California.

Clarke, Adele E. 2005. *Situational Analysis: Grounded Theory after the Postmodern Turn*. Thousand Oaks, CA: Sage Publications.

Cohen, Steven M., and Arnold M. Eisen. 2000. *The Jew Within: Self, Community, and Commitment among the Variety of Moderately Affiliated*. Bloomington: Indiana University Press.

Cohen, Steven M., and Leonard Fein. 2001. "American Jews and Their Social Justice Involvement: Evidence from a National Survey." Amos—The National Jewish Partnership for Social Justice. https://www.bjpa.org/search-results/publication/4692.

Coleman, James William. 2001. *The New Buddhism: The Western Transformation of an Ancient Tradition*. New York: Oxford University Press.

Cooper, David A. 2000. *The Handbook of Jewish Meditation Practices: A Guide for Enriching the Sabbath and Other Days of Your Life*. Woodstock, VT: Jewish Lights Publishing.

Cornille, Catherine. 2002. *Many Mansions? Multiple Religious Belonging and Christian Identity*. New York: Orbis Books.

Corrigan, Patricia. 2013. "Rabbi Introduces Calming Mindfulness Meditation to Parents." *St. Louis Jewish Light*. January 16. http://www.stljewishlight.com/features/health/rabbi-introduces-calming-mindfulness-meditation-to-parents/article_f44c6700-6022-11e2-93e6-0019bb2963f4.html.

Cox, Harvey Gallagher. 1973. *The Seduction of the Spirit: The Use and Misuse of the People Religion*. New York: Simon and Schuster.

Daniel Goleman (blog). n.d. "About Daniel Goleman." http://www.danielgoleman.info/biography/.

Das, Surya. 1998. *Awakening the Buddha Within: Tibetan Wisdom for the Western World*. New York: Broadway Books.

Davids, T. W. Rhys. 1893. *Journal of the Pali Text Society, 1891–3*. London: Oxford University Press.

Demerath, N. J., III. 2000. "The Rise of 'Cultural Religion' in European Christianity: Learning from Poland, Northern Ireland, and Sweden." *Social Compass* 47, no. 1 (March): 127–39.

DiMaggio, Paul, and Walter W. Powell. 1983. "The Iron Cage Revisited: Collective Rationality and Institutional Isomorphism in Organizational Fields." *American Sociological Review* 48 (2): 147–60.

Ecklund, Elaine Howard, and Kristen Schultz Lee. 2011. "Atheists and Agnostics Negotiate Religion and Family." *Journal for the Scientific Study of Religion* 50, no. 4 (December): 728–43.

Eisenberg, Ellen M. 2008. *The First to Cry Down Injustice? Western Jews and Japanese Removal during WWII*. Plymouth, UK: Lexington Books.

Emerson, Robert M., Rachel I. Fretz, and Linda L. Shaw. 2011. *Writing Ethnographic Fieldnotes*. Chicago: University of Chicago Press.

Everyday Zen Foundation. n.d. "Zoketsu Norman Fischer." http://everydayzen.org/about-everyday-zen/teachers/zoketsu-norman-fischer/.

Federman, Asaf. 2009. "His Excellency and the Monk: A Correspondence between Nyanaponika Thera and David Ben-Gurion." *Contemporary Buddhism* 10, no. 2 (November): 197–219.

Fields, Rick. 1981. *How the Swans Came to the Lake: A Narrative History of Buddhism in America*. Boston: Shambhala Publications.

Fischer, Norman. 1995. *Jerusalem Moonlight: An American Zen Teacher Walks the Path of His Ancestors*. San Francisco: Clear Glass Press.

Fischer, Norman. 2003. *Opening to You: Zen-Inspired Translations of the Psalms.* New York: Viking Press.

Fishman, Sylvia Barack. 2000. *Jewish Life and American Culture.* Albany: SUNY Press.

Fleisch, Eric. 2014. "Israeli NGOs and American Jewish Donors: The Structures and Dynamics of Power Sharing in a New Philanthropic Era." PhD diss., Brandeis University.

Fleishman, Joel. 2009. *The Foundation: A Great American Secret: How Private Wealth Is Changing the World.* New York: Public Affairs.

Fong, Colleen, and Judy Yang. 2000. "In Search of the Right Spouse: Interracial Marriage among Chinese and Japanese Americans." *Contemporary Asian American: A Multidisciplinary Reader,* edited by Min Zhou and James V. Gatewood, 589–605. New York: NYU Press.

Frankel, Ellen. 2013. "5 Reasons Jews Gravitate toward Buddhism." *Huffington Post,* January 24. https://www.huffpost.com/entry/5-reasons-jews-gravitate-toward-buddhism_b_2520948.

Frickel, Scott, and Neil Gross. 2005. "A General Theory of Scientific/Intellectual Movements." *American Sociological Review* 70 (2): 204–32.

Fronsdal, Gil. 1998. "Insight Meditation in the United States: Life, Liberty, and the Pursuit of Happiness." In *The Faces of Buddhism in America,* edited by Charles S. Prebish and Kenneth Tanaka, 163–80. Berkeley: University of California Press.

Galveston Daily News (Houston, TX). 1893. "J.W. Strauss of New York Has Been Converted to Buddhism." October 2, 4.

Glaser, Barney G., and Anselm L. Strauss. 1967. *The Discovery of Grounded Theory: Strategies for Qualitative Research.* Chicago: Aldine Publishing.

Glassman, Bernard. 1997. *Lessons to the Cook: A Zen Master's Lessons in Living a Life That Matters.* New York: Three Rivers Press.

———. 2018. "Bernie Glassman, Zen Master: Zen Peacemakers Founder (1939–2018)." Zen Peacemakers International. http://zenpeacemakers.org/bernie-glassman/.

Gleig, Ann. 2012. "Wedding the Personal and Impersonal in West Coast Vipassana: A Dialogical Encounter between Buddhism and Psychotherapy." *Journal of Global Buddhism* 13:129–46.

Goenka, S. N. 2000. "Superscience: An Interview by Helen Tworkov." *Tricycle* 10 (2): 44–50.

———. 2003. *Meditation Now: Inner Peace through Inner Wisdom.* Onalaska, WI: Vipassana Research Publications.

Goldberg, Michelle. 2015. "The Roots of Mindfulness." *Tablet,* October 8. https://www.tabletmag.com/jewish-life-and-religion/193989/the-roots-of-mindfulness.

Goldberg, Robert Alan. 1995. *Barry Goldwater.* New Haven, CT: Yale University Press.

Goldman, Ari L. 1989. "Dalai Lama Meets Jews from 4 Major Branches." *New York Times.* September 26. http://www.nytimes.com/1989/09/26/nyregion/dalai-lama-meets-jews-from-4-major-branches.html.

Goldstein, Eric L. 2006. *The Price of Whiteness: Jews, Race, and American Identity.* Princeton, NJ: Princeton University Press.

Goleman, Daniel. 1995. *Emotional Intelligence.* New York: Bantam Dell.

Gooren, Henri. 2007. "Reassessing Conventional Approaches to Conversion: Toward a New Synthesis." *Journal for the Scientific Study of Religion* 46, no. 3 (September): 337–53.

Granovetter, Mark S. 1973. "The Strength of Weak Ties." *American Journal of Sociology* 78, no. 6 (May): 1360–80.

Green, Arthur. 2003. "To Learn and to Teach: Some Thoughts on Jewish-Buddhist Dialogue." In *Beside Still Waters: Jews, Christians, and the Way of the Buddha*, edited by Harold Kasimow, John P. Keenan, and Linda Klepinger Keenan, 231–42. Somerville, MA: Wisdom Publications Inc.

Greenbaum, Jesse Linnell. 1890. "Eastern Religion a Science." *American Hebrew*, July 25, 226.

Greenfield, Sidney, and Andre Droogers, eds. 2001. *Reinventing Religions: Syncretism and Transformation in Africa and the Americas*. New York: Rowman and Littlefield.

Guruge, Avanda, ed. 1965. *Return to Righteousness: A Collection of Speeches, Essays, and Letters of Anagarika Dharmapala*. Ceylon: Government Press.

Heiftetz, Harold. 1978. *Zen and Hasidism*. Wheaton, IL: Theosophical Publishing House.

Heinze, Andrew. 2004. *Jews and the American Soul: Human Nature in the Twentieth Century*. Princeton, NJ: Princeton University Press.

Hervieu-Léger, Danièle. 2000. *Religion as a Chain of Memory*. New Brunswick, NJ: Rutgers University Press.

———. 2006. "The Role of Religion in Establishing Social Cohesion." *Transit* (August). https://www.eurozine.com/the-role-of-religion-in-establishing-social-cohesion/.

Hickey, Wakoh Shannon. 2015. "Two Buddhisms, Three Buddhisms, and Racism." In *Buddhism beyond Borders: New Perspectives on Buddhism in the United States*, edited by Scott A. Mitchell and Natalie E. F. Quli, 35–56. Albany: SUNY Press.

Hicks, Rosemary. 2010. "Saving Darfur: Enacting Pluralism in Terms of Gender, Genocide, and Militarized Human Rights." In *After Pluralism: Reimagining Religious Engagement*, edited by Courtney Bender and Pamela Klassen, 252–76. New York: Columbia University Press.

Hill, Tiffany. 2013. "Hawai'i's Japanese Buddhist Temples Are Struggling to Keep Ancient Traditions Alive." *Honolulu*, July 8. http://www.honolulumagazine.com/Honolulu-Magazine/July-2013/Buddhism-in-Hawaii-Fading-Tradition/.

Hollinger, David A. 2009. "Communalist and Dispersionist Approaches to American Jewish History in an Increasingly Post-Jewish Era." *American Jewish History* 95, no. 1 (September): 1–32.

Horowitz, Bethamie. 2000. *Connections and Journeys: Assessing Critical Opportunities for Enhancing Jewish Identity*. New York: UJA-Federation of Jewish Philanthropies of New York.

Hunt, Ernest. 1955. *Essentials and Symbols of the Buddhist Faith*. Honolulu: printed by the author.

Hutchison, William R. 2003. *Religious Pluralism in America: The Contentious History of a Founding Ideal*. New Haven, CT: Yale University Press.

IJS (Institute for Jewish Spirituality). 2019. "The Institute's History." http://www.jewishspirituality.org/about-us/history/.

Insight. 1996. "A Contemplative Intersearch in Jewish and Buddhist Traditions." Insight Meditation Center Newsletter (Spring): 6.

International Campaign for Tibet. n.d. "A Complete Seder for Tibet Haggadah." http://www.savetibet.org/action/seder/hagg.htm.

Jackson, Carl T. 2010. "D.T. Suzuki, 'Suzuki Zen,' and the American Reception of Zen Buddhism." In *American Buddhism as a Way of Life*, edited by Gary Storhoff and John Whalen-Bridge, 39–56. Albany: SUNY Press.

Jacobs, Janet. 1989. *Divide Disenchantment: Deconverting from New Religions*. Bloomington: Indiana University Press.

———. 2002. *Hidden Heritage: The Legacy of the Crypto-Jews*. Berkeley: University of California Press.

———. 2010. *Memorializing the Holocaust: Gender, Genocide, and Collective Memory*. London: I. B. Tauris.

———. 2014. "Sites of Terror and the Role of Memory in Shaping Identity among First-Generation Descendants of the Holocaust." *Qualitative Sociology* 37 (1): 27–42.

Jewish Criterion (Pittsburgh). 1896. November 27, 1.

Jewish Exponent (Philadelphia). 1889. "Buddha and Buddhism." October 4, 5.

———. 1893. "Lectures and Sermons: Rev. Israel Joseph on Buddhism and Catholicism." February 3, 7.

Jewish Messenger. 1874a. "Display Ad 3." February 6, 3.

———. 1874b. "Local Items." February 13, 2.

———. 1879a. "A Buddhist Idyl." September 17, 1.

———. 1879b. "The Chinese Question." February 21, 4.

———. 1895. December 13, 2.

Jewish South (Richmond, VA). 1893. "What Is Buddhism?" October 20, 4.

JMC (Jewish Meditation Center of Brooklyn). n.d. https://www.facebook.com/jmcbrooklyn/.

Kabat-Zinn, Jon. 2011. "Some Reflections on the Origins of MBSR, Skilled Means, and the Trouble with Maps." *Contemporary Buddhism* 12 (1): 281–306.

Kamenetz, Rodger. 1994. *The Jew in the Lotus: A Poet's Rediscovery of Jewish Identity in Buddhist India*. New York: HarperCollins.

———. 1999. *The Jew in the Lotus*. Toronto: Blind Dog Films.

Kaplan, Aryeh. 1978. *Meditation and the Bible*. York Beach, ME: Samuel Weiser, Inc.

———. 1982. *Meditation and Kabbalah*. York Beach, ME: Samuel Weiser, Inc.

———. 1985. *Jewish Meditation: A Practical Guide*. New York: Schocken.

Kaplan, Dana Evan. 2009. *Contemporary American Judaism: Transformation and Renewal*. New York: Columbia University Press.

Kashima, Tetsuden. 1977. *Buddhism in America: The Social Organization of an Ethnic Religious Institution*. Westport, CT: Greenwood Press.

Kasimow, Harold, John P. Keenan, and Linda Klepinger Keenan, eds. 2003. *Beside Still Waters: Jews, Christians, and the Way of the Buddha*. Somerville, MA: Wisdom Publications Inc.

Kasselstrand, Isabella. 2015. "Nonbelievers in the Church: A Study of Cultural Religion in Sweden." *Sociology of Religion* 76, no. 3 (Fall): 275–94.

Kaufman, Debra. 2007. "Post-Memory and Post-Holocaust Jewish Identity Narratives." In *Sociology Confronts the Holocaust: Memories and Identities in Jewish Diasporas*, edited by Judith M. Gerson and Diane L. Wolf, 39–54. Durham, NC: Duke University Press.

Kaufman, Jason, and Orlando Patterson. 2005. "Cross-National Cultural Diffusion: The Global Spread of Cricket." *American Sociological Review* 70, no. 1 (February): 82–110.

Kaunfer, Elie. 2010. *Empowered Judaism: What Independent Minyanim Can Teach Us about Building Vibrant Jewish Communities*. Woodstock, VT: Jewish Lights Publishing.

Keller, Rosemary Skinner, and Rosemary Radford Ruether, eds. 2006. *Encyclopedia of Women and Religion in North America*. Bloomington: Indiana University Press.

Kelner, Shaul. 2011. "In Its Own Image: Independent Philanthropy and the Cultivation of Young Jewish Leadership." In *The New Jewish Leaders: Reshaping the American Jewish Landscape*, edited by J. Wertheimer, 261–321. Hanover, NH: University Press of New England.

Ketelaar, James. 1991. "Strategic Occidentialism: Meiji Buddhists at the World's Parliament of Religions." *Buddhist-Christian Studies* 11:37–56.

Khema, Ayya. 1998. *I Give You My Life*. Boston: Shambhala Publications.

Kim, Helen Kiyong, and Noah Samuel Leavitt. 2016. *JewAsian: Race, Religion, and Identity for America's Newest Jews*. Lincoln: University of Nebraska Press.

Klassen, Pamela. 2011. *Spirits of Protestantism: Medicine, Healing, and Liberal Christianity*. Berkeley: University of California Press.

Knitter, Paul F. 2009. "Islam and Christianity Sibling Rivalries and Sibling Possibilities." *Cross-Currents* 59 (4): 554–70.

Kornfield, Jack. 1993. *A Path with a Heart: A Guide through the Perils and Promises of Spiritual Life*. New York: Bantam Books.

Kraut, Benny. 1979. *From Reform Judaism to Ethical Culture: The Religious Evolution of Felix Adler*. Cincinnati: Hebrew Union College Press.

Kucinskas, Jaime. 2019. *The Mindful Elite: Mobilizing from the Inside Out*. Oxford: Oxford University Press.

Leopold, Anita Maria, and Jeppe Sinding Jensen, eds. 2005. *Syncretism in Religion: A Reader*. New York: Routledge.

Lew, Alan. 1996. "It Doesn't Matter What You Call It: If It Works, It Works." In *The Way of Flame: A Guide to the Forgotten Mystical Tradition of Jewish Meditation*, edited by Davis Avram, 48–49. San Francisco: HarperSanFrancisco.

———. 2001. *One God Clapping: The Spiritual Path of a Zen Rabbi*. Woodstock, VT: Jewish Lights Publishing.

———. 2003. *This Is Real and You Are Completely Unprepared: The Days of Awe as a Journey of Transformation*. New York: Little, Brown and Company.

———. 2005. *Be Still and Get Going: A Jewish Meditation Practice for Real Life*. New York: Little, Brown and Company.

Lewis, James R. and Inga B. Tøllefsen, eds. 2016. *The Oxford Handbook of New Religious Movements*. Volume II. New York: Oxford University Press.

Lewis, Paul. 2000. "William Segal, Publisher, Who Painted Self-Portraits." *New York Times*, May 22. http://www.nytimes.com/2000/05/22/arts/william-segal-95-publisher-who-painted-self-portraits.html.

Lewis, Samuel. 2013. *Sufi Vision and Initiation: Meeting with Remarkable Beings*. San Francisco: Sufi Ruhaniat International.

Libin, Nicole Heather. 2010. "The Choosing People: Constructing Jewish Buddhist Identity in America." PhD diss., University of Calgary.

Linzer, Judith. 1996. *Torah and Dharma: Jewish Seekers in Eastern Traditions*. Lanham, MD: Jason Aronson.

Lion's Roar Staff. 2013. "Remembering Meditation Teacher Toni Packer (1927–2013)." August 24. https://www.lionsroar.com/remembering-meditation-teacher-toni-packer-1927-2013-2/.

Los Angeles Times. 1934. "Buddhists Ordain American." June 18, A5.

Madsen, Richard. 2009. "The Archipelago of Faith: Religious Individualism and Faith Community in America Today." *American Journal of Sociology* 114, no. 5 (March): 1263–301.

Magid, Shaul. 2005. "Jewish Renewal Movement." In *Encyclopedia of Religion*, 7:4868–74. 2nd ed. Detroit: Thompson Gale.

Marshall, Ruth. 2009. *Political Spiritualities: The Pentecostal Revolution in Nigeria.* Chicago: University of Chicago Press.

McAdam, Doug. 1995. "'Initiator' and 'Spin-off' Movements: Diffusion Processes in Protest Cycles." In *Repertoires and Cycles of Collective Actions*, edited by Mark Traugott, 217–41. Durham, NC: Duke University Press.

McGuire, Meredith. 2008. *Lived Religion: Faith and Practice in Everyday Life.* Oxford: Oxford University Press.

McIntosh, Janet. 2009. *The Edge of Islam: Power, Personhood, and Ethnoreligious Boundaries on the Kenya Coast.* Durham, NC: Duke University Press.

McMahan, David L. 2003. "Repackaging Zen for the West." In *Buddhism in the Modern World: Adaptations of an Ancient Tradition*, edited by Steven Heine and Charles S. Prebish. New York: Oxford University Press.

———. 2008. *The Making of Buddhist Modernism.* New York: Oxford University Press.

Metcalf, Franz Aubrey. 2002. "The Encounter of Buddhism and Psychology." In *Westward Dharma: Buddhism beyond Asia*, edited by Charles S. Prebish and Martin Baumann, 348–64. Berkeley: University of California Press.

Meyer, Michael. 1995. *Response to Modernity: A History of the Reform Movement in Judaism.* Detroit: Wayne State University Press.

Meyer, Wali Ali. n.d. "Murshid Samuel L. Lewis, Sufi Ahmed Murad Chisti, 1896–1971." Sufi Ruhaniat International. http://www.ruhaniat.org/index.php/lineage/murshid-samuel-l-lewis.

Michels, Tony. 2012. *Jewish Radicals: A Documentary History.* New York: NYU Press.

Moore, Deborah Dash, ed. 2008. *American Jewish Identity Politics.* Ann Arbor: University of Michigan Press.

Morgan, Bill. 2006. *I Celebrate Myself: The Somewhat Private Life of Allen Ginsberg.* New York: Penguin Books.

Moses, A. 1898. "From Selfishness to Benevolence." *American Israelite*, May 12, 5.

Muermel, Heinz. n.d. "Carl Theodor Strauss, Buddhist Activist and Author (1852–1937)." Speech at the eleventh annual International Conference on Sri Lankan Studies.

Nathan Cummings Foundation. n.d. "Our Focus." https://nathancummings.org/our-focus/.

New York Times. 1879. "Married: Strauss-Agatz." April 23, 5.

———. 1918. "Rev. Jenkin Lloyd Jones." September 13.

New York Times, Obituaries and Marriage Notices. 1981. "Katherine W. Strauss." July 11, 5.

New-York Tribune. 1893. "His Belief Not a Conversion." September 29, 10.

Niculescu, Mira. 2015. "Mind Full of God: Jewish Mindfulness as an Offspring of Western Buddhism in America." In *Buddhism beyond Borders: New Perspectives on Buddhism in the United States*, edited by Scott A. Mitchell and Natalie E. F. Quli, 143–60. Albany: SUNY Press.

Niebuhr, Gustav. 1997. "Adding a Contemporary Ring to an Ancient Story." *New York Times*, April 26. http://www.nytimes.com/1997/04/26/us/adding-a-contemporary-ring-to-an-ancient-story.html.

Nisker, Wes. 1994. *If You Don't Like the News Go Out and Make Some of Your Own*. Berkeley: Ten Speed Press.

Pew Research Center. 2013. "A Portrait of Jewish Americans." October 1. http://www.pewforum.org/2013/10/01/jewish-american-beliefs-attitudes-culture-survey.

———. 2014. "How Americans Feels about Religious Groups." July 16. https://www.pewforum.org/2014/07/16/how-americans-feel-about-religious-groups/.

———. 2019. Religion and Public Life. https://www.pewforum.org/.

Phan, Peter C. 2003. "Multiple Religious Belonging: Opportunities and Challenges for Theology and Church." *Theological Studies* 64 (3): 495–519.

Porterfield, Amanda. 2001. *The Transformation of American Religion: The Story of a Late Twentieth Century Awakening*. Oxford: Oxford University Press.

Prebish, Charles S. 1999. *Luminous Passage: The Practice and Study of Buddhism in America*. Berkeley: University of California Press.

Prebish, Charles S., and Kenneth Tanaka, eds. 1998. *The Faces of Buddhism in America*. Berkeley: University of California Press.

Prothero, Stephen. 1997. "Julius Goldwater: The Good Shepherd." *Tricycle* 7, no. 2 (Winter): 44–48.

———. 2010. *The White Buddhist: The Asian Odyssey of Henry Steel Olcott*. Indianapolis: Indiana University Press.

Putnam, Robert D. 2000. *Bowling Alone: The Collapse and Revival of American Community*. New York: Simon and Schuster.

Putnam, Robert D., and David E. Campbell. 2010. *American Grace: How Religion Divides and Unites Us*. New York: Simon and Schuster.

Queen, Christopher. 1998. "Buddhism, Activism, and Unknowing: A Day with Bernie Glassman (Interview with Zen Peacemaker Order Founder)." *Tikkun*, January–February, 64–66.

———. 2000. *Engaged Buddhism in the West*. Somerville, MA: Wisdom Publications.

Queen, Christopher, and Sallie King. 1996. *Engaged Buddhism: Buddhist Liberation Movements in Asia*. Albany: SUNY Press.

Rambo, Lewis. 1995. *Understanding Religious Conversion*. New Haven, CT: Yale University Press.

Rebhun, Uzi. 2016. *Jews and the American Religious Landscape*. New York: Columbia University Press.

Robbins, Joel. 2011. "Crypto-Religion and the Study of Cultural Mixtures: Anthropology, Value, and the Nature of Syncretism." *Journal of the American Academy of Religion* 79, no. 2 (June): 408–24.

Robbins, Thomas, and Dick Anthony. 1982. "Deprogramming, Brainwashing, and the Medicalization of Deviant Religious Groups." *Social Problems* 29, no. 3 (February): 283–97.

Roof, Wade Clark. 1993. *A Generation of Seekers: The Spiritual Journeys of the Baby Boomers Generation*. San Francisco: HarperSanFrancisco.

———. 1999. *Spiritual Marketplace: Baby Boomers and the Remaking of American Religion*. Princeton, NJ: Princeton University Press.

Roof, Wade Clark, and William McKinney. 1985. "Denominational America and the New Religious Pluralism." *Annals of the American Academy of Political and Social Science* 480, no. 1 (July): 24–38.

Rosenberg, Lisa. 2003. "Buddhist Heart—Jewish Soul: An Examination of the Phenomenon of Jewish Buddhists in the United States." Master's thesis, Dominican University of California.

Roth, Jeff. 2009. *Jewish Meditation Practices for Everyday Life: Awakening Your Heart, Connecting with God*. Woodstock, VT: Jewish Lights Publishing.

Sahagun, Louis. 2008. *Master of the Mysteries: The Life of Manly Palmer Hall*. Port Townsend, WA: Process Media.

Sangharakshita, Bhikkhu. 1983. *Anagarika Dharmapala: A Biographical Sketch*. 4th ed. Kandy, Ceylon: Buddhist Publication Society.

Sarna, Jonathan D. 2004. *American Judaism: A History*. New Haven, CT: Yale University Press.

Sautter, Cia. 2002. "Chochmat: Rhymes with Spirit Rock." *Journal of Religion and Popular Culture* 1, no. 1 (2002): 5–5.

Schmidt, Leigh Eric. 2005. *Restless Souls: The Making of American Spirituality*. New York: HarperCollins.

Seager, Richard. 1995. *The World's Parliament of Religions: The East/West Encounter, Chicago, 1893*. Bloomington: Indiana University Press.

———. 2012. *Buddhism in America*. New York: Columbia University Press.

Segal, William. 2003. *A Voice at the Borders of Silence*. New York: Overlook Press.

Seidman, Naomi. 1998. "Fag-Hags and Bu-Jews: Toward a (Jewish) Politics of Vicarious Identity." In *Insider/Outsider: American Jews and Multiculturalism*, edited by David Biale, Michael Galchinsky, and Susannah Heschel, 254–68. Berkeley: University of California Press.

Senauke, Alan. 2010. *The Bodhisattva's Embrace: Dispatches from Engaged Buddhism's Front Lines*. Berkeley: Clear View Press.

Senzaki, Nyogen. 1978. "What Is the Mentorgarten?" Sufi Ruhaniat International. http://murshidsam.org/Documents/Papers/Level1/What_is%20_the%20_Mentorgarten.pdf.

———. 2008. *Eloquent Silence: Nyogen Senzaki's Gateless Gate and Other Previously Unpublished Teachings and Letters*. Somerville, MA: Wisdom Publications.

Shoshanna, Brenda. 2008. *Jewish Dharma: A Guide to the Practice of Judaism and Zen*. Boston: Da Capo Press.

Sigalow, Emily. 2016. "Towards a Sociological Framework of Religious Syncretism in the United States." *Journal of the American Academy of Religion* 84, no. 4 (December): 1029–55.

———. 2018a. "Breaking down the Barriers: The Encounter between Judaism and Buddhism in the Late Nineteenth Century." *American Jewish History* 102 (3): 459–81.

———. 2018b. "From Jewish Prominence to Buddhist Prominence." *PaRDes: Journal of the German Association of Jewish Studies* 23:119–31

Silvers, Emma. 2013. "Seminar Will Connect Mindful Eating with Jewish Ideals." Jweekly.com. March 7. https://www.chabadcv.org/templates/articlecco_cdo/aid/2421439/jewish/Seminar-will-connect-mindful-eating-to-Jewish-ideals.htm.

Slater, Jonathan. 2004. *Mindful Jewish Living: Compassionate Practice*. New York: Aviv Press.

Smith, Tom. 2005. *Jewish Distinctiveness in America: A Statistical Portrait*. New York: American Jewish Committee.

Snow, David A., and Robert D. Benford. 1992. "Master Frames and Cycles of Protest." In *Frontiers in Social Movement Theory*, edited by Alcon D. Morris and Carol McClurg Mueller, 133–55. New Haven, CT: Yale University Press.

Stark, Rodney, and Roger Funke. 2000. *Acts of Faith: Explaining the Human Side of Religion*. Berkeley: University of California Press.

Staub, Michael E., ed. 2004. *The Jewish 1960s: An American Sourcebook*. Lebanon, NH: Brandeis University Press.

Stein, Arlene. 1998. "Whose Memories? Whose Victimhood? Contests for the Holocaust Frame in Recent Social Movement Discourse." *Sociological Perspectives* 41 (3): 519–40.

———. 2009. "Trauma and Origins: Post-Holocaust Genealogists and the Work of Memory." *Qualitative Sociology* 32 (3): 293–309.

Stewart, Charles, and Rosalind Shaw. 1994. *Syncretism/Anti-Syncretism: The Politics of Religious Synthesis*. New York: Psychology Press.

Strang, David, and John W. Meyer. 1993. "Institutional Conditions for Diffusion." *Theory and Society* 22 (4): 487–511.

Strang, David, and Sarah A. Soule. 1998. "Diffusion in Organizations and Social Movements: From Hybrid Corn to Poison Pills." *Annual Review of Sociology* 24:265–90.

Strauss, Charles. 1923. *Buddha and His Doctrine*. New York: W. Rider and Son.

Sun (New York). 1893. "Hebrew Turns Buddhist." September 26, 1893, 3.

Svonkin, Stuart. 1999. *Jews against Prejudice: American Jews and the Fight for Civil Liberties*. New York: Columbia University Press.

Taves, Ann. 2009. *Religious Experience Reconsidered: A Building Block Approach to the Study of Religion and Other Special Things*. Princeton, NJ: Princeton University Press.

Taves, Ann, and Courtney Bender. 2012. "Things of Value." In *What Matters? Ethnographies of Value in a Not So Secular Age*, edited by Courtney Bender and Ann Taves, 1–33. New York: Columbia University Press.

Tenenbaum, Shelly, and Lynn Davidman. 2007. "It's in My Genes: Biological Discourse and Essentialist Views of Identity among Contemporary American Jews." *Sociological Quarterly* 48 (3): 435–50.

Tipton, Steven M. 1982. *Getting Saved from the Sixties: Moral Meaning in Conversion and Cultural Change*. Berkeley: University of California Press.

Travisano, Richard V. 1970. "Alternation and Conversion as Qualitatively Different Transformations." *Social Psychology through Symbolic Interaction*, edited by Gregory Prentice Stone and Harvey A. Faberman, 594–606. Waltham, MA: Ginn-Blaisdell.

Tricycle. 1996. "End of the Story: An Interview with Toni Packer." Summer. https://tricycle.org/magazine/end-story/.

Trigilio, Tony. 2007. *Allen Ginsberg's Buddhist Poetics*. Carbondale: Southern Illinois University Press.

Tweed, Thomas A., ed. 1997. *Retelling US Religious History*. Berkeley: University of California Press.

———. 1999. "Night-Stand Buddhists and Other Creatures: Sympathizers, Adherents, and the Study of Religion." In *American Buddhism: Methods and Findings in Recent Scholarship*, edited by D. Williams and C. Queen, 71–90. Abingdon, Oxon: RoutledgeCurzon.

Tweed, Thomas A. 2000. *The American Encounter with Buddhism, 1844–1912: Victorian Culture and the Limits of Dissent.* Chapel Hill: UNC Press.

———. 2008. *Crossing and Dwelling: A Theory of Religion.* Cambridge, MA: Harvard University Press.

———. 2015. "Theory and Method in the Study of Buddhism: Toward 'Translocative' Analysis." In *Buddhism beyond Borders: New Perspectives on Buddhism in the United States*, edited by Scott A. Mitchell and Natalie E. F. Quli, 3–20. Albany: SUNY Press.

Tweed, Thomas A. and Stephen Prothero. 1999. *Asian Religions in America: A Documentary History.* New York: Oxford University Press.

Umansky, Ellen M. 2005. *From Christian Science to Jewish Science: Spiritual Healing and American Jews.* New York: Oxford University Press.

Unno, Taitetsu. 2001. "The Pure Land in the New World." *Tricycle* (Fall). http://tricycle.org /magazine/pure-land-new-world/.

Valisinha, Sri D., ed. 1955. "The Diary Leaves of the Late Ven. Anagarika Dharmapala." *Maha Bodhi* 63:53–56, 436–39.

———. 1956a. "The Diary Leaves of the Late Ven. Anagarika Dharmapala." *Maha Bodhi* 64 (8): 405.

———. 1956b. "The Diary Leaves of the Late Ven. Anagarika Dharmapala." *Maha Bodhi* 65 (6): 301.

———. 1958a. "The Diary Leaves of the Late Ven. Anagarika Dharmapala." *Maha Bodhi* 66 (3): 372.

———. 1958b. "The Diary Leaves of the Late Ven. Anagarika Dharmapala." *Maha Bodhi* 66 (11): 372.

van der Veer, Peter. 1994. *Religious Nationalism: Hindus and Muslims in India.* Berkeley: University of California Press.

Van Gelder, Lawrence. 1999. "'The Jew in the Lotus': A Journey Back to Judaism, Thanks to the Dalai Lama." *New York Times*, January 29. http://partners.nytimes.com/library/film /012999lotus-film-review.html.

Verman, Mike. 1996. *The History and Varieties of Jewish Meditation.* New York: Jason Aronson Incorporated.

Warner, Stephen. 1993. "Work in Progress toward a New Paradigm for the Sociological Study of Religion in the United States." *American Journal of Sociology* 98, no. 5 (March): 1044–93.

Watts, Alan W. 2011. *Beat Zen, Square Zen, and Zen.* New York: Literary Licensing.

Weinberg, Sheila. 1994. "Many Voices in One Mind." *Reconstructionist* 59, no. 2 (Fall): 53–58.

———. 2008. "Practicing and Teaching Mindfulness in a Jewish Context." Institute for Jewish Spirituality.

———. 2010. *Surprisingly Happy: An Atypical Religious Memoir.* Amherst, MA: White River Press.

Weitsman, Mel. 1999. "Zen in America." Unpublished lecture at Stanford University, October 23. Copy in author's possession.

Werner, Julian. 1877. "Correspondence: New York Letter Prof. Adler's Letters Fort-Fourth Street." *American Israelite*, February 2, 5.

West, Candace, and Don H. Zimmerman. 1987. "Doing Gender." *Gender and Society* 1, no. 2 (June): 125–51.

White, Christopher. 2008. *Unsettled Minds: Psychology and the American Search for Spiritual Assurance, 1830–1940*. Berkeley: University of California Press.

Williams, Duncan Ryūken. 2002. "Camp Dharma: Japanese-American Buddhist Identity and the Internment Experience of World War II." In *Westward Dharma: Buddhism beyond Asia*, edited by Charles S. Prebish and Martin Baumann, 191–200. Berkeley: University of California Press.

Williams, Richard. 2007. "Responses to the Holocaust: Discussing Jewish Identity through the Perspective of Social Construction." In *Sociology Confronts the Holocaust: Memories and Identities in Jewish Diasporas*, edited by Judith M. Gerson and Diane L. Wolf, 92–114. Durham, NC: Duke University Press.

Wilson, Jeff. 2009. *Mourning the Unborn Dead: A Buddhist Ritual Comes to America*. New York: Oxford University Press.

———. 2014. *Mindful America: The Mutual Transformation of Buddhist Meditation and American Culture*. New York: Oxford University Press.

Woo, Elaine. 2001. "Rev. Julius Goldwater; Convert to Buddhism Aided WWII Internees." *Los Angeles Times*, June 23. http://articles.latimes.com/2001/jun/23/local/me-13844.

Wuthnow, Robert. 1998. *After Heaven: Spirituality in America since the 1950s*. Berkeley: University of California Press.

Zuckerman, Phil. 2008. *Society without God*. New York: NYU Press.

INDEX